A collaborative work by Thomas Horn, Nita Horn, Gary Bates, Chuck Missler,
Gary Stearman, Fred DeRuvo, Russ Dizdar, Donna Howell,
Michael Hoggard, Noah Hutchings, Terry James

GOD'S
GHOSTBUSTERS

Vampires? Ghosts? Aliens? Werewolves?
Creatures of the Night Beware!

DEFENDER

CRANE, MISSOURI

God's Ghostbusters: Vampires? Ghosts? Aliens? Werewolves? Creatures of the Night Beware

Defender
Crane, MO 65633
©2011 by Thomas Horn
A collaborative work by Thomas Horn, Nita Horn, Gary Bates, Fred DeRuvo, Russ Dizdar, Donna Howell, Derek Gilbert, Sharon Gilbert, Michael Hoggard, Noah Hutchings, Terry James, John McTernan, Chuck Missler, Jeff Patty, Gary Stearman, and Douglas ·Woodward.
All rights reserved. Published 2011.
Printed in the United States of America.

ISBN 13: 9780983621652

A CIP catalog record of this book is available from the Library of Congress.

Cover illustration and design by Daniel Wright.
All Scripture quotations from the King James Version; in cases of academic comparison, those instances are noted.

ACKNOWLEDGMENTS

So many are deserving of acknowledgment without whose friendship, inspiration, assistance, and research this book would have simply been too challenging.

Many thanks are extended in particular to Gary Bates, Fred DeRuvo, Russ Dizdar, Donna Howell, Derek Gilbert, Sharon Gilbert, Michael Hoggard, Noah Hutchings, Terry James, John McTernan, Chuck Missler, Jeff Patty, Gary Stearman, and Douglas Woodward, for their outstanding chapter additions to this work, and to Daniel Wright for a superior cover design.

Of course editor, Donna Howell, must be shown gratitude for making all of us sound better than we are.

Finally, to the many thousands of friends who visit our websites and constantly express their love and support, please know how much your affection lifts us up in these critical times.

Contents

THE BOUNDARIES OF OUR
PHYSICAL REALITY

By Chuck Missler

Before we attempt to explore the fringes—and beyond—of our understanding of the physical universe (ghosts, aliens, vampires, etc.), it is of paramount importance to dispose of the baggage of our misconceptions and the mythology of what we have been erroneously taught in this age of deceit.

The puncturing of our delusions is what some might call "a painful blessing." That sounds like an oxymoron, but it is absolutely vital for well-being, and a prerequisite for maturity.

Much of what we have been taught is in error: some from disproven myths, others from an agenda of politics and "political correctness." In our current culture, even the very existence of "truth" has been abandoned rather than to persist in the search! When we don't fully understand a phenomena, we wrap it in clichés and techni-speak. Metaphors reign where mysteries reside.

(The search for truth was regarded, at one time, the primary goal of mankind; however, having taught our children that they are simply the result of a series of cosmic accidents, we then wonder why they have lost any sense of destiny or accountability!)

Elusive Concepts

There are several concepts in mathematics which seem to elude any actual discovery within our physical universe. One of these is randomness and the other is infinity. They both deserve some preliminary tutorial comment.

Randomness turns out to be a concept which is more elusive than most people realize. In 1955, the "grandfather" of the "think-tanks," the RAND Corporation,[1] made a technological milestone by publishing a book entitled, *A Million Random Digits with 100,000 Normal Deviates*. A layman might pick up a copy and discover that it was simply a collection of five-digit numbers, and would probably assume that this was some kind of joke or satire. Actually, it was regarded—at the time—as a useful, practical breakthrough.

It turns out that it is virtually impossible to obtain a significant supply of truly random numbers. Laboratory technicians have to resign themselves to dealing with what are actually *pseudorandom numbers*, because in the "real world," any algorithm (or procedure) to obtain a "random number" involves non-random elements.[2] The elusive quest for a supply of truly random numbers, by those pursuing extended simulations or other experimental pursuits, led to the RAND milestone publication. Relying on the most advanced computers available at the time, they exhaustively searched for—*and removed*—any traces of symmetry, patterns, repeatability, or predictability of any kind. To qualify as truly *random*, they had to remove any traces of *design*. In the information sciences, randomness and design are totally antithetical: they are definitively opposites. To attribute design to random processes is an ultimate absurdity.

We live in a culture that attributes the most elegant designs imaginable to totally random processes. A leaf, a bird's wing, the human eye, or our digestive system, are virtually impossible to exhaust in an investigation of their teleology, elegance, and function. The capstone example is the human cell: our explorations of the DNA are only preliminary glimpses into a design sophistication that continues to challenge the most talented experts. To attribute to randomness the elegance of a three-out-of-four, error-correcting code, that apparently underlies all of life, represents some kind of limit to credulity.

The other elusive concept we seem unable to encounter within our physical universe is *infinity*.

Our Finite Universe

The great discovery of twentieth-century science was the realization that the universe is not infinite: it is *finite!* (It may be expanding, but it has a finite size.) And it had a beginning. That's what gave birth to the various conjectures that deal with its inceptions: the "Big Bang": "First there was nothing; then it exploded." Metaphors reign where mysteries reside.

All "work" in the universe depends on a difference in temperature. From thermodynamics, we know that heat flows toward cold. And it does this with less than 100 percent efficiency. (These two sentences are simplifications of the first two "laws" of thermodynamics.) The resulting "inefficiency" is absorbed in raising the ambient temperature. If the universe was infinitely old, there wouldn't be any differences in temperature remaining. It appears to be in the process of winding down, but it hasn't completed that yet. Therefore, it had a beginning. And, inevitably, when the ambient temperature is uniform everywhere, it will, ultimately, have an end.

The inability to confirm the existence of infinity—in either the macrocosm of the astronomer or the microcosm of the quantum physicist—has placed an unwelcome limit on our cosmological speculations. Even the ambiguous comfort of any true randomness within the physical world has now been called into question by the new math of Chaos Theory. *(This, too, would also seem to pull the rug out from under those who insist on ascribing the creation to an accident of "chance.")*

It is in this dysfunctional culture, in which most people have been misinformed about foundational concepts, that we will be attempting to understand what we really know about the physical reality we find ourselves in. We are stumbling within this interval between the miracle of our origin and the mystery of our destiny. And we are now beginning to realize that the most critical aspects that impact our destiny lie just outside the ostensible boundaries of the veil surrounding only a "virtual" reality.

We will focus our inquiry in two primary directions: the macrocosm of our universe, and the microcosm of our existence. Using the idiom of Leonardo da Vinci's *Vitruvian Man* to represent our "anthropic reach," we will first explore the macrocosm—the largeness—of our known universe:

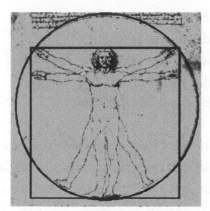

The Macrocosm:
(Our known universe)

Size, (Largeness)

As we explore "largeness"—the macrocosm[3]—we also discover that much of what we have been taught about astronomy is now known to be in error. Sir Isaac Newton's Laws of Universal Gravitation elegantly codified the mysteries of planetary motion postulated by Johannes Kepler. However, astronomers have subsequently become excessively addicted to looking towards gravity as the fundamental explanation for almost everything. Many of the contemporary speculations of astrophysics result from self-imposed myths inferred from *gravitational* hypotheses:

- "There is a black hole in the center of that galaxy" (otherwise we cannot explain its level of energy output).
- "There is invisible dark matter in that galaxy" (otherwise we cannot explain how it rotates the way it does).
- "There is 96 percent of the universe that is made up of dark energy and dark matter we cannot see" (otherwise clusters of galaxies would fly apart because gravity alone can't hold them together).

- "Pulsars are made up of strange matter" (otherwise we can't explain their oscillator-like behavior).
- "Photographs of connections between two objects that have different redshifts are only chance alignments"[4] (otherwise the Big Bang theories are refuted!).[5]

Unfortunately, most astronomers have never fully recognized the implications of James Clark Maxwell's equations summarizing *electromagnetism* which can have 10^{36} *times* the influence of gravity alone.

To gain a grasp of the immense distances involved, let's examine a scale model of convenience.

The Burnham Model

Robert Burnham Jr., in his *Burnham's Celestial Handbook: An Observer's Guide to the Universe Beyond the Solar System*,[6] suggests a convenient model to gain a grasp of the relative scales involved among the members of our celestial sky. (The distance from the sun to Earth is an accepted standard called an Astronomical Unit [AU]). The number of Astronomical Units in one light-year (63,294) happens to be approximately equal to the number of inches in a statute mile (63,360). In Burnham's suggested model: One inch in the model will represent the distance from the sun to the Earth; and one mile in the model will represent one light-year.

The sun is about eight hundred and eighty thousand miles in diameter. In the Burnham model, an AU (93 million miles) is represented by one inch. Thus, the sun would be represented by a speck .0088 in. (about 0.01 inch) diameter: a tiny speck smaller than the period at the end of this sentence.

All nine planets would thus fit inside a seven-foot diameter circle around that speck:

Mercury	0.4" radius
Venus	0.7" radius
Earth	1.0" radius (1 "AU" by definition)
Mars	1.6" radius
Jupiter	5.2" radius
Saturn	9.5" radius
Uranus	19.2" radius
Neptune	30.0" radius
Pluto	39.5" radius

The nearest star, *Alpha Centauri*, is about the same size as the sun, and is four-and-a-half light-years away. That equates to an equivalent tiny speck *4.5 miles away* in our model!

Let's remember that gravitational force between two masses equals the product of the two masses *divided by the square of the distance* between them. How much influence would *gravity* have on two specks of dust *4.5 miles apart?* Virtually, none. (If we visualized them as golf balls, they would have to be over seven hundred miles apart! Gravity between them would also be negligible.)

Incidentally, in the Burnham model, our Milky Way galaxy model itself would be *one hundred thousand miles in diameter!*

Obviously, the effects of gravity at such distances are miniscule. However, the *effects of electromagnetism can be 10^{36} times as great!* What the plasma physicists have maintained for years is that the entire volume of our galaxy is filled with diffuse clouds of magnetized *plasma*—the fourth state of matter—electrically charged, ionized particles: 99 percent of all matter in the universe is in the form of *plasma!*[7] They follow the non-intuitive laws of James Clark Maxwell which most astronomers have avoided as too awkward and inconvenient.

A Holographic Universe?

The GEO 600 is an ambitious project attempting to detect gravity waves located near Sarstedt, Germany.[8] Gravitational waves are extremely small ripples in the structure of space-time which had been predicted by Albert Einstein in 1916, but have *never yet been directly observed.* The GEO 600, a laser interferometer of 600 meters arm length, with its sister interferometric detectors, comprises the most sensitive gravitational wave detectors ever created. They are designed to detect relative changes in distance of the order of 10^{-21}, about the size of a single atom compared to the distance from the sun to the Earth.[9]

However, some yet unidentified "noise" present in the GEO 600 detector measurements might be due to the instrument's extreme sensitivity to small quantum fluctuations of space-time affecting the positions of parts of the detector.[10] It is now suspected, by some, that the Gravitational Wave Detector in Hannover may have detected evidence of a *holographic* universe, a concept that was originally advanced by David Bohm, a confrere of Dr. Einstein, who had a deep understanding of plasma physics.[11] His speculations may be on the threshold of confirmation (which would be a discovery that vastly exceeds the significance of what GEO 600 was designed for).

But these explorations of the "finite-ness" at the large end of things—the "macrocosm"—are only a beginning. Our discoveries of "finite-ness" on the *small* end of things—the "microcosm"— result in even more challenging and bizarre strangeness.

The Microcosm:
(The nature of our existence)

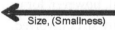

Size, (Smallness)

The Macrocosm:
(Our known universe)

Size, (Largeness)

The Microcosm

Do you have "faith" in the chair you're sitting on? Why are you confident it will hold your weight? It may seem solid enough, but suppose someone told you that essentially there was *nothing* there…that its ostensible firmness is the result of an electrical simulation creating only an illusion of "solid-ness"…

The molecules of the materials that make up the chair you're sitting on are collections of atoms (which, of course, we've never seen since they are smaller than a wavelength of light). Yet, let's try to comprehend the substance of what we are talking about: Again, let's attempt a simple illustration.

The simplest atom is that of hydrogen, which can be visualized as a nucleus (of one proton) encircled by a single electron.

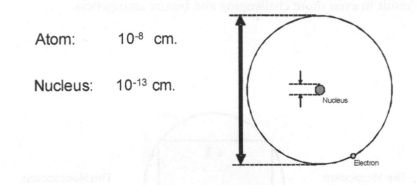

Atom: 10^{-8} cm.

Nucleus: 10^{-13} cm.

Nucleus

Electron

This sketch is, of course, not scale. It is useful, however, for us to attempt to gain an appreciation for the *relative* sizes involved. The hydrogen atom is approximately 0.00000001 centimeters in diameter, usually abbreviated as 10^{-8} cm. The nucleus, consisting if a single proton, is approximately 0.0000000000001 centimeters in diameter, usually abbreviated as 10^{-13} cm. In linear terms, that's a ratio of $10^{-8}/10^{-13}$ which means that the diameter is 10^5, or *one hundred thousand times the size of the nucleus!*

That may be a bit too abstract for most of us. Let's try to picture making a "model" of this. Let's take a golf ball to represent the nucleus; our "electron" would have to be over a mile, or eighteen football fields, away!

But that's just the *linear* differential. To represent this in terms of *area*, we would need square that distance: length times width. To represent this *volumetrically* (length times width times height), we need $(10^5)^3$ or 10^{15}, a numerical relationship which is virtually impossible for us to grasp! *It is the same relationship that one second would have to 30 million years!*

So as I confidently trust that my chair will hold my weight, and yet you might insist that there really "isn't anything there," you would be closer to describing the actual reality by that same physical relationship: the ratio of a mere second to 30 million years!

As atoms bond to other atoms to make up a molecule, it is their *electrical* relationships that create the ostensible solidity (or liquidity) that we sense in the apparent reality around us.

As we explore further the nature of the tiny particles that create the illusion of our reality, it gets worse. The world of "smallness" has its own, most peculiar, boundaries.

If we take any length, we assume that we can divide it in half. We could retain a half, and then divide it again, discarding the remainder. We take the remaining half, and divide it again, discarding the remainder. We naturally assume that we could—at least conceptually—do this forever, dividing ever smaller remainders, etc. However, we would discover that when we reach a defining minimum—known as the "Planck length" 10^{-33} cm.— we would encounter any attempts to divide that remainder would result in a property known as "non-locality": being connected to everywhere at once!

It has now been proven that all "non-local" particles throughout our apparent universe are somehow intimately, directly, connected simultaneously: negligible "travel time" is involved between them![12]

Everything we encounter: length, mass, energy, even time— are all composed of *indivisible* units, commonly designated "quanta." This field of study is called "Quantum Physics" and its philosophical implications can be shattering to our presuppositions about our "reality." We now discover that the physical reality that surrounds us is only a virtual *simulated* reality—made up of indivisible, electrically charged particles: in fact, we exist within a *digital electrical simulation!*

Hyperdimensional Implications?

One of the growing concerns, at the very frontier of our physical sciences, is the discovery that some of the "constants" of physics appear to be *changing*! The pursuit of measuring these ostensible changes is far more challenging than might first appear. One of the implications of such changes is that "Our universe may be but a shadow of a larger reality."[13] We will designate that "larger reality" the *Metacosm*.[14]

Dr. Einstein, while grappling with the nature of space and time, made history by recognizing that we live in four dimensions: three spatial dimensions plus time. The reality that time is a physical property—which varies with mass, acceleration, and gravity, among other factors—is not only what led to Einstein's Theory of Relativity, it was a discovery that totally alters our understanding of our own existence. We no longer are restricted to the myopia of Euclidean geometry of only three dimensions.

Einstein's four-dimensional space-time is curved by the presence of matter, producing a universe whose geometry is Riemannian rather than Euclidean, in which bodies travel in geodesics (shortest paths) which are the curved orbits interpreted by Newton as a result of some attractive force.

(It is interesting, and not without its own significance, that the Apostle Paul listed the *four* dimensions in his Epistle to the Ephesians.)[15]

It was tragic that Dr. Einstein went to his death frustrated that he was unable to reconcile his theories with light and other factors. If he had applied his fundamental insight by reaching to yet higher dimensions, he might have discovered what Theodor Kaluza and Oskar Klein (and, subsequently, Chen Ning Yang and Robert Mills) uncovered in the following years by going to five and higher dimensional equivalents. Kaluza noticed that when he solved Albert Einstein's equations for general relativity using *five* dimensions, then James Clark Maxwell's equations for electro-magnetism simplified elegantly.

Current assumptions among the quantum physicists today is that we live in (at least) ten dimensions—four are directly discern-able, but six are only inferable indirectly since they are "curled" in less than the shortest wavelengths of light.

(It is also rather provocative that Nachmonides, an ancient Hebrew sage writing in the thirteenth century, concluded, from his study of the text of the *Book of Genesis*, that our universe has ten dimensions; however, only four of them are "knowable" and six of them—in his words—were not directly "knowable." We have spent many millions of dollars on atomic accelerators to arrive at an equivalent conclusion.)

(It is corollary study to discover how the biblical text anticipates virtually all of our current technologies and predicaments; but that's another book for another time. There are some biblical scholars that attribute the fracturing of our ten-dimensional universe into 4 + 6 as a result of the curse in Genesis 3 which will be restored in Revelation 21. But that, too, is a topic for another time.)

It is difficult to identify practical examples of hyperdimen-sional excursions outside the conceptual regions of advanced mathematics. For example, a tesseract is a four-dimensional cube, unraveled into three dimensions. The only place I have found an actual use of one is in Salvador Dali's painting *Crucifixion* (*Corpus Hypercubus*). (I was startled to discover that he had the advanced mathematical insight so appropriate for that application!)

Encounters with hyperspaces—spaces with more than three dimensions—may involve phenomena which we call "paranormal" or "supernatural." Paranormal events may be the result of trans-dimensional interactions. Metaphors reign where mysteries reside.

Such themes have become popular in our entertainments, such as science fiction movies (*Thirteenth Floor*, *Matrix*, et al) where the participants discover that they are simply "program units" within a simulated virtual environment. However, it is disturbing to discover that we, too, are apparently in an equivalent predicament: being a pawn in a virtual reality, being caught in a game played by others from outside our own existence.

This puts an unusual premium on the tools and resources we need to evaluate our true condition, and to gain a glimpse into our own destiny. It translates our academic interest into a prerequisite for survival. How does one calibrate or evaluate trans-dimensional events from inside "the box"?

The Margins of the Metacosm

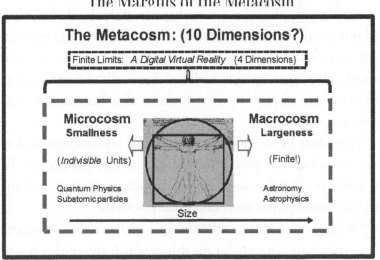

Does the "Paranormal" lie within the margins between the "Metacosm" and the virtual reality established by the digital simulation?

Which of apparent phenomena are trans-dimensional events? Why should we be surprised by trans-dimensional phenomena when we get glimpses of them in cloud chambers of the physicists? How much of our discounted history is the record of trans-dimensional events? How much of our understanding will rely on competence in hyperspatial constructs and characteristics? How will our Euclidian presuppositions limit our horizons when encountering Riemannian geometry? What are the tools to discern between insights and discoveries and the deceits and illusions?

Upon serious reflection, it becomes even more urgent: Is the "metacosm" a docile place, or is it the theater of a larger cosmic warfare? Are we the pawns or the prize? What are our resources? What are our risks? Is one of the principle weapons deceit? Delusions with their own agenda?

As we peruse the subsequent chapters of this book, let's blindfold our prejudices from the myths of the past, and let's approach these areas with a humility borne of a broader perspective. Let's, indeed, take a peak outside and look beyond the comfort of the four-dimensional playpen we've been confined to…but let's also appreciate the risks.

There may be an enormous amount of information available if we are to have the perceptions to gain a valid perspective. But the stakes may be far more significant than we suspect, and they also may preempt our most cherished priorities.

"While we look not at the things which are seen, but at the things which are not seen: for the things which are seen are temporal; but the things which are not seen are eternal" (2 Corinthians 4:18).

Good hunting.

CHAPTER ONE

THE SPIRIT OF NOSFERATU
AND THE
CHILDREN OF THE DAMNED

By Thomas Horn

Currently, America and much of the world is experiencing what would have seemed impossible just fifty years ago: an explosion of ancient occultism and wicked fascination with all things paranormal by today's spiritually abandoned public. In the United States alone, there are now more than two hundred thousand registered witches and as many as 8 million unregistered practitioners of "the craft." On college and high school campuses across the nation (and in homes via electronic media such as iPads and TV), ghosts, incubus, succubus, witches, vampires, werewolves, and other "creatures of the night" are popularly esteemed as objects of desire and idolized by young men and women who view them as cult icons of envious mystical power. Psychologists have long understood how women in general desire strength in men, but few could have imagined how this natural and over-riding need by young ladies would be used in modern times to seduce them of their innocence using mysteriously strong yet ever-lastingly damned creatures depicted in popular books and films like *Twilight*, *New Moon*, and *Eclipse*. Listing all of the related fan sites, music videos, magazines, television shows, and movies cur-rently dedicated to sexual (or romantic) obsession with alluring demons-in-flesh would require more space than can be allowed in a chapter of this nature. These would include television shows like *Being Human*, *The Gates*, *Underworld*, *The Vampire Diaries*, *True Blood*, and dozens of others (not to mention hedonistic gay-themed programs such as *The Lair*, a series that plays nationwide on all major cable systems based on a vampire-run sex club). Pop music idols including Lady Gaga, Natalia Kills, Jessie J, and even Britney Spears have likewise caught the demon-fever, and in recent years have used their music to increasingly deploy magic spells, occult words, and esoteric symbols. Even church leaders and Christian teens seem enchanted by the darkness. An April 13, 2011 article titled "Mysticism Infecting Nazarene Beliefs" was preceded only a few days before by a Telegraph article describ-ing how a "surge in satanism" including inside the church has sparked a "rise in demand for exorcists" within traditional reli-gious settings.[16]

Yet for some, focusing as we just have on pop-culture memes as a sign of deeper, culturally relevant consequences is an over-assessment of the danger. The present captivation with dark supernaturalism by this generation will eventually fade, people like this argue, so we should not worry, as the long-term effects of *Harry Potter's* witchcraft and *Twilight's* vampirism will be of no more significance in the years ahead than was the Cowboy and Indian games played by our grandparents.

As a doctor of theology with a past in exorcism, I couldn't disagree more. Mass media including the Internet, television, film, radio, and other mass communications systems have traded the Bela-Lugosi-like vampires of former years who could be vanquished with Christian symbols (and silly Abbott and Costello's Frankensteins and Mummies) for monsters of profound demonic character depicted as impervious to Christ's power. As a result, today's youth have exchanged yesterday's pigtails and pop-guns for pentagrams and blood covenants aligned with forces far stronger than former generations could have imagined. Under demonic influence, this age is systematically being seduced by a supernatural system, wherein *kosmokrators* (rulers of darkness who work in and through human counterparts) command spirits of various rank until every level of the material world, secular and religious, is touched by this influence. If we could see through the veil into this domain, we would find a world alive with good against evil, a place where the ultimate prize is the soul of this generation and where legions war for control of its cities and people.

Where Did "Creatures of the Night" Come From?

In what is considered to be one of the most important Scriptures having to do with *spiritual warfare,* the Bible lifts the curtain on this contest for man's spirit by supernatural realities in the tenth chapter of the book of Daniel. This is where the prophet Daniel is found fasting and praying for twenty-one days. He had purposed to chasten himself before the Lord in hopes that God would bless him with a revelation of Israel's future. On the twenty-first day of his fast, while he was standing on the bank of the Tigris River, an angel suddenly appeared to him and said, "From the first day that thou didst set thine heart to understand, and to chasten thyself before thy God, thy words were heard, and I am come for thy words" (Daniel 10:12).

If a messenger was dispatched from heaven "from the first day," why did it take three weeks before he arrived? The angel provided the answer by explaining that a powerful Persian demon had opposed him for twenty-one days. Not until the archangel Michael came to assist in the battle was he free to continue his journey. The book of Daniel also describes similar powers at work behind Babylon, Greece, and Rome, revealing an incredible tenet: Demons can control not only individuals, but entire societies, on a territorial scale.

In Persian theology, the spirit that opposed Daniel and his angel would have been identified as Ahriman, whose legend closely parallels the biblical fall of Lucifer. According to Persian religion, Ahriman was the death-dealer—the powerful and self-existing evil spirit from whom war and all other evils had their origin. He was the chief of the cacodemons, or fallen angels, expelled from heaven for their sins. After being kicked out of heaven, the cacodemons endeavored to settle down in various parts of the Earth, but were always rejected, and out of revenge found pleasure in tormenting the inhabitants of the Earth. Ahriman and his followers finally took up their abode in the space between heaven and the Earth, and there established their domain, called Ahriman-abad—"the abode of Ahriman." From this location, the cacodemons could intrude into, and attempt to corrupt, the governments of men.

Besides Persian Zoroastrianism and the mythos of Ahriman (and a host of other ancient origin myths for demons), scholars in the field of demonology offer various hypotheses they believe explain the origin and motivation of these malevolent spirits.

What follows is a brief examination of the seven most popular theories.

1) Demons—Spirits of a Pre-Adamic Race?

According to this field of thought, a pre-Adamic race existed on the original Earth before it became "dark and void" (Genesis 1:2). These humanlike creatures lived under the government of God and were presided over by Lucifer, the "anointed cherub that covereth" (Ezekiel 28:14). When these pre-Adamites joined Lucifer in revolt against God, a cataclysm fell upon Earth, physically destroying its inhabitants. Only the spirits of these beings survived to roam the Earth disembodied. This is offered as an explanation for why demons desire to possess humans, as they were meant to be "housed" in bodies of flesh and are uncomfortable otherwise.

2) Demons—Otherworld Beings?

Since little is known about life outside the limited sphere of our planet, a growing body of people contend that intelligent life forms may have been visiting Earth from distant worlds or parallel dimensions since the beginning of time. Some Bible expositors have picked up on this concept, blending it with traditional demonology and suggesting that demons are perhaps entities from another world (or reality) whose structure, like ultraviolet rays, are invisible to the human eye, but nonetheless distinct in atomic design.

Those holding this view note the universal consistency with which extraterrestrials and UFOs have been seen throughout history and that continue to be reported worldwide at a rate greater than six sightings per hour. Eric von Daniken's best-selling book *Chariot of the Gods?* gave international rise to this concept some years ago by speculating that Earth was visited by aliens in the distant past, leaving behind archaeological evidence that gave birth to legends and mythological gods. Unlike von Daniken, in demonology, these creatures are presented as invisible and menacing, the originators of evil supernaturalism.

3) Demons—Offspring of Angels and Women?

As far back as the beginning of time and within every major culture of the ancient world, the astonishingly consistent story is told of "gods" that descended from heaven and materialized in bodies of flesh. From Rome to Greece—and before that, to Egypt, Persia, Assyria, Babylonia, and Sumer—the earliest records of civilization tell of the era when powerful beings known to the Hebrews as "Watchers" and in the book of Genesis as the *b'nai ha Elohim* (sons of God) mingled with humans, giving birth to part-celestial, part-terrestrial hybrids known as *Nephilim*. The Bible says this happened when men began to increase on Earth and daughters were born to them. When the "sons of God" saw the beauty of the women, they took wives from among them to sire their unusual offspring. In Genesis 6:4, we read: "There were giants in the earth in those days; and also after that, when the sons of God came in unto the daughters of men, and they bare children to them, the same became mighty men which were of old, men of renown."

When this Scripture is compared with other ancient texts, including Enoch, Jubilees, Baruch, Genesis Apocryphon, Philo, Josephus, and Jasher, among others, it unfolds that the giants of the Old Testament such as Goliath were the part-human, part-animal, part-angelic offspring of a supernatural interruption into the divine order of species. The apocryphal *Book of Enoch* gives a name to the angels involved in this cosmic conspiracy, calling them "Watchers." We read:

> And I Enoch was blessing the Lord of majesty and the King of the ages, and lo! The Watchers called me—Enoch the scribe—and said to me: "Enoch, thou scribe of righteousness, go, declare to the Watchers of the heaven who have left the high heaven, the holy eternal place, and have defiled themselves with women, and have done as the children of earth do, and have taken unto themselves wives: Ye have wrought great destruction on the earth: And ye shall have no peace nor forgiveness of sin: and inasmuch as they delight themselves in their children [the Nephilim], the murder of their beloved ones shall they see, and over the destruction of their children shall they lament, and shall make supplication unto eternity, but mercy and peace shall ye not attain." (1 Enoch 10:3–8)

According to Enoch, two hundred of these powerful angels departed from "high heaven" and used women (among other raw material) to extend their progeny into mankind's plane of existence. The book of Jude describes the judgment the Watchers received for their actions, saying the "angels which kept not their first estate, but left their own habitation, he hath reserved in everlasting chains under darkness unto the judgment of the great day" (Jude 6).

Unlike these progenitor Watchers who are currently bound under darkness until the Day of Judgment, the spirits of their dead offspring, the Nephilim, continue to roam the Earth as cursed entities or demons, according to this theory.

Those holding this view also point to the historical connection between the Nephilim and the Rephaim, who were associated throughout the ancient world with demons, ghosts, hauntings, the "shades of the dead," and spirits in Sheol.

4) Demons—Spirits of Wicked Men Deceased?

This teaching, still popular with a fragment of modern theologians, seems to have its origin in early Greek mythology. The Homeric gods, who were but supernatural men, were both good and evil. The hypothesis was that the good and powerful spirits of good men rose to assume places of deity after experiencing physical death, while the evil spirits of deceased, evil men were gods, doomed to roam the Earth and its interior. At death, their spirits remained in an eternal limbo, unable to perish, yet incapable of attaining heaven. Besides Greeks, the ancient Jewish historians, Philo and Josephus, held similar views, as did many of the early Church fathers.

Hollywood often conveys this idea (that demons are the spirits of dead, wicked men) through box office hits such as *Child's Play* and *Nightmare on Elm Street*. In *Nightmare on Elm Street*, Freddy Krueger, played by actor Robert Englund, is the maniacal slasher and indestructible evil spirit of a deceased child-molester. In *Child's Play*, a doll possessed by the spirit of a deceased voodoo strangler calls upon Damballa, the serpent god, to give him the power of immortality. Warner Brothers, who, in association with Wonderland Sound and Vision, produces the popular television drama/horror series *Supernatural*, used our published work on the *strigae* (vicious owl-like affiliates of the goddess Hecate who flew through the night feeding on unattended babies and during the day appeared as simple old women) in the first season of their series in this regard. They invited us to join a panel of paranormal activity experts for the release of the fifth season. The series stars Jared Padalecki as Sam Winchester and Jensen Ackles as Dean Winchester, two brothers who, as demon hunters, often find themselves pursued by spirits of the wicked dead. While expert input is sought by the screenwriters in order to give series episodes a mode of believability, shows like *Supernatural* blend numerous religious concepts and worldviews inconsistent with orthodox faith and should not be taken seriously.

5) Demons—Fallen Angels?

Of the seven theories we are summarizing, this is the most popular among contemporary Christians. This teaching is based on the assumption that at some time in eons past, Lucifer rose up in great rebellion and declared war on the God of heaven. Somehow, he persuaded one-third of the angelic host to stand with him in insurrection (Revelation 12:4). At this point, God cast Lucifer and his rebellious angels out of heaven, at which time they became demons. Less in form and nature than they originally were, they brought darkness and chaos upon the virgin Earth. Some believe Ezekiel 28:13–19 is a record of this event:

> Thou hast been in Eden the garden of God; every precious stone was thy covering. Thou art the anointed cherub that covereth; and I have set thee so: thou was upon the holy mountain of God; thou hast walked up and down in the midst of the stones of fire. Thou was perfect in thy

ways from the day that thou was created, till iniquity was found in thee. By the multitude of thy merchandise they have filled the midst of thee with violence, and thou hast sinned: therefore I will cast thee as profane out of the mountain of God: and I will destroy thee, O covering cherub, from the midst of the stones of fire.

Isaiah 14:12–14 continues the record on Lucifer's fall:

How art thou fallen from heaven, O Lucifer, son of the morning! How art thou cut down to the ground which didst weaken the nations! For thou has said in thine heart, "I will ascend into heaven, I will exalt my throne above the stars of God: I will sit also upon the mount of the congregation, in the sides of the north: I will ascend above the heights of the clouds: I will be like the Most High." Yet thou shalt be brought down to hell, to the sides of the pit.

The apostle John records an event in the book of Revelation (12:7–9) that some believe refers to Lucifer's fall. John also tells of other angels:

And there was war in heaven: Michael and his angels fought against the dragon; and the dragon fought and his angels, And prevailed not; neither was their place found any more in heaven. And the great dragon was cast out, that old serpent called the Devil, and Satan, which deceiveth the whole world: he was cast out into the earth, and his angels were cast out with him.

6) Demons—Several of the Theories Above?

The proponents of this hypothesis believe a singular concept for the origin of "demons" is a mistake, that in fact what is routinely considered "the demonic realm" could be made up of several of the explanations above, and that this might demonstrate the hierarchy of demons as outlined in the book of Ephesians. In this view, "fallen angels" would rank above the "spirits of Nephilim" and so on, with each being part of the army of darkness. Just as privates in the United States military serve under sergeants who serve under majors, Satan's forces consist of wicked spirits (*poneria*: the mass of common demon soldiers comprising Satan's hordes) under rulers of darkness (*kosmokrators*: martial spirits that influence or administer the affairs of earthly governments) and powers (*exousia*: high-ranking officials whose modes of operation are primarily battlefield ops). Above these are principalities or archons (*arche*: brigadier generals over the divisions of Satan's hosts). Satan, who reigns as supreme commander and king, is the "prince of the powers of the air" (Ephesians 2:2).

7) Demons—None of the Above?

Some believe all of the theories above are erroneous and that demons exist only in the imagination. These note how primitive men interpreted inherent diseases such as epilepsy as demonic possession and saw volcanoes and other natural catastrophes as the manifested anger of gods. This illustrates a human psychological weakness, they say, which assigns "paranormal activity" to events that men cannot otherwise explain.

While this theory is considered incomplete by most demonologists, it is not without credible points. In addition to ailments that cause people afflicted with disorders such as schizophrenia to experience auditory hallucinations, the human imagination can be persuasive when "filling in the blanks" on unsolved mysteries, sometimes leaving people convinced that undefined activity is the presence of ghostly beings. For instance, people have reported spooky apparitions in areas where strong electromagnetic fields are discovered, suggesting to some researchers that persons who are sensitive to these fields may be confusing the effect upon them by electromagnetic frequencies (EMFs). Some years ago, scientist Vic Tandy's research into frequencies and eyeball resonation led to similar conclusions and a thesis called "Ghosts in the Machine," which was published in the *Journal of the Society for Psychical Research.* Tandy's findings outlined natural causes for certain cases of specter materialization. Using his own experience as an example, Tandy was able to show that 19 Hz standing air waves could, under some circumstances, create sensory phenomena in an open environment suggestive of a ghost. The third of Arthur C. Clarke's laws of prediction is also mirrored here, which concludes that "any sufficiently advanced technology is indistinguishable from magic."[17]

Toward a Supernatural End-Game

Regardless of the position one holds concerning the origin of demons—whether they are spirits from a pre-Adamic race, offspring of angels and women, fallen angels, or a mixture of several theories—as Carol Anne so ominously expressed in the 1982 film *Poltergeist,* "They're here." Demons and their militaristic interest in people and geography are ontological facts, according to the Bible. In the Old Testament, demons are seen as the living dynamic behind *Twilight*-like idolatry (i.e., Deuteronomy 32:17), and in the New Testament, every writer refers to their influence. Extrabiblical texts including ancient pseudepigraphical works like the first *Book of Enoch* and post-New Testament writings such as the *Didache, Ignatius' Epistle to the Ephesians,* and the *Shepherd of Hermas* agree with this concern. Early Church fathers also reinforced the belief that evil spirits not only exist everywhere around us, but unseen intermediaries—both good and evil—interlope between spiritual and human personalities at home, in church, in government, and in society. Understanding how and why this is true is defined in demonological studies including those based on the *divine council* (a term used by Hebrew and Semitic scholars to describe the pantheon of divine beings or angels who administer the affairs of heaven and Earth), where experts typically agree that, beginning at the Tower of Babel, the world and its inhabitants were disinherited by the sovereign God of Israel and placed under the authority of lesser divine beings that became corrupt and disloyal to God in their administration of those nations (Psalm 82). Following Babel, these beings quickly became idolized on Earth as gods, giving birth to the worship of "demons" (see Acts 7:41–42; Psalms 96:5; and 1 Corinthians 10:20) and the quest by fallen angels to draw mankind away from God.

Although the Bible warns against inviting such supernaturalism into one's life via fascination with the occult, the revival of ancient paganism and the experiences being drawn from them are especially seductive curiosities for people today. Sociologists understand that the public's demand for pop-media material such as we started this chapter discussing—*Twilight, New Moon, Eclipse, Ghost Hunters, Paranormal State, Psychic Kids: Children of the Paranormal,* Animal Planet's *The Haunted,* and more—may be evidence of something far deeper than today's entertainment fads; it could be indicative of a new preferred spirituality, an informal consensus toward a post-New Testament theological condition, which, unfortunately, has been helped as much by Gospel-depleted modern churches as anything else. As such, it may not be unreasonable to believe today's culture is rapidly approaching a prophetic end-times conflict known to Christians as "Armageddon": a time in which the demonic influences behind the gods and idols of *Twilight*, *The Vampire Diaries*, *True Blood*, and *Harry Potter* actually go to war with Jesus Christ. "The LORD will be terrible unto them: for he will famish all the gods of the earth" says Zephaniah 2:11 of this time. "The LORD of hosts, the God of Israel, saith; 'Behold, I will punish the...gods'" (Jeremiah 46:25). Human followers of the pagan deities will join this conflict, calling upon their idols (Revelation 9:20) to convene their powers against the Christian God, uniting with "the spirits of devils working miracles, which go forth unto the kings of the earth...to gather them to the battle of that great day...[to] a place called in the Hebrew tongue Armageddon [Megiddo]" (Revelation 16:13–14, 16).

If the world's current fascination with creatures of the night—from demons and werewolves to vampires and ghosts—is indicative of this timeframe, a deal with the devil has been struck by society and every man, woman, boy, and girl had better quickly choose whose side they are on... *because things may be about to get ugly.*

CHAPTER TWO

INTERVIEW WITH A
(MODERN) VAMPIRE

By Donna Howell and Nita Horn

(NOTE: To avoid the confusion and awkward reading flow of an entire chapter written in first-person with the pronoun "we" [as there are two authors of this chapter], all references to the authors' persons will be simply, "I.")

Children, teens, and adults alike have flocked to the nearest book retailer upon the release of every *Harry Potter* volume since the character's origin. At midnight, July 21, 2007, crowds large enough to justify the temporary installation of theme park line partitions throughout the inside of Barnes & Noble in Bend, Oregon lead all the way around the building and back and forth through the parking lot. Hundreds of fans stood in their wizard costumes, glasses, and the quintessential black lightning-bolt on their foreheads, chanting "Harry, Harry" and repeating well-known spells to their comrades while waiting in suspense to crack open the cover of J.K. Rowling's final episode. It was a memorable night for a record-breaking number, who would return home to their cozy beds and couches, and dive, eagerly and open-mindedly, into the intoxicating world of incantations, witchcraft, wizardry, and magic.[18]

Friends and neighbors gathered in common interest of werewolves, vampires, and half-human, half-vampire hybrid offspring in the sensual, tantalizing, sexual-tension-inspiring *Twilight* series, the first volume of which was a proud winner of the *Publisher's Weekly* "Best Children's Book Award" and the *School Library Journals* "Best Books" in 2005.[19] If you have somehow managed to miss all the posters, articles, sale banners, advertisements, press releases, promotions, and word-of-mouth exposures on this series, and you happen to be one of the very few who don't have some immediate level of familiarity with the series merely by title, you will likely recognize it by the cover. The brilliant contrast of the black background with the pale, white hands holding the bright, red apple (admittedly said by Stephenie Meyer to represent the "forbidden fruit" of the Book of Genesis, symbolizing the "forbidden" relationship between main characters Bella [human] and Edward [vampire], similar to the fruit of the Tree of Knowledge of Good and Evil, and Bella's deliberate choice to partake of said "forbidden fruit" by choosing to be with Edward)[20] is eye-grabbing, even amongst all other titles across the visually chaotic and colorfully competitive layout of your average local book retailer. The record-breaking opening day box office sales (on a regular Thursday night) for the latest movie to be released, *Twilight Saga: Eclipse*, was an eye-opening 24.2 million, reaching 178 million by the end of the July 4th holiday weekend (only second place in cinematic history for that weekend just under *Spiderman 2*).[21]

And why not? What's wrong with children and teens reading, dreaming, and filling their head with romanticized concepts about such content? Wouldn't the life of a wizard, werewolf, demon hybrid, vampire, or vampire's child be filled with excitement, festivity, romance, and fantasy? What's wrong with that?

What One Generation Allows in Moderation, the Next Allows in Excess

The purpose of this chapter will be to address the high disregard for the importance of traditional family values, and to help readers become aware of how far out of control some things in American culture have become in the last few decades.

Remember as you read on, that I am very aware that iconic role-models of bad or evil behavior have existed as far back in history as anyone can possibly calculate. This compilation of notes and facts has not been gathered to prove that evil never existed prior to our culture today. I would only like to bring to light that, until recently, most acts or obsessions of a strange or corrupt nature were not broadcast or carried out in public; contrarily, though they existed and were very real, they were considered shameful, and therefore happened behind closed doors. (Additionally, the details listed below represent the overall change in American culture from decade to decade *as a whole*,[22] they are not meant to classify each individual, family, or geographical area during that time.)

1900-1909:
A New and Innocent Beginning

To make my point ultimately more clear, it is important to begin by taking a moment to reflect on what life was like prior to media influence, and then break down the behavioral patterns that crept into culture gradually as a result of radio, stage, and television.

At the start of the twentieth century, American culture reflected a wholesome, healthy, modest, and honest way of living.

Women flirted and showed their availability to a man of their interest by wearing a slightly more decorated hat with more provocative ornaments, such as wax cherries or peacock feathers. In an extreme situation, they might wear shoes where the buttonhooks only climbed ankle-high instead of the standard shin-length. They sometimes participated in "unladylike" activities such as riding a bicycle or working in the fields, though you would have only seen a woman in these cases wearing a ground-length skirt. Clothes for the family were handmade by mothers until their daughters were old enough to learn to stitch. Meals were prepared in the house, and served family style, on a spotless tablecloth.

Entertainment consisted of books, community events, and of course, visiting with family. Men and women knew, understood, and had time for their spouses, resulting in a mere 0.7 percent of divorce cases throughout the entire decade.[23] People in the neighborhood baked pies for the elderly and visited them in person. Children often made their own games from fabric dolls, wooden planes and trains, and invented playful scenarios out of nothing more than their imagination and a few props. Public advertisements and posters often depicted delicate women posing with a bottled beverage or baking soda, small children sipping tea or holding flowers, and gentlemen shaking hands or building muscle with a miracle tonic.

From this decade came several notable book titles including *The Wonderful Wizard of Oz, The Call of the Wild, The Jungle,* and *Anne of Green Gables* to name a few. Many early invention concepts were drawn during these years, and technological achievements included the typewriter, portable camera, alkaline battery, and probably most memorable was the first Ford vehicle (costing the consumer seven hundred and fifty dollars and reaching a top speed of twenty-eight miles per hour), and the Orville and Wilbur "Flying Machine."

The country was founded on a belief in God. Schoolhouses would begin their day with a prayer. Business transactions were conducted between parties with an open consideration of "God's will" in the matter. "May God bless you," and similar sayings, were often heard in passing in the middle of town. People often couldn't afford the time and travel arrangements it would take to attend church more than once per week, so Sunday church was an all-day meeting focused on the Lord's good blessings and fellowship within the community. Members of the congregation prepared a large meal spread and carried it to church with them in the back of their wagons, laying it out on tables for all to share. These potlucks were a weekly event that lead to the solidified friendships and shared prayers between family, community, and friends. Everybody knew the names and faces of those in their area and relied on their neighbors for support and guidance in their daily lives, all the while visiting the sick, feeding and sheltering the needy, and most living in prayer and obedience to God.

1910-1919:
A Decade of Promise and Unforeseen Loss

When looking back to this cluster of years, one's mind is flooded with visions of loss, sadness, and death as the tragic sinking of the *RMS Titanic* was followed shortly by the even more catastrophic beginning of World War I. There have been full volumes written on the incomprehensible impact that these two historical events had on the Western world, so to try and describe the changes to culture as a result of this era in time would be impossible in this chapter. Suffice it to say that more households and communities than we could ever possibly count suffered the loss of loved ones. Hearts cried out to God on lonely nights for husbands, fathers, and sons to return home safely from war, and communities traded their happy-go-lucky, whistling tunes in for somber, hopeful hymns of protection. The "Dear God, bless this food," dinner prayer quickly became a prayer of survival in times of unfathomable misfortune. Headlines in local newspapers evolved into an everyday war and destruction update, with an ever-growing list of soldier's names who would never see their wives, mothers, and children again.

Knees bent at the bedside at night.

Children developed a faith in God beyond their years.

America was united as one nation, *under God*.

When the war was over, and those who had survived were allowed to come home, praises were sung toward the heavens and thanks were given to a faithful God as families reunited, tearfully and gratefully.

1920-1929:
The Roaring Twenties/The "Showbiz" Decade

The Roaring Twenties was a time of celebration, wealth, and excess, and it is an important decade for the purpose of this study.

Although many women outside the major cities continued to maintain more modest attire (and lifestyles) from years past, the fashion industry boomed (as a result of this eras deep increase in live stage productions and show business) with flapper dresses and other shocking apparel that allowed the entire arm, armpit, neckline, and almost the entire leg to show. Shoes no longer covered the ankle, and women bobbed their hair and took up smoking in public places. The average woman in the city wore makeup to accentuate (or completely fabricate) their facial features, living in the fantasies of the stars on the screen or stage. (Motion pictures were now being synchronized with sound.)

Entertainment exploded into daily life in the cities. Because of new exposure and advertising on the now-existing radio broadcasts, talent was being discovered and glorified nationwide. Musical performers were taking center stage, and dreams of fame and name-in-lights ignited in the hearts of youth. People laughed, dined, bought into many forms of artistic expression, and the economy thrived.

As a result of the merry, lighthearted, and carefree lifestyle that swept the nation during this "showbiz" era, a certain liberal and lurid behavior began to emerge. Cartoon pornography books called "Tijuana bibles" (drawings by mostly-unknown artists portraying popular cartoon characters, movie stars, and important political figures engaging in sexually explicit encounters) began their "under the table" circulation.[24] A new awareness for the previously harder-to-find burlesque nightclubs and gentlemen's clubs gave more opportunity for public temptation (although this kind of attraction did suffer *some* drawback in the '20s during the prohibition). Both women and men became looser with their sexuality and more open-minded to having "relationships on the side" while married. Crimes of passion made headlines, and the divorce rate grew to 1.6 percent, ensuring more broken families than before.

On Black Thursday, October 24, 1929, the stock market began its historical crash, bringing countless numbers of people to an instant, penniless status, and heralding in the start of the Great Depression.

1930-1939:
Seeking an Escape from Depression

Suicides, murders, and general acts of desperation were carried out as a result of the stock market crash. People ate from garbage cans on the street and considered themselves blessed to wrap a baby in nothing but a thin blanket with no clothes underneath. Farmlands dried up and were abandoned, adding to the wreckage of the Dust Bowl that spread like a disease across American soil. The overnight cutoff of vegetation, mixed with seemingly endless drought, led to a period of starvation that had never been seen before and hasn't been seen since in the United States. Unemployment was at an all-time high. Fathers couldn't find (or keep) jobs and mothers listened to children's growling, empty bellies as they waited in lines outside shelters for hours for sometimes only a single crust of bread for the whole family to share. Daily life was hard and stressful, and once again, we found ourselves only surviving by the grace of God.

With many hurting and struggling to stay afloat in a time remembered as devastating and depressing, movies and radio started to play a larger role in daily lives. For some, this was merely a way to keep updated on the global crises and stock market fluctuations (and other current events). For others, it had become the escapist material that fed their souls with the kind of meat you couldn't find in the best of butcher shops. With actual moving, speaking pictures on the television and thrilling tales of wonder and mystery on the radio, men, women, and children alike sighed, swooned, and felt their heart pummeling their throats with every cinematic or auditory adventure. Despite the troubles they faced, television and radio provided a cheap, wonderful diversion from the worst of times for those that had access.

As the economy slowly improved for some by the late '30s, life gradually climbed out of the daily gloom and despair (though the Great Depression was not over for the country until the mid-'40s, and often individuals effected by this financial and economic collapse lived the rest of their life in futile attempts of climbing out). Women's fashion broke away from the vaudeville style (mostly due to the elaborate and glamorous dresses worn by actresses on screen), and returned to lower hemlines for a time, though the fabrics were still suggestive, resembling that of nightwear and bedroom laces. Men's fashion was also influenced by the entertainment industry. Gone were the days of strong, military-style or Edwardian clothing, and in its absence came floods of slick, debonair zoot suits (between the '30s and '40s), the kind likely to be seen on a Tommy-Gun-sporting, cigar-chewing, no-goodnik gangster in an action film, holding up a group of lawmen with the line, "You'll neva get da money, see," just before diving into the getaway car. Children's playtime was still very innocent, though it had now begun to reflect imaginary games with plots similar to what they had heard or seen on television or radio.

Most American citizens still believed in, and prayed to, the Christian God for help and solace in times of need, but with the rise of hope for a better life through fantasies as depicted on television and in movies, there were those that traded time on their knees in prayer for a good show.

The First Cinematic Vampire

Noteworthy to this chapter (aside from the glaring evidence that our country had already begun to fantasize about, and mirror the behavior of, fictitious characterizations from the media) is the first English-speaking, sound-synchronized film with a plot surrounding a vampire. The movie *Dracula*, starring Bela Lugosi, was released into theaters in 1931. I could go on and on describing, in tedious detail, all the facts about this film that I have researched and the mind-boggling and hard-to-believe effects this (totally corny) movie had on Americans after its release, and compare those facts to those of modern day, but that is a book entirely by itself. To summarize:

> When the film finally premiered at the Roxy Theatre in New York on Feb. 12, 1931, newspapers reported that members of the audiences fainted in shock at the horror on screen. This publicity...helped ensure people came to see the film, if for no other reason than curiosity. *Dracula* was a big gamble for a major Hollywood studio to undertake. In spite of the literary credentials of the

source material, it was uncertain if an American audience was prepared for a serious full length supernatural chiller. Though America had been exposed to other chillers before…this was a horror story with no comic relief or trick ending that downplayed the supernatural.[25]

In this one paragraph alone, we can see the following things:

1. Americans in the 1930s were absolutely terrified to the point of fainting upon viewing Bela Lugosi's vampire depiction on the big screen. (To the modern-day, twenty-first-century moviegoer, this seems downright silly.)
2. Because frightening visuals on screen were in their infancy, the visual stimulation needed to activate fear within the imaginative human brain via the movie screen was also in its infancy. (Nobody in the movie business had yet been challenged to "raise the bar" of visual fear stimulation in the movies and make something "more frightening" than the other films had been, because there was not, as of yet, much basis of comparison.)
3. The publicity of a "film so scary, people are fainting" stirred such a curiosity within people that it drove them to the theaters to see for themselves. (It has always been human nature to chase after a thrill.)
4. It was uncertain that Americans were ready for something so scary. (When would we be "ready" for something so scary, and whose job is it to determine when we [as a country, population, individual, put whatever label you want on it] would be ready? The movies decided we were ready, so, ready or not, we "were ready.")

5. When the supernatural or paranormal is not "played
    down" by "comic relief" (or a *Scooby Doo*, kid-in-a-
    mask, "trick ending"), a further sense of fearful reality is
    implied in the plot of a film that sticks with the viewer,
    probably, in most cases, past the credits at the end of
    the film. If something ever scared me so bad that I had
    fainted as a result, I would likely carry it with me for
    a long time. (Now that it had been decided that the
    viewers of 1931 were ready for this level of stimulation,
    you can clearly see how, through a short online search
    of film history, it was quickly decided that they would
    soon be ready for the next level of visual fear stimulation
    that *would* "raise the bar" and require a movie to be
    "more frightening." In later films, just as "frightening,
    yet comical" wasn't enough stimulation until the comic
    relief was stripped from the plot in 1931, "frightening"
    by itself would someday no longer be enough
    stimulation for the human brain. Sex quickly became a
    requirement.)

While we are on the subject of the human brain, I would like
to briefly share a piece of science with you:

The brain is not the unchanging organ that we might
imagine. It not only goes on developing, changing and,
in some tragic cases, eventually deteriorating with age, it
is also substantially shaped by what we do to it and by
the experience of daily life. When we say "shaped", we're
not talking figuratively or metaphorically; we're talking
literally. At a microcellular level, the infinitely complex
network of nerve cells that make up the constituent parts

of the brain actually change in response to certain experiences and stimuli.

The brain, in other words, is malleable—not just in early childhood but right up to early adulthood, and, in certain instances, beyond. The surrounding environment has a huge impact both on the way our brains develop and how that brain is transformed into a unique human mind.[26]

1940–1949:
Seeking Distraction from World War II

The 1940s brought the end of the Great Depression (on a national level, not on an individual basis), and just as the world started to become an easier, cushier place to live again, World War II began. Again, Americans fell to their knees in prayer. Again, a time of extreme survival slapped our country (and many others) with a cold serving of hard-to-digest reality just as things started to look promising. Again, women and children cried out in loneliness for their husbands and fathers.

Again, we were a united nation, under God.

However, movies (and radio shows) became an even greater importance during this time. Such dramas as, *In Which We Serve*, *Casablanca*, and *The Way Ahead*, gave a more momentous portrayal of war, taking seriously the trials military families would face, while offering hope and inspiration through their patriotic imagery of national unity and social cohesion within the context of war. Comedies such as Abbot and Costello's *Keep 'Em Flying* and the Three Stooges' *Boobs in Arms* brought humor, relief, and laughter to the constant and inescapable truth of the draft, with memorable quotes such as, "'Greetings little shut-in. Don't you weep or sigh. If you're not out by Christmas, you'll be out the Fourth of July!' N'yuk n'yuk n'yuk!"[27] Radio programs featured such personalities as the Andrews Sisters, who brought many tired and weary soldiers (and Allied forces) through WWII with their swing and boogie-woogie-style "victory" songs. (These songs were aired and performed in person in Army, Navy, Marine, and Coast Guard bases, as well as war zones, hospitals, and munitions factories.)

The Big Screen—"Fantastical"? Raising the Bar?

If one was seeking to distract themselves from the subject of war and tragedy entirely, they may find it difficult to accomplish such a task with that subject being the first thing on everyone's mind in any social situation in WWII. (How often since then have people become desperate with the circumstances of their life, sometimes merely out of boredom, and sought a temporary escape into a different life through fantasies on screen, radio, or in books? Isn't that what we all do? You might even say, "That's what they're there for." Hmm… Let's continue.) Nonetheless, once again, the movie screen delivered. Not only was the still-young, revolutionary "world of media" a natural go-to for temporary happy-fixes (like a drug perhaps?), but something else started to happen around this time. To be brief: "The strictures of wartime also **brought an interest in more fantastical subjects**…including *The Man in Grey* and *The Wicked Lady*…and films like *Here Comes Mr. Jordan, Heaven Can Wait, I Married a Witch* and *Blithe Spirit*… [Also produced during this time was] a series of atmospheric and influential…horror films, some of the more famous examples being *Cat People, Isle of the Dead* and *The Body Snatcher*"[28] (bold added).

These titles above are only to name a few that resulted when the world needed a fantasy. However, since this list was already so conveniently provided by *Wikipedia*, let's elaborate a little on what occurred here. Although some movies did exist from the earliest stages of film-making on the subject of bad behavior, the paranormal, and the supernatural, there is a significant increase in moviegoers' interest in these subjects when the need to "escape" or become "distracted from" their everyday lives is desired. The more people "need" to fantasize, the more the industry responds by "raising the bar" of the purchased fantasy.

Suddenly, movies with strange or brooding plots or focus that would have been only minimally successful during happy times become hugely successful. (Such plots as the haunting spirits of dead wives [*Blithe Spirit*]; women who can't be intimate with their partners because they may turn into half-human, half-feline hybrid species [*Cat People*]; cruel and pre-planned adultery and infidelity [*The Man in Grey* and *The Wicked Lady*]; people visiting Hades to discuss their afterlife in the underworld [*Heaven Can Wait*]; ancient witches who were burned at the stake, and whose ashes were buried beneath a tree to imprison their evil spirits, coming back from the dead to marry and then torment the descendants of their original Salem-witch-trial-persecutors [*I Married A Witch*]; a surgeon who hires a cabman to dig up graves to provide him with fresh corpses for dissection [*The Body Snatcher*]; and people dying one by one as a deadly plague breaks out near the location of a *vorvolakas*, a kind of vampire [*Isle of the Dead*].)[29]

Nobody can deny that the media began introducing more "fantastical" plots in comparison to previous decades around this time. The bar was raised. The people were hungry for a bigger, better escape, a heavier dose of the mental drug called "media," and the fantasies delivered.

Still notable, however, is the *representation* of such material. Morally concerning *ideas* and *implications* could be brought very openly into a plot during the movies of that time, and yet there was nothing specifically alluring or glorified about the way it was represented. Monsters, vampires, creatures of the night, and weirdoes that dissected people were NOT attractive or sexy; nor were they just "confused" or "brooding" "good guys at the core." (Also note that, usually, any seductive power they held over people was only by the supernatural powers they were given as said monster, not because they were seductive by nature; I have seen many "Come to me my dear" scenes where some bad guy wiggles his long, pointy fingers at a defenseless woman who follows his order against her will because she physically cannot stop herself. This is not the same "power" or "seduction" over someone being depicted in today's modern vampire or monster flick.) "Sex scenes" began and ended with the simple candle blow-outs while the camera directed itself to a slow fade-out past the curtains and some campy, "I'll see you in the morning Frank," "Perhaps sooner than that, Darling," conversation exchange, and then the movie blipped to the next day or "later that night," skipping over the intimacy entirely. Scenes of graphic violence were implied, but the camera angles always switched just in time to divert from the impending neck-breaking or stab scene. Roles of bad behavior (supernatural or otherwise) almost always ended wherein the responsible party were made to face justice and punished for their wrong-doing by death, the justice system, or being given an ironic taste of their own medicine. The Christian God was never portrayed as less powerful as, or not effective against, the bad guys.

All in all, despite the evolution during this period of cinematic history, an overall respect for God, modesty, decency, and reserved behavior was still present in film.

1950-1959:
The Crooners and Their "Mini-Me"s

Two words: Elvis. Monroe.

Parents weren't crazy about the rock and roll singin', hip-swingin' "hound dog" at first. Yet, slowly over a period of years, through his charm and electric stage presence, parents could no longer continue to resist their teenager's tireless requests for his albums and movies. In comparison to modern times, Elvis is nothing but a completely innocent, charming, and absolutely fun historical figure whose iconic paraphernalia surrounds such themes as soda shops, sock hops, and poodle skirts. At the peak of his popularity, though, there were mothers that covered their daughters' eyes to "shield them" from the sinful, lustful, dance moves that he so shamelessly performed, all the while shakin' to a worldly rock and roll beat. Teen girls wanted to date him and teen boys wanted to be him. Within only a few months of his first appearances in the media, little Elvis look-alikes popped up all over the place and lowered their voices, spoke with one lip crooked and hips loose, and ruled the school with each pomaded hair in the perfect "swoop." (People still follow his influence today...years after his death. It just goes to show what a powerful influence on society can really become.)

For the more mature audiences, Monroe packed a wallop. If you were a woman, she either offended you with her ostentatious and brazen sexuality, or you donned a similar blonde, wavy 'do and thick eyeliner and spoke in seductive tones to "keep up with the times." If you were a man, you likely found it almost impossible not to look (out of temptation or shear shock) when passing the famous subway-grating-blows-the-skirt-up photo that has become the staple image locked in our memories of the lethally flamboyant actress. Either way, she definitely had a strong impact on our culture and helped to set the standard that many celebrities would follow, therefore also influencing our country further. Her nude appearance in *Playboy Magazine* was only two years ahead of another well-known sexual icon: Bettie Page. (Bettie Page is considered to be one of the main role models behind today's punk, gothic, and vintage fashion styles worn primarily by teens.)

The Latter Half of the Century

As we approach the later decades of the twentieth century, much less need be said about the steady change of culture, for two reasons: first, the general public has much more familiarity with the latter part of the century and the role the media played in culture; second, the pattern of people mirroring the media in fashion and behavior and becoming rapidly desensitized from one "shock" to the next in our culture as a result of the fantastical developments in the media has been well established by this point in the chapter. Let's speed things up.

Bewitched and The Beatles

Probably the most eye-opening happenings in and around the '60s to paint a clear picture of how much society really had changed were the show *Bewitched,* which single-handedly introduced the idea of a "good witch" (and an attractive one) and this famous quote by The Beatles' member John Lennon, regarding their worldwide fame: "Christianity will go," Lennon said. "It will vanish and shrink. I needn't argue about that; I'm right and I will be proved right. We're more popular than Jesus now."[30] Clearly, when a music group is "more popular than Jesus," we have arrived at a time when the media has dominated the world beyond the wildest dreams of someone living in the potluck Sundays lifestyle at the beginning of the century. Granted, there were many religious groups and activists that rejected The Beatles after Lennon's offensive statement, but the idea that a performer felt comfortable to say that in an interview tells a lot about what our country had become in comparison to what it was.

The Exorcist

In 1973, we saw the release of *The Exorcist*, which was the forefather of countless other horror movie titles well-known for their blasphemous scenes and overall disregard for the power of God. Bela Lugosi (and his collaborators in the making of the *Dracula* depiction of 1931) chose not to make fangs a part of his Dracula costume. If you watch the movie from beginning to end, you will see this for yourself. His character is 100 percent the full-fledged granddaddy of all vampires, and yet he doesn't even sport fangs. The moviemakers of 1931 evidently thought that the movie would be frightening and edgy enough without them. Were they correct in that assumption? I believe the fainting audiences would attest to that (as addressed earlier in this chapter). Now, here we are in 1973 (only a mere forty-two years later, a short time considering the fluctuation of an entire nation's culture), where demon-possessed, twelve-year-old girl, Regan, is depicted as bathed in her own blood from stabbing herself between the legs with a crucifix while shouting an exclamation so blasphemous and vulgar (including the name of Jesus, Himself) that I can't even include the words in this writing. When the girl's mother tried to intervene on her daughter's behalf, the possessed child grabbed her mother by the head and, with supernatural force, pressed her mother's face into the bleeding area and then slapped her across the room, just before Regan turned her head 360 degrees to face her mother again and speak the following in a strong, male voice: "Do you know what she did? Your [expletive] daughter?"[31]

This time, not only did audiences faint at the shocking and frightening display, they vomited in the halls of the theater, tore at curtains, damaged doors, and even trampled the landscapes of nearby buildings. The following quote was taken directly off of the Warner Brothers website:

> "My janitors are going bananas wiping up the vomit," complains Frank Kveton, manager of the United Artists Cinema 150 in Oakbrook. Kenton [sic] also has had to replace doors and curtains damaged by unruly crowds, and even relandscape the McDonalds plaza a cross the street where moviegoers park their cars. "I've never seen anything like it in the 24 years I've been working in movie theaters," says H. Robert Honahan, division manager at the ABC/Plitt theaters in Berkeley. "We've had two to five people faint here every day since this picture opened. More men than women pass out, and it usually happens in the evening performance, after the crucifix scene involving—"[32]

I have intentionally cut off the quote above. The original quote included a term that does not need to be in this book for the reader to get the idea, especially since I already described the scene in focus. I only wish that I had the time and space to really address, at length, the effects the release of this movie had on American culture (and the spooky events that happened in association to the making, and premier, of this film). Yet, without digressing from the point, one can easily see that the movies once again decided we were ready for the next level of horror, and the bar was once again raised. (Despite this raising of the bar, however, *The Exorcist* is now simply a classic on the movie shelves with many others, as we wait with baited breath for the next thrill to once again exceed our expectations.)

Where Will We Be in a Century from Now?

As shown above, since the start of the twentieth century, cultural evolution hasn't stopped for anyone to take a breath. One shock after another after another has fallen into the archives of history, as the ever-steady desensitization of society has paved the way for the next gravely worrisome social issue to also evaporate into nothing but a memory of yesterday's statistics. The greatest fears of concerned parents traveling to church in their covered wagons for potluck Sunday in the year 1900 would have seemed like nothing compared to the woman shielding her daughter's eyes from the worldly and lustful dance moves of Elvis Presley. The modern-day father concerned about his self-proclaimed, thirteen-year-old vampire daughter only *wishes* he had Elvis' hip-swingin' to worry about.

Modern Vampires

Everything I have said up to this juncture, points to a very alarming phenomenon. Some readers may be aware of this, and others may not: Modern vampires exist, and they are seducing our youth. One search online will refer you to a cesspool of links and websites connecting you (or your daughter or son) to well-established vampire covens anywhere in the world.

Albeit, they don't turn into bats or mist, they don't "infect" humans with the soul-sucking bite on the neck as depicted in books and movies, and they aren't afraid of garlic. However, they absolutely *do* drink human blood, wear fangs (permanent implants by a cosmetic dentist [or "fangsmith"], but they are often used to bite), hang out in places away from sunlight, sleep in coffins, and participate in dark rituals such as astral projection. Most importantly, they do acknowledge themselves (often quite openly) as vampires and are accepting new young recruits everyday with open arms.

When I first started to see actual cases of people claiming to be vampires, I originally thought it nothing more than a cliché gang of confused gothic kids trying to make a statement to society by wearing dark clothes and false fangs. However, as I searched online and read more information (available everywhere) about the modern vampire, I realized that, despite what reality may be for any one vampire on a case-by-case basis, many of them truly believe themselves to be a bona fide creature of the night. Donors, known among most vampire subcultures as "Swans," are happy to join in a bloodletting encounter for the sanguinarius (blood-drinking) family by baring various body parts to razorblades, scalpels, and sharp teeth, but the most common is letting blood flow through a needle in the vein of the arm and into some kind of ritualistic wineglass for the vampire's feeding.

In October of 2008, Tyra Banks invited several real vampires on her show[33] in an episode called "Vampires: Tyra Investigates the Vampire Culture." (The episode is available online on several websites, including YouTube.)[34] After watching Don Henrie, also known among his circles as "The Emperor," share details of his blood-drinking lifestyle with Tyra (and a clip was shown from his circle in which human blood was drained from the arm of a young girl and ingested by Don Henrie), I found myself rethinking my theory that vampires are a myth. A quick search online about real vampires rendered many videos and articles proving my suspicion about the "modern vampire" too true for comfort. "Like Dracula and other literary vampires, some traditions of modern vampires drink blood, either animal or human, although human is preferred. They claim they need blood to make up for a deficiency of proper energy processing within the body."[35] Additionally, the majority of them are very young. Websites all over the internet reflect this. "The majority of modern vampires are teenagers and young adults...they tend to see vampires as 'everything the young adult is not and everything they aspire to be,' such as being 'suave, sophisticated, certain of himself [or herself], rooted in history, poised to take the future with neither fear nor reluctance, self-possessed, sexual, powerful...not possessed by doubts, not burdened with conscience, cool and resourceful, supremely intelligent and, best of all, immortal'"[36] (brackets in original).

Not only do they exist, but they are being very well excepted into society today; not only are they being excepted into society, they're being glorified as celebrities! Real modern vampires are making guest appearances on talk shows, landing featured interviews in high-profile magazines, and developing flashy websites to give testimonials of their awakening experiences. Any young person lured in by the glamour of such media as *Twilight* and *True Blood* these days have an easy-access list of ways to find themselves a part of this ever-growing community.

They're Hot—They're Sexy—They're Undead

It didn't take an enormous amount of research to connect the vampire appeal to the subject of sex. "This focus on sex and sexuality stems from vampire literature. In fact, sexual attraction was the most frequent response in a survey conducted among a group of 574 college and high school participants, where the participants were asked what they found most appealing about vampires and vampire literature."[37]

The cover of the *Rolling Stone Magazine* September 2010 issue[38] made one of the strongest statements I have seen in a long time, and it accomplished such a task from every major newsstand in the country. The magazine hasn't exactly been shy about its cover design in the past, having already released several previous issues with fully nude, strategically posed celebrities. However, this one had more than just the sex appeal. *True Blood* stars Anna Paquin, Stephen Moyer, and Alexander Skarsgård may not have known, or perhaps didn't care, how many people would be affected by their stirring display. Happily, they tossed their clothing aside and hugged their nude bodies together, Moyer's right hand cupping Paquin's left breast, Skarsgård's chest pressed into her other, suggesting among other things a *ménage à trois* and once again, strategic poses just barely obscuring genitalia from view. The nudity, by itself, was far more risqué than other nudes the magazine had featured before. The fact that the actors were dripping in what was characterized to be fresh, human blood added to the offense for many. "It's the cover controversy some say goes one step too far... Fans of the series say the cover is an accurate reflection of the show...but *E!*'s Ryan Seacrest asks whether or not the stars have gone over the line. He points out *Rolling Stone* is not *Hustler Magazine*, and that's concerning because kids can buy it in stores."[39]

At the bottom/left of the cover, the words, "True Blood: They're Hot—They're Sexy—They're Undead," make very clear the popular connection between sex and vampirism. If, however, one had not yet arrived at that conclusion based on the cover alone, the article would be sure to fill in the blanks. "If we go from a base level, vampires create a hole in the neck where there wasn't one before... It's a de-virginization—breaking the hymen, creating blood and then drinking the virginal blood. And there's something sharp, the fang, which is probing and penetrating and moving into it. So that's pretty sexy. I think that makes vampires attractive."[40] (Other forms of sexual deviation within the show, too graphic to describe in this book and which would shock many parents, is pushed way past the limits of decency in many of the television series including werewolf gang rape scenes, necrophilia, intercourse while blood-feeding, etc.)

Join Us... We're a Family...

Assuming that you don't already have real vampire acquaintances to ask, think back to every depiction of vampires you have ever seen, heard, or read. Notice how they almost always talk about the "family"? I can't think of a single flick in history where the leader or recruiting vampire character didn't lure the victim in at some point in the story by appealing to their sense of need for a tight family setting. Like a gang, vampire "families" stick together. You pick on one, you pick on the family. For the real vampires in the twenty-first century, often coming from broken or estranged families themselves, they are all the more willing to listen to, be there for, be close to, and welcome in the new family member. In a world where even a family with the best intentions to know one another is still going here, running there, talking on the phone, texting, checking email, etc., a feeling of separation can still manifest itself, especially for the youth who have influences all around them and don't always feel that their family will understand the way a group of dark, brooding people will who are extending the open ear and hand of friendship.

Speaking from personal experience (author Donna Howell, in this case), my family was extremely close my entire life. I went through a period around the time of the sixth or seventh grade where I truly believed that none of them understood me. I fantasized several times about running away. Now that I am an adult, I look back, and I'm being perfectly honest when I say that I only felt alone because I was bored, a little more mature and analytical than the average kid so my friends often didn't think like I did, I sought after a bigger thrill than the typical afternoon at home, and the friends I did have had the bad habit of getting together and sharing their depressing, adolescent "nobody understands me, I think I'll eat worms" routine, which rubs off on the most sincere of youth after a while. At this time and in my area, the go-to for kids who felt alone and disconnected from their family was the Wicca and New Age circles. Thank God (literally) that when I was welcomed by them with open arms and befriended by them, I thanked them for their friendship, but something in my gut (which I believe to be the deep instillation of biblical teachings all those one-on-one days from my parents) told me to keep them at a distance. Parents: "And these words, which I command thee this day, shall be in thine heart: And **thou shalt teach them diligently unto thy children, and shalt talk of them when thou sittest in thine house, and when thou walkest by the way, and when thou liest down, and when thou risest up**" (Deuteronomy 6:6–7, bold added).

Interview with a Vampire

During the research for this chapter, I stumbled upon many social websites for real vampires to meet and mingle online. Desperate for the real story from the night crawlers themselves, I invited several chat opportunities with young "vamps." From the beginning, I was honest with them, letting them know that I was researching the change in American culture, and that I was not a vampire. One after another, I chatted with people who claimed to be between the ages of twelve and thirty, and who had stories ranging anywhere from "I was bit on the neck and I have no soul" to "I'm regular, just like you, but I drink blood." Although their stories varied intensely (some were raised in a Christian church by Christian parents and attended church regularly and others had parents who practiced witchcraft and drank blood at the dinner table), one thing remained the same case after case: they felt rejected or misunderstood by family and/or society, and felt welcomed by "friends" into their darker lives and new "families."

I asked many of them what the appeal had been for them prior to their initiation, and that list was consistent in each case and dead-on accurate to my suspicions. Other than the obvious draw of sharing your misunderstood life with those that understand and have dark secrets and problems of their own, the following things were attractive: Today's modern vampire has no shame and answers to no one. Vampires have gone from being inferior, damned, subhuman creatures of the night hunted by mad mobs with pitchforks to superior beings who no longer have to hide. They're macho. They're cool. They're envied by many young people. They're faster, stronger, and physically perfect, shedding away the mortal imperfections of their days as a human, not sharing in the weaknesses that mankind suffers for merely being mortal such as cancer, sickness, loss of loved ones, and here's a biggie, imperfect bodies. (Whether it's true or not, many of the stories I heard from these chat sessions, and several of the online testimonies on vampire sites, claimed that after they discovered what they were meant to be and officially became a vampire, they lost all their weight or their cancer disappeared or they believe they truly "became immortal," etc. If they are giving themselves over to dark influences, the changes they face after their initiation doesn't surprise me at all. They are dealing with powerful, deceptive forces that can mimic miracles.)

More frightening than anything else, there was the perk of obtaining eternal life without accountability to God (everlasting life without a SAVIOR?).

Because online chat isn't the utmost reliable and verifiable way of gathering truthful details and facts, I will not spend a lot of time regaling all of the conversations I had (most of which were webcam friendly, so I could see the young gothic on my end, though I chose to keep my webcam off). However, one girl in particular (we'll call her "Vamp"), age twenty-seven, looked very normal to me. She was a pretty, thin brunette with a natural, no-fangs smile and no makeup, and whose desk and living room were decorated with pink flowers and posters of Broadway musicals. If I had met this girl in public, I would have never been able to tell she was a self-proclaimed vampire. Open-minded to telling me anything I wanted to know (and less vulgar than many others had been), in a four-hour chat session, I discovered that she was ten years old when her "awakening" took place.

Her whole life prior had been "haunted" by the spirits of dead people or lost souls of the spirit world (which she can still see and hear). She told me that she hung out with another girl down the road who seemed like a normal girl. She liked to play with dolls and stuffed animals. One night when she was spending the night with said friend, the girl started acting very strange and mature, "like a forty-year-old woman all of a sudden or something." Friend approached her, gave her a hug, and told her she was "one of the few." Awestruck and captivated by Friend's odd and "strangely calming" behavior, Vamp hugged Friend and remained still. A sharp pain surged in her shoulder, caused by a stab with a knitting needle. Instead of freaking out, Vamp waited patiently while Friend drank her blood. Vamp said, "After that, I don't really remember what happened. I just woke up the next morning and I had a strange, new sensitivity to blood. I can smell it on other humans, and it makes it very hard to be close to people."

As the conversation continued, she shared with me that when she was a little girl, she tried to "get help" with the "hauntings" she had been having, but nobody would believe her and she eventually started talking back, initially in an attempt to rid herself of these spirits, but eventually to help them when they no longer posed a threat to her life. "I had read several books about helping those poor souls stuck in the afterlife, and I figured I may as well be useful, ya know?" Her family was terribly dysfunctional and she never felt close to anyone, and when she tried to gain assistance from a local church, they welcomed her until she shared a few secrets with a woman at the church, and then they "cast me out and the demons with me. That's what they said. I was 'possessed.' I have never believed I'm possessed though. I just hear and see things." After her "awakening," she left her family almost completely, and they didn't stop her. At the age of ten, she basically lived with this other family who didn't fear her spiritual-world contact, and drank blood from them and their "Black Swan" donors on a regular basis.

When Vamp met her husband, she didn't know him for long before she decided to level with him and tell him she was a vampire. When I asked whether that was appealing to him or not, she explained that "at first, he didn't know how to react, but then on one of our earlier dates, we got together and watched a bunch of vampire movies and after a while he started looking at me differently from across the couch. The first time I drank from him, it was very sexual." They have been married for several years now, and she drinks from him regularly (he is not a vampire).

I asked if she needed human blood to live, and she seemed honest enough: "No, that's all the make-believe stuff you hear about in the movies. I need it to get through the day, but I wouldn't starve to death without it. If I go two or three weeks without human blood, I have absolutely no energy. Blood is like coffee or an energy drink. Shortly after drinking, I perk back up to my normal self and I can accomplish things again, but also, there's something spiritually gratifying about the feeding. Sometimes it's the drinking in itself that I need, not so much the effects of the blood." To clarify, I asked her about all the other movie-related clichés. She confirmed that real modern vampires do not turn into bats or mist or have magical powers over other people, and "the biting on the neck thing is just a corny deal. Some do it for the thrill or the closeness, but there is no infectious bite that converts an unwilling person into a vampire. We're not immortal and we're not afraid of crosses and all that garbage. We are just regular, human people with unique needs." However, like many others, she did reveal that her awakening led to the ability to smell blood in other humans, and she suddenly noticed that she sunburns very easily (once again, changes that do not surprise me when you open yourself up to dark influences).

Lastly, as I was wrapping things up, I asked her if she would have ever "awakened" another person the way she had been awakened at the age of ten by her neighbor. She answered, "No, certainly not. I would wait until they were at least sixteen. Then, if I sensed they were one of us, I would ask them if they wanted to be awakened. If they did, I would awaken them, but only then." When asked if she was happy she had been "awakened," she merely said, "No. I would give anything in the world to be normal right now. I don't want to hear spirits anymore, and although I enjoy drinking blood, I wish I could feel I had more of a choice. Espresso tastes better anyway, haha. Seriously though, I'm miserable being who I am right now, and my [vampire] family is, too. I can't think of any one of us that have ever been happy. It's too late for us now, though."

I wish someone would have responded to Vamp's cries for help early on, but as Keith Green so articulately put it in his song, "The world is sleeping in the dark / that the Church just can't fight / 'cause *it's asleep* / *in the light*."[41] Some readers might be thinking that because this was merely a chat session, Vamp could have made this whole thing up. Possibly so. Yet, for all *she* knew, I could have been a sixteen-year-old girl looking to be "awakened" myself, and she was giving me all kinds of tips on how to go about it. Whether her story was 100 percent true or not, this girl (poor girl if her story is true) represents a predator online that your family can easily meet for free. No registration required.

They *are* out there.

Blood Is Currency in the Spiritual World

When Christ instructed His disciples at the Last Supper to eat of His flesh and drink of His blood in "remembrance" of Him, He used bread and wine, not actual flesh and blood. Getting straight to the point, why would He do that? Jesus, in the testimony of His ultimately sacrificial death, could have easily opened a vein and tore small pieces of flesh and given His disciples real blood to drink and flesh to eat. It was nothing in comparison to the amount of blood and flesh He would willingly lose upon being flogged and hung on the cross in the hours to come, and He knew that.

In Ephesians 1:7, Hebrews 9:12, Romans 3:24, and dozens of other places in the New Testament we are told that Christ, through the shedding of His blood, "redeemed" us (same meaning of word "redemption" in Old Testament). This is the Greek word *apolytrōsis* and it means to purchase or pay a ransom, thus His blood was the currency used to pay a necessary price. Strong's Greek Concordance describes this word as meaning: 1) a releasing effected by payment of ransom; 2) redemption, deliverance; and 3) liberation procured by the payment of a ransom. *Barnes' Notes on the Bible* addresses Galatians 3:13 ("Christ hath redeemed us from the curse of the law…") and shows how it had a specific meaning of "purchase" as opposed to a general meaning of "purchase" otherwise used in the Bible:

> Christ hath redeemed us—The word used here εξηγόρασεν *exegorasen* is not that which is usually

employed in the New Testament to denote redemption. That word is λυτρόω *lutroo*. The difference between them mainly is, that the word used here more usually relates to a purchase of any kind; the other is used strictly with reference to a ransom. The word used here is more general in its meaning; the other is strictly appropriated to a ransom. This distinction is not observable here, however, and the word used here is employed in the proper sense of redeem. It occurs in the New Testament only in this place, and in Galatians 4:5; Ephesians 5:16; Colossians 4:5. It properly means, to purchase, to buy up; and then to purchase anyone, to redeem, to set free. Here it means, that Christ had purchased, or set us free from the curse of the Law, by his being made a curse for us. On the meaning of the words redeem and ransom, see my notes at Romans 3:25; Isaiah 43:3, note; compare 2 Corinthians 5:21.[42]

BLOOD EQUALS CURRENCY IN THE SPIRITUAL WORLD. The antithesis then would be any way by which occultism uses blood for making an oath or otherwise securing favor with the dark side. We are commanded not to partake of the lifeblood: "But flesh with the life thereof, which is the blood thereof, shall ye not eat" (Genesis 9:4); "And whatsoever man there be of the house of Israel, or of the strangers that sojourn among you, that eateth any manner of blood; I will even set my face against that soul that eateth blood, and will cut him off from among his people. For the life of the flesh is in the blood: and I have given it to you upon the altar to make an atonement for your souls: for it is the blood that maketh an atonement for the soul. Therefore I said unto the children of Israel, No soul of you shall eat blood, neither shall any stranger that sojourneth among you eat blood" (Leviticus 17:10–12).

When vampires drink of real lifeblood, what exactly are they "purchasing"? This kind of partaking of blood is a blatant demonization of the Holy Communion at the Last Supper of Jesus Christ, where "spiritually" we partake of his body and blood. When a young guy or girl, mesmerized by the human/vampire relationship in stories like *Twilight*, partake of the blood (or donate blood) in a real setting, do they even think of such things?

Candy Blood Bags and Bottles of "Human Blood" Beverages

"Train up a child in the way he should go: and when he is old, he will not depart from it" (Proverbs 22:6). On an immediate level, this verse makes a strong parenting calculation. A secondary point in the verse is also clear: Whatever you "train" your child to be when they're young is likely what they will be when they grow up. Even if you do not have children of your own, you are, right now, an influence on somebody who is watching what you do, and what you support. In addition to turning your cell phone off once in a while and KNOWING YOUR FAMILY (and friends), you have a duty to be careful of how loosely you handle certain potentially dangerous things of this world. A candy blood bag or a bottle of "human blood" beverage, available right this minute in candy stores and shopping malls all across the United States, inspires a number of different reactions. Of course, many just scoff and say it's gross. Others say it's just a harmless toy. Perhaps *today*, that might be all it is. I think it's quite alarming and disgusting to be honest. As you can see by the information given in the first half of this chapter, what is harmless yesterday is tomorrow's out-of-control reality.

Where do you draw the line between too overprotective and too open-minded? So much depends on the person in question and your relationship to them. Balance and prayerful consideration is needed in each case, and at the risk of sounding redundant, knowing and being involved with those important to you is the key to keeping balance. Clearly, most people will still grow up to be healthy, regular adults if they watched the Count on *Sesame Street* as a child counting cookies on a plate with the Cookie Monster and Big Bird. However, buying a candy blood bag for a child to go home to their bedrooms, snip the tip off, put their plastic vampire fangs in, and fantasize while the fake blood drips slowly from the pretend IV bag into their mouth, is different. If you "train" your child in the ways of healthy eating and fitness, it's less likely that you will be "training" tomorrow's couch potato. If you "train" your child in the ways of the vampire, what do you think they will become? Even if their infatuation with vampires fades and reveals itself (thank goodness) to be nothing more than a kick they were on, by supporting that "kick," you have given their next unhealthy phase a major boost. You may not stand in public with picket signs and point a judgmental finger at others for what they do (trust me, there's enough of that going around right now), but even if you do it quietly and one-on-one with your family, think twice about what you allow in your house (monitor your internet!) and around your children, and remember that your values and balance will be inherited to a large degree. You always have the right to say, "As for me and my house, we will serve the LORD" (Joshua 24:15b).

Amish Vampires?

Living in Missouri, I see the Amish quite frequently. Interested in their lives (and appreciative of their outstanding hand-made furniture), I did some reading on them.

In the book, *The Amish In Their Own Words: Amish Writings from 25 Years of* Family Life *Magazine*,[43] compiled by Brad Igou, the beliefs and traditions of the Amish are explained. One who reads this whole book will see that, collectively, Amish beliefs are widely misunderstood. Overall, it's not the surface-level "electricity and colorful clothing is sinful" summary that most people quickly proclaim. It's more the fact that if they strictly maintain order and tradition within their communities and forbid the use of modern technology, keeping only to modestly covering clothing in tasteful or natural colors, etc., they will preserve godliness and space between their community and the temptations of this world. It might seem silly or perhaps a little "overboard" to most people who see them struggling to compete for the road in their covered wagons on a hot day while we cruise in our air-conditioned cars, but essentially, it makes sense. We have *become* the world they will never be a part of, and if they allow a light bulb today, it will be a TV tomorrow, because *what one generation allows in moderation, the next allows in excess.*

In a world without television or movies, no beepers or texts interrupting their dinner, no internet, no porn, no young girls letting their "goods" hang out the bottom of a miniskirt, etc., all the while handing down the skills of raising crops, sewing, caring for livestock, etc. (which also results in almost all of their time spent with the family, Amish community, and in service to God), let me ask you this: How many Amish vampires do *you* know?

Conclusion

Get involved. Know your children and family, and get to know the children in your community. When I (Donna Howell) had my baby dedicated, the pastor first challenged us, the parents, then he challenged himself, promising to help my husband and I raise this baby in the ways of the Lord and to be there for him when he feels misunderstood or needs help, and then he challenged the congregation to all be responsible for that one child's soul…

You have a place in someone's heart and a responsibility to them to try as hard as you can to know them, accept them, love them, and truly be there for them when they need you (and not by wagging a finger of judgment at them when they're down). The love of Christ is stronger than any other force on this Earth… Satan is after our youth and those who are hurting and looking for a hand to hold, but he cannot cross the barrier of Christ's blood.

CHAPTER THREE

THE BLOOD IS THE LIFE

By Derek Gilbert

Vampires are hot. There is no question about it; over the last quarter century, the mythological stuff of nightmares has been transformed from "scary" into "sexy." Somehow, the monstrous image of the vampire has been rehabilitated to the point that, today, they are more often than not portrayed as sympathetic, if not downright heroic.

If you know a young woman, you've probably witnessed first-hand the powerful appeal of the vampire. Author Stephanie Meyer's immensely popular *Twilight* series has drawn millions of predominantly female fans, not all of them still in their teens, into the saga of protagonists Bella, an awkward teenage girl, and her love interest, the painfully handsome, virtuous (by human standards), 108-year-old but eternally young, Edward.

HBO's popular *True Blood* takes the vampire to the American South (and to a more adult audience), and other popular television series like *Buffy the Vampire Slayer*, *Buffy* spin-off *Angel*, and

Being Human have helped popularize the idea that vampires are more to be admired than feared.

This is the culmination of a trend that began in the mid-1970s with the *Vampire Chronicles* novels of Anne Rice. Rice, the premier vampire storyteller of our generation, succeeded in adding a seductive veneer to a creature that had terrified us for millennia.

How has the ghoulish become genteel? Why is our culture awash in entertainment based on the exploits of the formerly cursed undead? These are not idle questions. For Christians, this trend should be disturbing. Vampirism, which has become so appealing that it's spawned an active and growing subculture (that sometimes insists on the alternate spelling *vampyre*), is nothing less than an absolute mockery of the central tenet of the Christian faith: salvation by the shedding of blood.

The transformation of the vampire from monster to hero reflects the gradual decay of the Christian faith into an anemic shell of its former self. The critical role of the blood shed by Jesus Christ for the redemption of our sins has been replaced in many churches today, either by an emphasis on our own works, or by a kinder, gentler Jesus for whom the greatest sin is being untrue to our innermost desires.

Against such a spiritual backdrop, it is much easier to portray the vampire as a sympathetic, even noble, character. Modern vampires, especially as portrayed in the *Twilight* series, are angst-ridden, struggling against their omnipresent thirst for human blood and striving for redemption through moral behavior.

Further, vampires are agents of transformation who can free us from the often painful limitations of our humanity—which is, perhaps not coincidentally, the alluring goal of the growing transhumanist movement.

The precise origin of the vampire is shrouded in the mists of history. The first recorded use of the word from which "vampire" is derived, the Old Russian *Upir'*, is found in a manuscript of the *Book of Psalms* translated into Cyrillic in 1047 AD. However, demonic, blood-sucking creatures resembling the modern vampire, evil spirits called Edimmu, were part of the cosmology of ancient Mesopotamia.

More recently, vampire hysteria erupted in the well-documented eighteenth century cases of Arnold Paole and Peter Plogojowitz[44] in Serbia and Mercy Brown in 1890s Rhode Island, all of whom were believed to have returned from the grave. Paole and Plogojowitz appear to have been accused posthumously due to an imperfect understanding of the process of decomposition. Miss Brown, who succumbed to tuberculosis along with her mother and two siblings within the span of four years, was the inspiration for the character Lucy Westenra in Bram Stoker's *Dracula*.

Our modern concept of the sophisticated, aristocratic vampire began to develop in the early nineteenth century. Dr. John Polidori, an associate of Lord Byron and Mary Shelley (the author of *Frankenstein*), published a novella in 1819 titled *The Vampyre*. The villain of the tale, Lord Ruthven, is clearly a precursor to Count Dracula, the central character of Bram Stoker's 1897 novel which defined the character and mythology of the vampire as we know it today.

But even in the works of Polidori and Stoker, the vampire was, like its ancient predecessors, absolutely malevolent; a parasite on the body of humanity that was exterminated only with extreme difficulty—and divine assistance. The most effective weapons against the vampire, as conceived by Stoker, were symbolic of key elements of the Christian faith: holy water (representing baptism), and a sharpened piece of wood: an analog for the cross.

A variety of theories have been put forward to explain the origins of the vampire myth. Some suggest that it was a primitive attempt to explain the mystery of death and decomposition; others believe that premature burials might be the source of stories of revenants, animated corpses that returned from the grave to terrorize and prey on the living.

The truth behind the stories is nigh impossible to ascertain, forever lost in the archives of years gone by. What we do know is that God placed special significance on blood, especially human blood, from the very beginning. Note the Lord's reaction to the murder of Abel by Cain: "And he said, What hast thou done? the voice of thy brother's blood crieth unto me from the ground. And now art thou cursed from the earth, which hath opened her mouth to receive thy brother's blood from thy hand; When thou tillest the ground, it shall not henceforth yield unto thee her strength; a fugitive and a vagabond shalt thou be in the earth" (Genesis 4:10–12).

God elaborated to Noah: "And surely your blood of your lives will I require; at the hand of every beast will I require it, and at the hand of man; at the hand of every man's brother will I require the life of man. Whoso sheddeth man's blood, by man shall his blood be shed: for in the image of God made he man" (Genesis 9:5–6).

A search for the word "blood" finds nearly four hundred mentions in the Bible. A surprising number of those references deal with exactly when and how the blood of sacrificial animals was to be shed for the remission of the sins of the Hebrews. The specific nature of the instructions God gave to Moses is a clue to the special significance of blood—for example: "And the priest that is anointed shall take of the bullock's blood, and bring it to the tabernacle of the congregation: And the priest shall dip his finger in the blood, and sprinkle of the blood seven times before the LORD, before the vail of the sanctuary. And the priest shall put some of the blood upon the horns of the altar of sweet incense before the LORD, which is in the tabernacle of the congregation; and shall pour all the blood of the bullock at the bottom of the altar of the burnt offering, which is at the door of the tabernacle of the congregation" (Leviticus 4:5–7).

And it is in the very first book of the Bible, chapter 9 of Genesis, that God makes clear to Noah that blood has a unique property. "Every moving thing that liveth shall be meat for you; even as the green herb have I given you all things. **But flesh with the life thereof, which is the blood thereof, shall ye not eat**" (Genesis 9:3–4, bold added).

The Lord emphasized this point of the Law, which Moses repeated to the Hebrews no fewer than half a dozen times:

Notwithstanding thou mayest kill and eat flesh in all thy gates, whatsoever thy soul lusteth after, according to the blessing of the LORD thy God which he hath given thee: the unclean and the clean may eat thereof, as of the roebuck, and as of the hart. **Only ye shall not eat the blood; ye shall pour it upon the earth as water...** When the LORD thy God shall enlarge thy border, as he hath promised thee, and thou shalt say, I will eat flesh, because thy soul longeth to eat flesh; thou mayest eat flesh, whatsoever thy soul lusteth after. If the place which the LORD thy God hath chosen to put his name there be too far from thee, then thou shalt kill of thy herd and of thy flock, which the LORD hath given thee, as I have commanded thee, and thou shalt eat in thy gates whatsoever thy soul lusteth after. Even as the roebuck and the hart is eaten, so thou shalt eat them: the unclean and the clean shall eat of them alike. **Only be sure that thou eat not the blood: for the blood is the life; and thou mayest not eat the life with the flesh.** Thou shalt not eat it; thou shalt pour it upon the earth as water. Thou shalt not eat it; that it may go well with thee, and with thy children after thee, when thou shalt do that which is right in the sight of the LORD. (Deuteronomy 12:15–16; 12:20–25, bold added)[45]

In *Dracula*, Bram Stoker put the words, "the blood is the life," into the mouth of Dracula's victim and servant, Renfield. In the 1931 film, with which more of us are familiar, the scripture is quoted by the Count, himself.

Why this special emphasis on blood? In our modern society, we tend to assume that the ancients were ignorant of modern physiology. How did Moses know thirty-five hundred years ago that "the blood is the life"? Is there significance to circulatory fluid that goes beyond simply oxygenating tissue?

The answer is yes. For reasons that are not clear, blood is required in our universe to redeem mankind from sin.

And whatsoever man there be of the house of Israel, or of the strangers that sojourn among you, that eateth any manner of blood; I will even set my face against that soul that eateth blood, and will cut him off from among his people. **For the life of the flesh is in the blood: and I have given it to you upon the altar to make an atonement for your souls: for it is the blood that maketh an atonement for the soul.** Therefore I said unto the children of

Israel, No soul of you shall eat blood, neither shall any stranger that sojourneth among you eat blood. (Leviticus 17:10–12, bold added)[46]

The author of Hebrews writes that the mission of Christ was the offering of His own blood as a sacrifice. Just as the blood of bulls and goats provided temporary purification of the flesh, so the shed blood of Jesus of Nazareth, God in the flesh and the only Man in history to live a sinless life, provided eternal redemption to those who confess Him as Lord and ended the need for animal sacrifice (Hebrews 9:11–28).

The Lord emphasized His warnings against consuming blood to the Hebrews, presumably because at least some of the Hebrews' neighbors were doing just that. Indeed, the Lord told Moses that He intended to clear the land of its inhabitants precisely because of their abhorrent practices (Leviticus 18:24–25).

It is simple logic to deduce that since the consumption of the blood of animals was forbidden by God, a prohibition repeated by the apostolic council in Jerusalem (Acts 15:20), and the mere shedding of human blood requires a reckoning even from animals, then the consumption of *human* blood must be doubly abhorrent in His eyes.

Dr. Judd H. Burton[47] theorizes that vampire legends may have originated with the Nephilim, the "the mighty men who were of old, the men of renown."[48] While the Bible tells us little about this mysterious race, which is mentioned only in Genesis 6:4 and Numbers 13:33, the non-canonical books of Enoch, Jasher, and Jubilees, all referenced in the Bible, expand on the little we're told in Scripture. The picture that develops is of a world terrorized by the giant Nephilim, who "consumed all the acquisitions of men." And when that wasn't enough, they turned to eating mankind, and even one another.

Significantly, Enoch also records that they began to drink the blood of their victims.

While the historicity of Enoch is debatable, there is no question that the pages of history are stained with human blood. Setting aside warfare and criminal activity, cultures have engaged in ritual human sacrifice since the beginning of recorded history. Given that God, Himself, told the first son born on the planet, Cain, that the blood of a human victim cried out to Him from the very ground on which it was spilled, why did mankind so soon forget?

If the apostle Paul knew what he was writing about (and given that the apostles in Jerusalem gave him their stamp of approval, I personally assume that he did), then our world is inhabited not just by our human neighbors, but by powerful entities that seek our destruction. Paul called them $\rho\chi$ (archē), $\xi ov\sigma\alpha$ (exousia), and $\kappa o\sigma\mu o\kappa\rho\tau\omega\rho$ (kosmokratōr), translated into English as "principalities," "powers," and "rulers." Is it possible that these entities, perhaps ranks of angels who rebelled against God, saw a purpose in persuading our ancestors to shed human blood in sacrifice?

"The blood is the life," God told Moses. If true for the blood of animals, how much more so the lifeblood of those created in God's image?

Dr. Michael Heiser[49] and the Divine Council Research Group[50] have demonstrated that the cosmology of the Ancient Near East, including that of the Hebrews, understood that the chief deity was served by a council of small-G gods—angels, if you prefer. Dr. Heiser believes that after the incident at the Tower of Babel, where God personally intervened to stop Nimrod's plan to build a means to access the abode of the gods, the Lord placed seventy "sons of God" (*bene elohim*) over the nations. "When the Most High divided to the nations their inheritance, when he separated the sons of Adam, he set the bounds of the people according to the number of the children of Israel ["sons of God" instead of "children of Israel" in the English Standard Version]" (Deuteronomy 32:8).

Dr. Heiser believes that the ESV has it right. His paper, "Deuteronomy 32:8 and the Sons of God," is a scholarly explanation of why "sons of God" is the correct translation. This has profound implications for our cosmology,[51] but getting into those nuts and bolts is way outside the scope of my chapter here. I strongly suggest those reading this book now to take a minute to read Dr. Heiser's article at the following:[52] http://www.thedivine-council.com/DT32BibSac.pdf.

This is a reference to the seventy people-groups described in the Table of Nations recorded in Genesis 10. According to Heiser, the seventy *bene elohim* to whom the Earth was delegated apparently rebelled and allowed themselves to be worshipped. They were perhaps known to the neighbors of the one nation God called to Himself, the Hebrews, by names recorded in the Bible: Molech, Chemosh, Dagon, Ba'al, Asherah, Adramelech, Anamelech, Marduk, Nabu, Tammuz, Nergal, Zeus, Apollo (Apollyon), Diana, Hades, and others.

Not all of these false gods were worshipped through human sacrifice, but some most definitely were. Molech in particular was singled out by God: "And the LORD spake unto Moses, saying, Again, thou shalt say to the children of Israel, Whosoever he be of the children of Israel, or of the strangers that sojourn in Israel, that giveth any of his seed unto Molech; he shall surely be put to death: the people of the land shall stone him with stones. And

I will set my face against that man, and will cut him off from among his people; because he hath given of his seed unto Molech, to defile my sanctuary, and to profane my holy name" (Leviticus 20:1–3).

Other references to making children "pass through the fire to Molech" appear in Leviticus 18, 2 Kings 23, and Jeremiah 32, indicating that this was a widely known practice for centuries in the Levant, since Moses and Jeremiah were probably separated by six hundred years or more. And the ritual sacrifice of children was clearly known centuries before Moses' day; Abraham appears to have been familiar with the concept when the Lord tested his faith by asking Abraham to offer up Isaac at Mount Moriah.

Despite God's stern warnings against performing these rites, the Israelites persisted in these detestable offerings at least through the reign of Jehoiakim, king of Judah at the time of Nebuchadnezzar's invasion of Judah around 598 BC.

Other cultures around the world are also known to have sacrificed human victims to their gods. Roman historians reported that the Carthaginians offered up infants on a bronze statue of Cronos, beneath which the children were dumped into a gaping fire pit. The Romans, however, were guilty as well; they buried prisoners of war alive as an offering to the *Manes*, or spirits of the dead, and archaeologists have found sacrificial victims entombed in the foundations of Roman buildings.

Ancient Celts from France to Britain apparently engaged in ritual sacrifice—beheadings, hangings, drownings, and the infamous Wicker Man described by Julius Caesar in his history of the Gallic War (a giant wicker figure filled with people who were burned alive). Ritual sacrifice, including cannibalism, was practiced in Tibet prior to the arrival of Buddhism in the seventh century.

Some of the best-documented examples of human sacrifice are found in the Americas. The Mayans, Toltecs, Incas, and Aztecs sent victims into the afterlife well into the modern age. Aztec practices are particularly well-documented (and gruesome); their eighteen-month calendar demanded specific rituals for the various gods of their pantheon, each with a different type of victim and method of execution, which included beheading, drowning, bludgeoning, immolation, and extraction of the heart.

Now, it is noted that these sacrifices did not specifically involve the consumption of human blood, except for those cases in which victims were cannibalized as part of the rite. Still, the question must be asked: When it is fundamental, human nature to shrink from death, why was religious significance attached to the shedding of human blood in so many places for so long? Why did parents consent to the slaughter of their children in cultures on opposite sides of the globe? Is it possible that a compelling, external force—in other words, "divine revelation" from fallen angels masquerading as gods—is responsible for this legacy of bloodshed?

Further, is it beyond imagining that "the blood is the life" is more than a simple statement of biological fact—that there are spiritual properties to blood that we don't understand? Can it be that the ritual spilling of blood actually results in some sort of supernatural transference of energy?

In other words, is blood, and especially human blood, intrinsically sacred?

One could devote an entire book to a psychological analysis of the reasons for the vampire's redemption in the collective consciousness—and indeed, many have. Such a study is beyond the scope of this book (and the academic qualifications of this author). It's not difficult to reason that the otherworldly nature of the vampire appeals to the innate human desire for eternal life. The "kiss" of the vampire offers that link to eternity; submitting to that kiss is the price of admission to the next life.

In modern television of cinematic portrayals, vampires are typically played by model-gorgeous young men and women. This appeals to our prurient desires, which makes it easier to draw us into the stories and cast vampires as benign and empathetic. This admixture of the divine and the carnal has been so appealing that it's birthed an active vampire subculture.

Vampires believe they need to feed on the life-energy of others. That doesn't necessarily involve drinking blood; some call themselves psychic vampires, or "psy-vamps," and believe they draw their strength from the aura, life force, or "pranic energy," of others. Sanguinarians are those within the vampire subculture who *do* drink blood. These modern-day vampires typically consume small quantities offered by "black swans" (willing non-vampire donors).

It's easy to write off this recent outgrowth of the Goth movement as a group of mentally disturbed people who find odd comfort in emulating the morbid and unhygienic practices of their literary heroes. Indeed, in a recent survey of 950 self-identifying vampires conducted by the vampire community, 30 percent reported being diagnosed with depression, 16 percent suffered from panic disorder, and more than 15 percent had been diagnosed as bipolar.[53]

But before we write this off as a manifestation of psychological issues, we should note that the majority of people who suffer from panic, depression, or bipolar disorder, and the alienation and rejection that can result, do not always turn to a parasitic lifestyle for comfort alone. And this subculture has only emerged within the last twenty-five years, in the wake of the aforementioned *Vampire Chronicles*. Could there be another cause for this unusual cultural phenomenon? Are the same principalities and powers that presumably lured our ancestors into practices condemned by God now using pop culture to glorify bloodshed?

It's difficult to get to the heart of the appeal of the vampire lifestyle, and understanding their beliefs and practices is somewhat constrained because there is no central authority on doctrine to codify vampire theology. That said, there are some very broad and basic conclusions that can be drawn about the recent emergence of the vampire subculture and the vampire's sudden rock-star status.

FIRST: the vampire represents the polar opposite of Jesus Christ. Simply put, Jesus shed His blood so that others may have eternal life. The vampire sheds the blood of others so that *he* can have eternal life.

SECOND: the eternal life promised by the vampire is a cheap imitation of that offered by Jesus Christ. The vampire lives in eternal darkness, fleeing the light, always seeking new victims to prolong its dark and bloody half-life. Those redeemed by partaking of the shed blood of Christ drink from "living water" and their thirst is eternally quenched (John 4:14). They will know darkness no longer, as the glory of the Lord Himself will illuminate the New Jerusalem (Revelation 21:23).

It will be difficult to convince girls who have been drawn into the story of Bella and Edward that their fantasy love-interest stands diametrically opposed to God, but in very basic terms, it's true. Similarly, adults eagerly awaiting the next episode of *True Blood* may be unwilling to give up their weekly dose of vampy titillation. Nosferatu has been replaced by sexy sanguinarians to a growing audience of vampire romance fiction—and a shadowy subculture of those who emulate their literary heroes.

We Christians can pretend it doesn't matter. It is, one may argue, only fiction—imaginative, entertaining stories that have inspired some harmless fantasy role-playing. And on one level, that's correct.

On a deeper level, however, we must be wise enough to understand that stories affect our worldview in ways that non-fiction does not. For example, Dan Brown's *The Da Vinci Code* compelled hordes of pilgrims fascinated with the legend of the Holy Grail to visit Scotland's Rosslyn Chapel, a site that's featured prominently in the novel. The (allegedly) non-fiction book from which Brown lifted his Gnostic theology, *Holy Blood, Holy Grail*, had far less effect on the masses.

It should be no surprise that Meyer's *Twilight* series has inspired a disturbing new trend: teens are literally biting one another—drawing blood—as a sign of affection.[54]

So we should recognize the spirit that inspires these modern stories of hunky, virtuous vampires. Blood is the central element of the biblical narrative—why blood had to be shed, how blood had to be shed, and especially *whose* blood had to be shed. Christ's blood, and His alone, was the only human blood God ever intended to shed on planet Earth.

The blood is the life. Consuming blood, even animal blood, is an unholy act, condemned in the Old and New Testaments because it was to be reserved for the altar and atonement for sin.

Thus, by its very nature, the vampire, no matter how glamorous, represents nothing less than the spirit of antichrist.

CHAPTER FOUR

DO YOU BELIEVE IN DRAGONS?

By Gary Stearman

In that day the LORD with his sore and great and
strong sword shall punish leviathan the piercing
serpent, even leviathan that crooked serpent; and
he shall slay the dragon that is in the sea.

ISAIAH 27:1

Virtually every culture on Earth has some sort of belief in dragons. The dragon of the Far East flies the skies of the Earth in
search of his lost wisdom. The gods of the Aztecs and Incas took
the form of a flying serpent. Some scaly monsters are even said
to live in the waters of our planet. They are often referred to as
dragons.

The so-called "Loch Ness Monster" of Scotland is perhaps the
best-known of them all, but there are many, many more. They
are commonly reported from all parts of the globe. From Lake
Champlain in New York, to Lake Okanagan in British Columbia
and the lakes at the base of Mount Fuji in Japan, occasional

sightings are reported. These monsters seem, in some ways, to be related both to the biblical descriptions of the dragon, and the numerous, historical, pagan objects of worship that have survived the fall of nations. When seen on land, they appear to scuffle along on their bellies like giant snakes, but without the usual reptilian grace. Their clumsiness is quite well-documented. In the water, their fierce heads are borne aloft upon a train of sinewy and scaly humps. Witnesses are frozen with fear.

At this point, you may object, saying that sea monsters are merely the product of excited imaginations. After all, their existence is hardly well-documented. Or, you may be of the opinion that if monsters such as Nessie really do exist, they are holdovers from a prehistoric era, trapped in inland lakes. Naturalists usually depict them as the offspring of ancient *plesiosaurs*—marine lizards—which somehow survived to the present day. Those who admit their existence say that their skill at hiding is the chief attribute of their survival. In Europe, they are often called "water horses," because their heads closely resemble the head of a horse, with a coarse "mane" and long snout.

Legions of eyewitnesses say that they give the impression of having an extraordinary level of intelligence. Furthermore, there are literally hundreds, if not thousands, of recorded sightings in every ocean of the world. What are these modern sea monsters, and what does the Bible say about them?

The Lord's Revelation to Job

Let us begin by examining a chapter in the Bible that is wholly devoted to a certain "Leviathan." Chapter 41 of the *Book of Job* gives mind-boggling detail and intriguing life to this bizarre creature that, in every way, seems to fit the description of the classic sea monster. The Lord gives Job a detailed picture of the "undocumented" (he doesn't appear in zoology textbooks) monster that is reported again and again by sea captains, vacationers, and fishermen the world over.

The Lord's revelation to Job comes at the conclusion of His first-person declaration concerning the glories of His creation. Every one of this chapter's 34 verses reveals remarkable aspects about a creature that mankind regards as merely a fabulous tale, or myth. Clearly, however, the Lord presents Leviathan as a tangible, physical creature; an animal that He considers to be the king of the waters.

After Job's severe suffering, during which he attempted to understand the cause and effect of his plight, the Lord appears to him in a whirlwind. A sort of divine debriefing follows, in which Job is given a running narration of the glories of creation. The purpose of the Lord's divine monologue is to restore Job's lost perspective. In the end, he is made acutely aware of his diminutive place in the universe. He is filled with wonder at God's creation and unfathomable grace.

Concerning Leviathan, the Lord gently chides Job. He asks whether Job can fish for the great sea-monster with a hook or string him up with a hook through his nose. (Of course not!) He asks whether Job can tame the beast, or talk sweet words with him. (In no way!) He inquires of Job about the possibility of making an agreement that the monster may serve him...or that he might toy with Leviathan as he would a little bird. These verbal images present a powerful case; Job must have gotten the point immediately. His perspective about his place in the universe achieves a new clarity.

As the Lord continues to paint the ludicrous picture of mere man vanquishing the great sea monster, it becomes clear that His intent is to educate Job about his position in this universe, including aspects of the amazing physical creation that includes such animals as Leviathan.

The Lord's description of Leviathan reveals an appearance so fierce that men are plunged to defeat even at the sight of him. They drop to their knees in fear. He reminds Job that if men can't stand before one of His creatures, they surely will not be able to stand before God, Himself.

On the other hand, the Lord regards Leviathan as being beautiful in his own way, even though he has a fierce array of frightening teeth, purposefully set in a jaw with ferocious power.

He has scales so tightly sealed against each other that they are completely airtight. Apparently, he is capable of deep diving. Furthermore, they are so strong that they resist barbed harpoons made of iron. The Lord shows the amazed Job that Leviathan's scales are so tightly joined that nothing can pry them apart. Truly, they are a living armor.

When Leviathan sneezes and snorts, light shines from his nostrils! Is this some sort of self-contained combustion? In conjunction with this revelation, the Lord says that even his eyes glow like the sunrise. Sparks and fire blaze from his mouth and his nose belches forth smoke and vapor, like steam from a boiling cauldron. His very breath can start a fire!

Leviathan's internal conformation is the picture of strength. His musculature is of a peculiar sort that forms an immovable structure. His heart is stout as stone.

When Leviathan rouses, strong men become weak and seek the Lord's mercy. Assorted swords, spears, and blades are useless against him. He breaks iron and brass as easily as rotted wood. Slings and arrows are nothing; he laughs at darts and stones. As a matter of fact, the Lord says his very nest is made up of sharp stones.

When he moves, the deep waters boil and churn. He leaves a long, foaming wake that gleams mysteriously. He invokes fear in all who see him. Verse 34, the concluding verse of Job, Chapter 41, says: "He beholdeth all high things: he is a king over all the children of pride."

What Is Leviathan?

Biblically speaking, Leviathan is certainly presented as a real and living animal. In Job's day—probably around the time of Abraham—Leviathan seems to have been a thriving reality, generally known by the people of that time.

Traditional expositors have attempted to explain away Leviathan as the ancient crocodile of Middle-Eastern waters. But this common explanation quickly folds in the face of the text, itself. First of all, no crocodile ever breathed fire and smoke. Secondly, the crocodile can easily be harpooned. Thirdly, crocodiles don't leave a foaming wake, nor are they covered with interlocking scales.

Though their toothy aspects bring great respect, men do not fall to the ground in fear at the sight of the mighty crocodile. In fact, crocodile skins were bought and sold by men in the ancient world.

So what is this amazing animal in Job 41? If we didn't know better, it would appear to be the classic, fire-breathing dragon. Does this mean that dragons really exist? And if so, what is their relation to "the great dragon," called in Revelation 12:9, "That old serpent, called the Devil, and Satan, which deceiveth the whole world…"?

Scripture makes it plain that the Lord created the original serpent, who was once called "the anointed cherub that covereth," as noted in Ezekiel 28:14. In fact, there is no evidence that Lucifer was ever anything other than a serpent being of some sort. Thus he appeared before Eve in the garden. But once, he was glorious. Since then, he and his kind have been placed under a curse. Their glory has been replaced by a hideous and repulsive appearance.

From Job 41, it is obvious that the Lord created Leviathan as a fierce, fire-breathing serpent armored with scales. It cannot be overemphasized that he is presented as a living, physical creature.

But wait; there is another clue to Leviathan's identity. It is found near the beginning of the book of Job, in chapter 3, as the afflicted Job sits on an ash heap, accompanied by his three friends. In this, his first discourse, he eloquently curses the day of his birth, saying that it would have been better if he had never been born in the first place. His language is a malediction of day, of light, and of blessing.

After this opened Job his mouth, and cursed his day.

And Job spake, and said,

Let the day perish wherein I was born, and the night in which it was said, There is a man child conceived.

Let that day be darkness; let not God regard it from above, neither let the light shine upon it.

Let darkness and the shadow of death stain it; let a cloud dwell upon it; let the blackness of the day terrify it.

As for that night, let darkness seize upon it; let it not be joined unto the days of the year, let it not come into the number of the months.

Lo, let that night be solitary, let no joyful voice come therein.

Let them curse it that curse the day, who are ready to raise up their mourning.

Let the stars of the twilight thereof be dark; let it look for light, but have none; neither let it see the dawning of the day:

Because it shut not up the doors of my mother's womb, nor hid sorrow from mine eyes.

Why died I not from the womb? why did I not give up the ghost when I came out of the belly? (Job 3:1–11)

In this passage, Job rues the day of his birth. Judging himself to be accursed, he calls for a darkness that he deems suitable for his condition. He begs for God to leave him alone.

But, in the eighth verse, he makes a special (and quite revealing) imprecation. He calls for those who "curse the day" to go ahead and curse it. Then, he calls for them to raise the power of Leviathan!

The English phrase, "who are ready to raise up their mourning," actually states in the Hebrew text, "who are skilled in stirring up Leviathan"!

According to the Old Testament Commentary of Keil and Delitzsch:

Those who curse days are magicians who know how to change days into *dies infausti* (a day accursed) by their incantations. According to vulgar superstition, from which the imagery of v. 8 is borrowed, there was a special art of exciting the dragon, which is the enemy of sun and moon, against them both, so that, by its devouring them, total darkness prevails. The dragon is called in Hindu *rahu*; the Chinese, and also the natives of Algeria, even at the present day make a wild tumult with drums and copper vessels when an eclipse of the sun or moon occurs, until the dragon will release his prey. Job wishes that this monster may swallow up the sun of his birthday.[55]

Thus, at the very beginning of his torments, Job foolishly cries out of his anguish for a dark and evil curse, involving the appearance of the dragon...Leviathan. Thirty-eight chapters later—in chapter 41—the Lord shows Job what he had been wishing for. The Lord tells him that indeed, there is a real Leviathan.

It is only through His grace that Leviathan remains at a safe distance. Once Job realized this truth, he must have been filled with enormous gratitude, even to his dying day.

The Beast That Isn't There

Today, reports of dragonlike lake and sea monsters come from the British Isles, Sweden, Russia, Siberia, Argentina, Tasmania, Canada, and the U.S., to name but a few locations.

The late naturalist, Dr. Ivan T. Sanderson, wrote in 1968:

> Today, there are three basic schools of thought about these creatures; I should here emphasize that we *now have absolute proof that they exist and that they are animals.* There need no longer be—nor, in fact, should there ever have been—any argument about this; and for one very simple reason. This is a straightforward question: "What can roar about the surface of any body of water at ten knots, without a sail, leaving a clear V-shaped bow-wave but no prop-wash?" Yet this is just what these things have

not only been reputed to do, but have been filmed doing. And once you have but one film of a "Something" so propelling itself across one lake without leaving a prop-wash, there can be but one inference—to wit, that it *was* an animal.[56]

Sanderson goes on to cite many examples of sightings, including the famous one by Captain Rostron of the Cunard Lines. He and dozens of others once tracked just such a monster for many hours in mid-ocean. It was said to be about a block long!

In the Middle Ages, when knights went about slaying dragons (the lake and river monsters), these were collectively termed, "worms." The Anglo-Saxon word, *wyrm*, was a collective term, meaning "dragon," "serpent," or "worm." These evil worms (in English, the term is shortened to "orm"), were thought to be the spawn of the devil, and were said to bring curses to nearby towns and villages, accompanied by a great appetite for livestock.

Marine Orms of two hundred to three hundred feet are occasionally spotted. The Loch Ness Orm is usually reported at about eighty feet in length. Medieval Orms—today called "dragons"—are referred to in literally hundreds of local chronicles that molder away in dank libraries, ignored by practically everybody. But if one is interested, there are many books on the subject.

One famous account of a dragon encounter is quoted by naturalist F. W. Holiday, writing in *The Great Orm of Loch Ness.*[57] In about 1420, one John Lambton, a noble knight, defended his property in County Durham beside the River Wear. The site is still well-known, near the modern village of Fatfield, England.

It seems that as a youth, John had snagged a young Orm while fishing. It resembled, "a worm, of most unseemly and disgusting appearance."[58] He threw it into a nearby well, where it was said to have quickly grown large enough to escape and crawl back into the river, where it was seen for many years thereafter. Eventually, it "had grown prodigiously and was now grew to enormous size and was fond of making periodic forays into the countryside,"[59] where it made a pest of itself, by raiding the livestock of nearby farms. The farmers were frightened nearly to death by its appearance.

Meanwhile, John, now a man, had taken Christian vows and become a crusading knight in the King's service. He decided to defeat the beast, and was advised to stud his armor with spear points, so that the pestilent worm would cut itself as it tried to eat him. According to history, the stratagem worked and he finally hacked the dragon to pieces. An old ballad commemorating the event is preserved to this day:

> The Worm shot down the middle stream
> Like a flash of living light,
> And the waters kindled around his path
> In rainbow colors bright.
> And when he saw the armed Knight
> He gathered all his pride
> And coil'd in many a radiant spire,
> Rode buoyant on the tide.
> And when he darted at length his Dragon strength,
> An earthquake shook the rock;
> And the fire-flakes bright fell around the Knight
> As unmov'd he met the shock.
> Tho' his heart was stout, it quiver'd no doubt,
> His very life-blood ran cold,
> As around and around the wild worm wound
> In many a grappling fold.[60]

In those days, men were often reported killed by these medium- to small-sized dragons. As in this ballad, many of the attributes of Leviathan are repeatedly mentioned. What animal flashes light, or leaves a shining path in the water, or belches fiery sparks? Only Leviathan fits this description.

Such accounts are legion. And they are presented not as myths, but as absolutely true. One Lord Conyers is said to have slain a "fiery, flying serpent which destroyed man, woman and child."[61] His reward from King Edward III was the Manor of Sockburn, held by his family to this day. Then there was the Worm of Linton, and the dragon of Ruardean.

St. George may be the most popular figure in the long line of dragon slayers, but others who came later are much better documented. As Holiday writes:

> These slayings of the Worm cannot be doubted. We know the names of the men concerned and where the encounters took place. These details are supported by documentary as well as monumental evidence. In England, various tympana [carved reliefs, usually at the top of arches] survive showing Worms being killed. Typical of these are the ones in churches at Ruardean, Gloucestershire; at Moreton Valence, in the same country; and at Brinsop near Hereford.
>
> It seems significant that these tympana occur on the banks of rivers. The Lambton worm was slain on the river Wear; the Worm of Sockburn on the River Tees and the Worm of Linton on a tributary of the Tweed. The Ruardeen, Moreton and Brinsop tympana are on the banks of the River Wye. The Worm or dragon, like the Orm in the River Ness, was clearly a denizen of the water.[62]

Denizen, yes, but is the Orm merely a historical phenomenon...a myth, born out of tales around the family fires of a thousand evenings? Hardly, since history of the dragon goes back over four thousand years, through the cultures of Europe, Sythia, Mongolia, and China. Archaeologists have discovered beautifully-executed dragon sculptures on the walls of ancient Babylon.

And of course, anyone who has ever eaten in a Chinese restaurant knows that the peoples of the Far East revere the divine creature that they call the "fortunate dragon." This flying creature is regarded by them as the keeper of wisdom and blessing. He is always preceded by a fiery disc or ball, which he is trying to catch and swallow. Their homes and businesses are profusely decorated with dragons in various settings.

Twentieth-Century Dragons

Those who allow for dragons in ancient history are merely giving surface consent to the Bible's clear teaching about the "old dragon." While believing that such a creature exists on the spiritual level, they hesitate to give credence to a whole family of such creatures, some of which are seen in the present day.

Writing in *Unexplained Mysteries of the 20th Century*, Janet and Colin Bord note:

In the Northern hemisphere, a line joining Canada, Ireland, Scotland, Norway, Sweden, Finland and the northern USSR indicates where lake monsters are most likely to be seen, all these countries having an abundance of sizable lakes. Canada's best-known monster is Ogopogo, who lives in Lake Okanagan in British Columbia... The

Indians who lived in British Columbia before the white settlers arrived included a giant serpent in their legends about the lake, and Arlene Gaal, who has been investigating Ogopogo since 1968, has on record over 200 sightings. A recent one was made by Lionel Edmond, who was fishing on the lake on 20 July 1986 when he heard a loud rushing of water behind him. "It looked like a submarine surfacing, coming up toward my boat. As it came up perpendicular to the boat we could see six humps out of the water, each hump about 10 inches out of the water and each one creating a wake." He estimated it at about 50 or 60 feet long.[63]

In County Galway, Ireland, there is a lake called Lough Nahooin. It is a small lake, measuring only eighty by one hundred yards. Yet, on February 22, 1968, Stephen Coyne watched a small Orm, or water horse, for several hours as it frolicked around the lake. He saw it from as close as twenty-five feet, estimating its length at twelve feet. It revealed two humps, a flat tail, and a long neck. Its head was about a foot in diameter, with horn-like projections and an open mouth.

At different times, several other witnesses saw the Orm. They commonly reacted to it with revulsion, as witnessed in 1954 by one young woman (identified as Georgina Carberry) who said it had, "two humps, a long neck, and a big open mouth. She remembered that 'the whole body had movement in it'—it was 'wormy,' 'creepy,' and made a vivid impression on Miss Carberry, so much so that it was six or seven years before she went back to the lake, and she never returned alone."[64]

In the U.S., many have labored long and hard to document the monster of Lake Champlain, on the border between New York and Vermont. This huge beast is known as "Champ." Hundreds of reports reveal Champ to be a classic Orm, or dragon. He is well over a hundred feet long, with many humps, a horned head and bristling mane. Furthermore, witnesses have reported huge, glowing eyes and fearsome teeth.

In Africa, a river creature called "Mokèlé-mbèmbé" has been reported many times in the twentieth century. Natives in the Congo region say that the long-necked, small-headed animal swims the waters of Likouala swamp and nearby Lake Tele. Locals say that the creature looks very much like the picture of a Brontosaurus they were shown. But he disappears underwater when spotted.

Their reports go back at least two hundred years. Farmers and hunters regard the creature with awe and outright terror, saying that to merely see it is to bring a curse upon yourself. If you venture into his territory, they say, you will die. Efforts by naturalists to document the creature have all failed.

This brings us to the crux of the matter. Countless thousands of dollars and observational hours have been devoted to the study of suspected waters. But nothing has been sighted that can be documented as evidentiary or even unusual.

Those who have devoted entire careers to studying these obscure creatures have come up empty-handed. They have labeled themselves "cryptozoologists," or those who study secretive animal forms. Theirs is a frustrating life, indeed.

For example, in 1987, a highly technical assault was launched on Loch Ness in Scotland. Called "Operation Deep Scan," it was comprised of a literal armada of boats, cruising in line abreast down the loch. Millions of dollars were spent in the process. They were equipped with amazing arrays of the latest in sonar equipment, some of which was capable of literally visualizing an underwater scene. Had the Loch Ness Monster swum past, he would have been seen and recorded on television screens from many angles.

As one might imagine, cryptozoologists, sonar analysts, and biologists from all over the world went home disappointed. Only once during the entire operation were they were tantalized by a large, fast-swimming underwater "something" that quickly evaded their gaze.

Ironically, Japanese scientists had come to Scotland to participate in the exercise. While they were there, a group of amazing sightings of water horses were reported in Japan, around Mt. Fuji. Again and again, the phenomenon makes fools of serious men. Occasionally, however, it is caught on film.

In 1976, off Falmouth, Cornwall in England, a long-necked sea monster was repeatedly sighted. A photo of it reveals a shape that dragon-hunters have come to expect. The unidentified photographer wrote, "It looked like an elephant waving its trunk, but the trunk was a long neck with a small head on the end, like a snake's head. It had humps on the back which moved in a funny way. The colour was black or very dark brown, and the skin seemed to be like a sealion's… the animal frightened me. I would not like to see it any closer. I do not like the way it moved when swimming."[65]

This dragon was given the name "Morgawr." For a while, he became something of a local celebrity in the area.[66]

What Are We Dealing With?

Certainly, Leviathan is a real creature—a marine reptile of some sort. But let's be honest, in this age of exotic observational equipment and low-light cameras, it seems highly unlikely that any animal of this size could escape detection and cataloging.

Furthermore, biologists can estimate the kind of food supply necessary to sustain a creature whose weight is measured in tons. Most of the lakes where sightings are made simply do not have enough food to support even a breeding pair of such huge animals. Don't forget, down through the ages, Orms, dragons, and water-horses have been known for their voracious appetites—stealing chickens, sheep, and cattle. For such misdeeds, they have earned the wrath of generations of common folk.

Yet they live on in secret, leaving no traces. No boney remains of their meals, excrement, or even tracks are seen. Perhaps—and this seems most likely—in this age, they are a kind of spiritual creature, capable of becoming visible for brief periods, then slipping back into their mysterious lairs.

One thing more needs to be said. In the rare event that an Orm is seen on shore, witnesses agree that it is most repulsively ugly. It scuttles along on stumps that suggest feet where there are no feet. Yet it can still wriggle along with remarkable speed.

In ancient narratives, where myth blends with real observation, dragon sightings are recounted in which the huge creatures not only had feet, but wings. And rather than being reported as hideously ugly, dragons were said to be the most beautiful and intelligent of creatures.

One is reminded of the Bible's early reference to this creature, seen throughout Scripture as the hissing serpent, the old dragon, or Satan:

> Now the serpent was more subtle than any beast of the field which the LORD God had made. And he said unto the woman, Yea, hath God said, Ye shall not eat of every tree of the garden?

And the woman said unto the serpent, We may eat of the fruit of the trees of the garden:

But of the fruit of the tree which is in the midst of the garden, God hath said, Ye shall not eat of it, neither shall ye touch it, lest ye die.

And the serpent said unto the woman, Ye shall not surely die:

For God doth know that in the day ye eat thereof, then your eyes shall be opened, and ye shall be as gods, knowing good and evil.

And when the woman saw that the tree was good for food, and that it was pleasant to the eyes, and a tree to be desired to make one wise, she took of the fruit thereof, and did eat, and gave also unto her husband with her; and he did eat. (Genesis 3:1–6)

If you read Scripture as divinely-inspired, you must believe this account of an intelligent, talking serpent, which deceived Eve into the forbidden act that resulted in man's downfall.

Traditionally, this serpent is identified as the devil, himself, called the dragon. His form was once attractive, and his approach was said to be clever beyond human resistance.

But you must also believe that the serpent was cursed.

"And the LORD God said unto the serpent, Because thou hast done this, thou art cursed above all cattle, and above every beast of the field; upon thy belly shalt thou go, and dust shalt thou eat all the days of thy life" (Genesis 3:14).

The nature of this curse implies that the serpent and all his kind were sentenced to an ignominious defeat. The clear implication is that once, they could walk, perhaps even fly, but now would have to crawl. Or perhaps, we should say that, like the modern dragons, the serpent would be reduced to scuffling awkwardly along on his belly. "Eating dust" suggests skulking along the ground without arms or legs, being forced to muck along in dirt and mire.

Some have suggested that this is simply a reference to common snakes. And it surely applies to them. But at the moment, we're considering the dragon of history and culture. As we have suggested in the past, the "serpent class" of creatures—the saurians or lizards—seem to have been led by their own overseer, called in Ezekiel 28:14, "the anointed cherub that covereth."

His downfall marked the progressive downfall of all his kind, so that all serpents have become furtive creatures who live in seclusion...in the "dragon's lair," so to speak.

Leviathan's Future

It must be concluded that Leviathan, the fearsome original form of the dragon, is now merely a shabby, broken-down, and decaying shadow of his former self. But Leviathan as an accursed animal is one thing; Leviathan, the symbol of Satan's behind-the-scenes spiritual manipulation, is quite another.

The Leviathan of prophecy evokes a picture of global power in the kingdom of darkness. In Psalm 74, for example, Leviathan is mentioned by name. The context of this Psalm is a *Maschil*, or "lesson" of Asaph.

Here, the evil world system is pictured as vicious and despotic. In verses 10 and 11, the psalmist asks a rhetorical question: "O God, how long shall the adversary reproach? shall the enemy blaspheme thy name for ever? Why withdrawest thou thy hand, even thy right hand? pluck it out of thy bosom."

This question states the obvious; namely, that the enemy seems to be advancing without restraint. The psalmist asks why God, given His great power, would allow this. This question having been put forward, the psalmist gives the answer: "For God is my King of old, working salvation in the midst of the earth. Thou didst divide the sea by thy strength: thou brakest the heads of the dragons in the waters. Thou brakest the heads of leviathan in pieces, and gavest him to be meat to the people inhabiting the wilderness" (Psalm 74:12–14).

Here, the dragons are the Hebrew *tanninim*. They are the monsters of the sea. In this context, Leviathan seems to be their leader, with many heads. In retrospect, this action addresses God's defeat of Satan's world kingdom. It is also a prophecy of His future victory.

But Leviathan, the spiritual beast, is the symbol of that system. As the dragon of reality, he is the degenerate monster of global power and control. The lesson of this Psalm is that the Lord, having vanquished the old dragon, will one day entirely eliminate his realm of control.

There is also another mention of Leviathan in the Psalms. It, too, speaks prophetically of Leviathan. This time, he is shown frolicking with the great ships of the merchant trade.

"There go the ships: there is that leviathan, whom thou hast made to play therein" (Psalm 104:26).

As we have pointed out in many past studies, these sea traders are the merchants of Tarshish. They are the global wholesalers, upon whose international traffic is based the Law Merchant. It is the all-powerful law of the sea. It ignores the needs of those who produce its multitudinous quantities of trade goods.

It enslaves men, and is pictured as a huge sea monster that rises in the latter days. Of course, it will be destroyed at the beginning of the Kingdom Age. The death of commercial Babylon is seen in Revelation 18:10, where it is seen as "that great city Babylon, that mighty city!" Of course, it is global in scope.

Before that, in Revelation 13:1–2, John witnesses the rise of Leviathan from the sea, a symbol of the final world power: "And I stood upon the sand of the sea, and saw a beast rise up out of the sea, having seven heads and ten horns, and upon his horns ten crowns, and upon his heads the name of blasphemy. And the beast which I saw was like unto a leopard, and his feet were as the feet of a bear, and his mouth as the mouth of a lion: and the dragon gave him his power, and his seat, and great authority."

Revelation 13:4 adds, "And they worshipped the dragon which gave power unto the beast."

Here is the ultimate blasphemy! Those alive on Earth during the Great Tribulation will actually come to worship the ancient dragon—Leviathan will at last come to realize his ancient desire: to be worshipped as God.

No wonder his destruction is prophesied so often and so firmly. As Isaiah writes, "In that day the LORD with his sore and great and strong sword shall punish leviathan the piercing serpent, even leviathan that crooked serpent; and he shall slay the dragon that is in the sea" (Isaiah 27:1).

According to Michael Strassfeld, writing in *The Jewish Holidays: A Guide and Commentary*, the feast of Sukkot (Tabernacles) is concluded with a powerful ritual that commemorates the destruction of Leviathan's power.

"The afternoon of Hoshana Rabbah is the winding down of Sukkot. Some people visit the sukkah [booth] one last time and recite the following prayer: 'May it be that we merit to dwell in the sukkah made of leviathan.' "[67]

He adds, "According to legend, God will make a sukkah [tentlike shelter] out of the body of the leviathan at the end of days and will place the righteous there. The leviathan is a mythical beast of enormous dimension who will be killed by God at the end of days."[68]

Mythical? Hardly. Even now, he swims the seas and lakes of the world, accursed and isolated from humanity. He is real to be sure; he is also the symbol of utmost evil…a model for the world government of the great dragon.

Yes, I believe in dragons. Even more, I believe in the great Dragon Slayer, the Lord Jesus Christ.

CHAPTER FIVE

A WALK IN THE PARK

By Fred DeRuvo

Thousands of years ago, during the time of the placid beauty of Earth's early days, Adam and Eve enjoyed that peaceful time on Earth, not yet marred by sin. We do not know for how long they relaxed, worked, and played in the middle of God's completed creative work, but we do know that at first, there was nothing to fear and nothing to run from in God's Edenic wonder.

It was not long before another being walked into the same Garden of Eden, uninvited, with evil on his mind. Interestingly enough, this entity did not enter Eden showing himself as he *was*, but as he wanted to be *seen*, hiding his actual identity under the guise of a reptile. Perhaps his reasoning for appearing to Adam and Eve as a snake (as opposed to his true, physical form) was because of the familiarity they had with that species prior to his arrival. One can only wonder.

As the serpent walked[69] into Eden, he caught Eve's attention. It was she that he decided to deceive, because he knew that if he could cause *her* to trust him first, it was likely that Adam would follow.

Within a short time, he had not only captured her attention, but her mortal sense of desire. He teased her with flights of fancy and the dream of becoming a god in her own right. According to the serpent, God was jealous of her and Adam and did not want them to eat of the Tree of the Knowledge of Good and Evil, because it would turn them into gods who no longer needed the true God.

It was with this temptation that our first parents succumbed, through the deception of the serpent. Because of it, evil was introduced into the world, which became a fallen mass of untimely and eventual death. What had been created to the praise of God's glory would now sink into a morass of sin, pain, suffering, and loss, stolen by a reptilian, who was alien to the environment God had created.

The most intriguing part of this entire set of events found in Genesis 1–3 is the fact that Satan (Lucifer from Isaiah 14 and Ezekiel 28), felt it necessary to clothe himself in a skin that was not his own. Why the need to hide? Why bury himself beneath the body of a serpent?

Genesis 3:14–15 tells us, "And the LORD God said unto the serpent, Because thou hast done this, thou [art] cursed above all cattle, and above every beast of the field; upon thy belly shalt thou go, and dust shalt thou eat all the days of thy life; And I will put enmity between thee and the woman, and between thy seed and her seed; it shall bruise thy head, and thou shalt bruise his heel."

In the above verses, God is speaking to both the actual serpent and to Satan himself. God cursed the *serpent* because he allowed Satan to use him and his body to create a situation in which humanity fell through sin. Satan, as the main instigator, also had to deal with God's judgment by hearing that one day he would be dealt a fatal blow by a Savior who would come from the *seed of the woman.*

The Nephilim

It would appear from Scripture that Satan is the consummate *performer*, able to deftly take on an identity that best suits him for the moment. Paul tells us that Satan can transform himself into an angel of light (2 Corinthians 11:14). It appears that being able to transform is key to Satan's success, though we know from Scripture that his "successes" are kept fully in check by God, Himself. One day, Satan will reach the end of his career as tormentor of this world and will find that there is plenty of room for him in the Lake of Fire, which was created with Satan and his angels in mind (Matthew 25:41).

Jumping ahead to Genesis 6, we learn that after Enoch lived and was taken to heaven, one of his descendants (named Noah) lived who was considered to be righteous in God's eyes. In fact, the text tells us that Noah was "perfect in his generations" (Genesis 6:9). A number of biblical scholars believe that this may, in fact, be referencing Noah's very DNA; the text is not using the term "perfect" to reference a kind of standard of good behavior that Noah upheld, but a non-corrupt DNA pattern in his physical makeup.

In verse 4, we learn that there were Nephilim on the Earth, and these Nephilim were the result of fallen angels who had somehow found a way to comingle with human women. The guise that Satan first used in the Garden of Eden by hiding his own true identity under the skin of a serpent may have been contin-ued here by fallen angels, literally by mixing their DNA with the DNA of women. The result was catastrophic to God's creation, requiring extreme judgment. This is likely one of the first his-torical instances of the *incubus*: demons masquerading as human men in order to copulate with human women.

The Nephilim that resulted from this unholy union were half-breeds: part angel, part human, yet with a fallen soul, incapable of redemption. Even though God wiped out all living creatures on the Earth with the Flood of Genesis 9, these same creatures appeared again hundreds of years later after God promised Abraham that He would use him to bless all the nations of the world (Genesis 12; 15; 17). Seemingly right on cue, as Moses attempted to lead the chosen race of Israel into the Promised Land following their escape from Egypt, the sight of gigantic people proved too much for the faith of the Israelites and they refused to go in. God forced them to wander the wilderness for forty years because of their rebellion (Numbers 13).

Goliath

Possible Nephilim appeared again later as well. When David was but a young shepherd boy who brought food to the Israeli army led by Israel's first king Saul who stood against the Philistines, he wondered why no one was willing to go out and fight the giant Goliath, who was the shortest of four brothers standing just less than ten feet tall according to the Scripture (1 Samuel 17). Ultimately, God used David to slay Goliath, showing that it was by faith, not by might, that the enemies of God are destroyed.

Though Satan has attempted to overcome humanity through

a variety of means (at times using lies, while at other times, using brute force), the reality stands that faith in God will overcome whatever Satan throws in our path. Even with all his masquerades included, Satan is absolutely no match for God's power.

Satan has worked some of his best deceptions by presenting himself as something he is not and that fact seems to continue to this day. Whether he is working through a serpent, the Nephilim, Goliath, fallen angels, or what appear to be aliens, the reality is that he will don whatever costume suits him for that purpose.

However, in present day, except for true Satan-worshippers and authentic Christians, it is the rare case that a person would believe in Satan or in fallen angels at all. This is exactly what Satan prefers, because it allows him to operate out in the open, in front of non-believers, whilst effectively remaining completely hidden in the shadows. As long as he appears in the camouflage of something or someone more intriguing (and sometimes even more terrifying) than the traditional Satan image associated with religion, he will continue to escape the attention or focus of his prey. In today's day and age, the more seemingly scientific (or Sci-Fi) the camouflage, the better.

There are multitudes of people who believe that there are entities among us known as "reptilian shape-shifters." These shape shifters allegedly have the power to cloak their own identity with the genetic shell of what outwardly appears to be a normal human being. These shells allow them (through the use of *energetic* [or *energy*] *transformation*, using realms of light outside a human's ability to perceive) to either take over physical bodies, possessing their mental and emotional processes, capabilities, and manifestations, or to create the *illusion* that they have a physical body. Who they are and what they want are the urgent questions, which must be answered.

Master of Disguise and Deceit

Satan truly has something for everyone. He does his best to keep as many people as possible under his control. When dealing with a person who is *religious*, even one who believes themselves to be Christian, he will often visit them as an *ascended master*, or *spirit guide*, speaking articulate and religiously resonating verbiage to draw them into his snare. For a *superstitious* person who believes in ghosts or poltergeists, he may opt for a disguise that conjures up images of long-departed friends or relatives, appealing to their sense of familiar association, which is a powerful tool of entrapment.

Even to those who merely have a seemingly innocent fascination into the Sci-Fi world, Satan may cloak himself or his minions as a variety of alien beings coming to this planet on missions of good will. Through circulating stories of aliens who have allegedly manifested themselves to earthlings, we have learned about complete races of separate and distinct aliens. Reptilians are merely one race of many in the alien world. There are Pleiadeans, Greys, and others, all with a type of hierarchy similar to that found within human societies.

Of course this sounds strange unless the discussion involves the latest episode of some Sci-Fi show or movie. The fact of the matter, though, is that there is a large (and growing) group of people who have catalogued many instances of what they believe to be actual situations in which some of these reptilian shape-shifters have momentarily allowed their mask to fall away, revealing their true identity. There are videos and photos on the Internet, along with books filled with research. Whether they are actual or not is another question. The more important point for this writing is that many *believe* these shape-shifting alien beings do exist.

If we simply peruse the succession of movies and TV shows within the past few years alone, we will see a plethora of projects dedicated to the concept of aliens or demons infiltrating the human race, either through direct possession, or through some type of physical interaction, such as mixing DNA. *Splice* is one such film, starring Adrien Brody, in which scientists strive to "achieve fame by successfully splicing together the DNA of different animals to create incredible new hybrid animals."[70] Not willing to rest on their laurels, they then seek to do the same thing with human DNA and animal DNA. What they create, though seemingly far superior to humanity, winds up being thoroughly deadly.

Other movies have not only broached this type of theme, but have gone well beyond it to inculcate into the depths of humanity's thinking the concept that genetic manipulation should be seen as *normal*. All of this is done, I believe, to desensitize people to the idea that, though fiction, it *could* possibly happen in future sciences and should not be avoided in the interest of humanity-benefitting breakthroughs.

First Stage

How did all this start? How did we get here at this particular point in time? Consider the fact that decades ago, the idea of demonic possession in movies was certainly not the norm. The whole idea of someone being possessed by another entity was not really discussed outside of religious circles until *The Exorcist* came to the screen. Here, we witnessed the epic struggle between human beings and other-dimensional entities so powerful that, in the process of attempting to force their extrication, people died in the process.

The Exorcist opened the floodgates and numerous production companies immediately began pumping out Sci-Fi thrillers that went from believable to bawdy, and some to completely laughable. It did not matter, though, because Satan was getting precisely what he wanted (and planned). The market was being flooded with a subject that had heretofore been relatively unknown, and once the *fear* of it was gone, the *desensitization* could begin.

If we look to other movies like *Galaxy Quest* or *Men in Black*, we see a trend where aliens are shown as somewhat whimsical. If you shot one in the head, it would hurt, but they'd grow another head back in short order. Sure, they lived among us, but unlike the spate of alien-type movies from the 1950s, it was the unconventional alien that truly wanted to harm or destroy us. Like humans, there were bad aliens around, but we were never to fear, because the brave *Men in Black* would take the challenge and face down any real alien threat with aplomb. Most of the time, these aliens simply wanted to live peaceably among us. They wanted to be left alone, having escaped a situation on their own planet that caused them to run for their lives. Relocating to Earth gave them the opportunity to start over without drawing unwanted attention to themselves, because they easily disguised themselves as human beings. Interestingly enough, one scene in *Galaxy Quest* implied a comingling between one of the female aliens and one of the crew of NSEA Protector *after* the alien returned to her original non-human, alien form.

Of course, plenty of movies have been made that show a side of aliens in which they are *seemingly* malevolent, or at the very least, powerfully realistic. The movie *Knowing*, starring Nicolas Cage, immediately comes to mind. Here, we encounter aliens that are quite capable of taking on forms that resemble humans in order to promote their own agenda undercover. For them, it is merely a matter of shifting light, energy, and particles to create a form that offers a recognizable disguise to humans.

The blockbuster movie *Avatar* is another case in point. Here, through available scientific technology, people are enabled to enter the worlds of aliens, *as* an alien themselves. In this particular movie, the main character, Jake Sully (a marine), is wheelchair-bound due to a war injury. Through the newly available technology, he is able to enter an electronic, foreign-body simulation device, allowing him to enter the genetically engineered, reptilian-type, Na'vi-human hybrid body to interact with the natives of Pandora, a land of peaceful, giant, blue individuals who simply want to be left alone. These individuals are very reminiscent of Native Americans, when America was first settled, and the storyline seems to follow a similar pattern of beliefs. The problem, of course, is that Sully learns of the corporate greed behind the military mission for which he volunteered. The primary issue surrounds the technology that allows human beings to become their own "avatar" in the world of Pandora. As such, they are taller, blue, and *reptilian*. It should interest the reader to know that the word "avatar" is from the Hindu religion and it means the *appearance, manifestation*, or *incarnation* of deity into a human form. The storyline of *Avatar* follows the New Age line of thinking, with the planet Pandora being *alive* and interconnected through the trees on the planet's surface, just as many believe the Earth to be "Gaia," with a living, breathing soul.

Succubus

Another movie of late that has tongues wagging is *Jennifer's Body*, starring Megan Fox. The basic outline here is that Jennifer becomes possessed and begins to dispatch male classmates, by first seducing them, then killing them. Like the scene in *Galaxy Quest,* this harkens back to the medieval idea of the *succubus,* a demon that takes on the form of a woman in order to seduce men.

As far as the reptilian shape-shifting theory goes, coupled with more of the *succubus* imagery, in recent years the movie *Species* probably best portrays this concept. In this movie, the alien is located by the SETI (Search for Extra Terrestrial Intelligence) program. Scientists back on Earth receive communication from an alien source telling them how to create an endless supply of fuel. The second transmission explains how to splice human DNA with alien DNA.

The alien in *Species* comes to Earth and begins mating with human men, after adorning itself with a human being's voluptuous female skin. Like the female praying mantis, the alien-turned-attractive-woman kills the men when she is finished. The obvious message is that reptilian aliens have come here to Earth to mate; to mix their DNA with ours and have done so under the guise of the *succubus.*

Incubus

The movie *Starman,* starring Jeff Bridges and Karen Allen, concerns an alien who comes to this planet, takes on the form of a man (Bridges), hooks up with a woman (Allen), and then winds up mating with her before the movie ends. What is interesting is how the producers of the movie crafted a contemporary love story throughout, weaving a web that captures the mind and emotions of the viewer.

Satan has a multitude of tricks that he has used and continues to use to gain the upper hand over humanity. He will do whatever is necessary to bring his schemes to fruition. He has no qualms whatsoever in crafting a lie that is so large and multi-faceted, that it is seen as truth.

The subject of aliens is very large, and interest in this area of the paranormal has been growing exponentially for decades. With the recent release of classified documents through Wikileaks, the world has gained a good deal of information concerning documentation of alleged contact with UFOs, aliens, and other entities. For decades, the world guessed as much, but under the guise of national security, governments continued to deny that fact.

It Gets More Intense

It is impossible in one or two chapters to fully outline all of the information we have learned about aliens. We know that since time immemorial, civilizations have noted strange travelers who went from place to place sometimes in flying carriages, while at other times, simply appeared. These individuals were seen and worshipped as gods by the Ancient Egyptians and others. The information these beings are believed to have provided these ancient civilizations is very likely what allowed them to be the dominant societies of their day, with technology that far surpassed neighboring and developing empires.

As time moved forward, other creatures became known to humanity. Creatures that live within the whimsical boundaries of fairytales and ancient writings of the Greeks (among others) may well have their origins in actual creatures who revealed themselves to them.

We know that through generations of time, humanity has written about satyrs, fauns, unicorns, giants, ogres, cyclops, and many other creatures that are known to us today. It is very likely that, within the kernel of many of these stories related to creatures this modern world has never seen, lays the fact that they *did* exist in some form. Could they have been demons in disguise?

Modern-day sightings of what is believed to be the teratorn[71] have generated tremendous fear in the individuals who have allegedly seen it. Standing six to eight feet tall as it sat, this bird has been described as brooding like a vulture, waiting to swoop in to begin eating prey that has recently died.

But why do these creatures such as the teratorn, chupacabra, Mothman, and others generate such horror in people? Is it solely because of the myths surrounding them, or is there something more at work here?

What if Satan, in wanting to create the concept that terrible, other-worldly creatures exist in our world now, did so by having some of his minions impersonate them? What if he had some of his fleet of fallen angels taking care of that aspect, while others built up an entire realm of aliens within aliens to impress their false ideologies on an unwary humanity? Is it possible? It would certainly seem so.

Satan's chief aim is to cause all people to worship *him* as god, correct? If this is so, then as long as he keeps people from worshipping the true God of the Bible, then he has succeeded in some way. What better way to distract God's people from Him than by replacing God with something else that appears to be intelligent and, in some cases, even superior to the antiquated "myth" of the Christian God?

Going to the Source

Whether the entity in question appears to be a reptilian shape-shifter, one of the Greys or Pleiadeans, or something else, aliens, it is said, have been slowly and consistently revealing themselves to humanity in order to gain our trust. It is easy to spot, in documented cases of alien contact, how they seek to assist us through what is now a very difficult period of our earthly history, in order to bring us to a point of *self-sufficiency*, beyond wars, hatred, and especially beyond the narrow-mindedness that is often revealed through a variety of religions. Many of these are described as *legalistic*.

Of course, it goes without saying that in all cases, Christianity is the single most attacked religion on the face of the planet by these other-dimensional beings. It is usually described by aliens in these accounts as being completely misunderstood and, therefore, misappropriated or simply wrong. Jesus either *did* exist, but whose reputation was completely blown out of proportion, or He *did not* exist, and sometimes, in association with this claim, He was merely a holographic image created by these higher beings in order to instruct us. In any case, the intended result is to indirectly destroy Christianity, and to cause the hearer(s) to doubt what they have always heard about Jesus and Christianity by redirecting their attention to superior intelligence, and other ideas about Jesus and Christianity. It is interesting that people will question the Bible without mercy, in spite of any proof provided as to its veracity. However, when an alien being (who, by the way, is *never* asked or expected to offer proof as to its real identity) comes along and promotes the idea that Jesus was something else entirely, or that Christianity is merely the result of wishful thinking on the part of the original twelve disciples, these words alone are sufficient to be accepted as truth. People sit in awe of these beings, holding onto every word, as messages are channeled through human beings to their audience, which waits with baited breath for new revelations.

Because of the impact they have had and continue to have on society, the overwhelming question becomes: *Why would aliens be concerned at all with what occurs on this planet?* The answer seems to be that these aliens want us to believe that they have either had a hand in creating (*seeding*) life on this planet to begin with, or *their* continued existence is somehow connected to humanity's continued existence.

Decades ago, aliens impacted society through what has become known as "alien abductions." These abductions were carried out, it was said, in order for the aliens to learn and study humanity. People were purportedly taken aboard some ship (or arrived to some place seemingly out of this world) and examined "medically." In some cases, both women and men were raped (*incubus/succubus* again), and in the case of some women, alien matter was at times planted in the womb. These same women have stated that they were brought back to these ships months later to have the alien matter removed.

Clearly, these types of stories and narratives indicate a certain interest in humanity on the part of the alien that goes well beyond simply getting to know us or desiring to help us. There is a message being propagated here that aliens not only want to "get to know" us, but want to somehow dominate or overtake us. If these experiments actually happened as many attest to, then it is evident that aliens are up to something far more sinister. What still remains of the issue, is who (or what) these beings really are.

Many UFOlogists like Jacques Vallée have come to a point of believing that there is something not merely superior about these aliens, but *malevolent*. He also believes them to be inter-dimensional as opposed to simply being from outer space.

With all these stories of abductions and visitations by aliens of all sorts, it has become clear that something is obviously going on behind the scenes. Yet, with Satan and his minions so willing and quick to approach us with alternative identities, it must be seriously considered that he and his troops of fallen angels may, in fact, be the ones behind this entire alien phenomenon.

Back to the Beginning

Why would aliens today be carrying out nearly the same acts that we read about in Genesis, perpetrated first by Satan, and then by fallen angels known as the "Watchers"? Genesis 6 tells us of events that are extremely difficult to believe: fallen angels (*incubus*) procreating with human women. What was the purpose behind this unholy and corrupt relationship?

I believe there are a number of reasons why fallen angels participated in such acts. (For a more extended account of this, the reader is encouraged to pick up a copy of the *Book of Enoch*. This may also provide insight as to why the same thing appears to be happening today.)

As soon as God pronounced judgment on Adam, Eve, the serpent, and Satan, it is clear that Satan knew immediately how his future and ultimate downfall would occur. From God's own lips, Satan was made aware of the fact that the woman's *seed* would strike the fatal blow against him. In others words, somewhere in the future, the woman would give birth to a male child (and this is where we get the idea of a virgin birth because women do not have *seed*, but *eggs*, so the implication is that a "male being" would overshadow the woman: the virgin birth). When and where he would be struck down by a male child born of a virgin, Satan did not know, but he was willing to accomplish whatever was necessary to prevent it from happening.

The answer soon became very clear: Destroy the genetic base of humanity so that it no longer resembled God's original creation. If Satan could modify human DNA by combining or integrating it with "alien" DNA, he would alter the bloodline of Adam and Eve's descendants, literally putting a stop to this Savior from ever being born into this world as a pure, perfect, sinless human with a soul, because there would be no pure human being left through which that birth could occur.

The Watchers

According to the Apocryphal Book of Enoch, two hundred powerful angels "descended in the days of Jared on the summit of Mount Hermon" (Enoch 6:6). These fallen angels lusted after women and found a way to procreate with them. How they did it is impossible to know, but we *do* know that every time an angel appears in Scripture, the angel appears in male form. It is also clear that from various places in the Bible, angels can not only walk through walls, unlock chains, and open gates with a thought, but are also capable of eating. It would appear that angels' bodies are similar to ours.

So, if these watchers found a way to impregnate human women, either directly or through manipulation of DNA or something else, the result as has been stated was the *Nephilim*. Down through the biblically recorded lineage (or commonly, "begats"), by the time one arrives at Noah, only he and his immediate family were spared from DNA manipulation. Satan would have succeeded with his plan, had he been able to change Noah's DNA. Through the Flood, God destroyed every thing and being on Earth whose DNA had been affected (and infected).

Noah and his family, along with the animals they took with them in the Ark (and the existing creatures in the seas), started civilization all over again. Still, Satan *infected* again, either through the use of the souls of Nephilim (whose bodies had been destroyed in the Flood but who remained alive as wandering souls), or by direct interference. The result was seen in people like Goliath, a giant just short of ten feet tall, who was the smallest of his brothers.

What does that have to do with today? It would appear that Satan is at it again. Does it not seem strange to you that the aliens of today appear with a message that bears remarkable similarity to the New Age movement (which has its roots in Babylon's Tower of Babel in Genesis 11), and seem to be performing the same genetic modification sciences that the Watchers of old were guilty of?

Think about it. There is a real possibility that beings are now walking around that *look* like actual people. This is where the similarities stop. The costume they wear is on the outside, while the real entity exists within. Their façade of being reptilian may also be just that, a façade, used as a smokescreen, or to redirect. While we are busy thinking of reptilian aliens living among us on this planet, the real problem is what is going on behind the scenes that has absolutely nothing to do with real aliens, because real aliens do not exist, but are merely entities fashioned by demons.

I watched a movie a number of months ago called *They Live*, a 1988 schlocky Sci-Fi thriller. The main premise was very interesting. Aliens existed and lived and worked among society. The only way one could see their true identity was by wearing a special pair of sunglasses. In addition to revealing the aliens as what they really were, the sunglasses also allowed the wearer to see all the signs and billboards that contained the subliminal messages printed into them by these invading beings. These messages were designed to make humans complacent and obedient, so that when the aliens opted to take over the Earth, they would be met with less resistance. There are people alive today who firmly believe that this planet will be taken over by aliens. In truth, this is a con, by the oldest and most intelligent con artist ever created, Satan himself.

In today's world, Satan has endeavored to make himself completely outmoded. In spite of his narcissistic nature, he is not interested in having a world that believes in him *as* Satan: the age-old evil one. He much prefers to create a world in which technological advances have catapulted our society to the far reaches of space where aliens of all sorts are the norm, and in some cases, exalted. As he has worked to accomplish this, the Bible's literal meaning falls by the wayside for a growing number.

When comparing the interest between discussions of Christ's return or the latest UFO sighting, today's obvious commonplace in conversation of the supernatural is more comfortably placed in what new excitement the Greys will bring. The belief that Jesus Christ will return to Earth as Savior and Judge is too much for many (including some Christians). This new age of Star Trekian inventions and revelations is far superior, because it is largely unknown and far more "interesting." The thought of Jesus puts us back in the first century. *Star Trek, Star Wars,* and other Sci-Fi topics push us into the technological future! People have been hearing for generations that Jesus will be returning. The question that naysayers are asking is, "Well, where is He?"

This coming new age promotes another concept, one that, for many, is far more believable. With reptilian aliens among us (and other aliens in the wings), the world is simply waiting for that right moment when the "big reveal" takes place, and those aliens who have spent generations helping humanity adjust to the idea that they exist, will actually be able to physically step onto this planet from their hiding places in order to help man "achieve."

Who *doesn't* want to be able to travel other galaxies? Who *doesn't* wish to learn the secrets of the ancient gods (demons clothed in alien skins) in order to evolve to the next spiritual plane?

In the Garden of Eden, Satan not only used the deception of words to enthrall and trap Eve and then Adam, but he also chose to use a deceptive disguise, one in which Eve would not be afraid to approach. The serpent had been around Eden. Eve had likely seen it, and didn't feel that it had posed a threat. Maybe, as the days passed, the serpent became more familiar to Eve until such a time as he sidled up to her to speak with her one-on-one. Once that gap was bridged, it all seemed normal. Maybe, as the serpent had moved around the garden, he was there just enough to pique Eve's curiosity, much the way we tend to listen harder when we hear someone whispering.

If biblical history is any indication, this seems to be exactly what demons have done and *are* doing. Eons ago, they approached humanity in a guise, from a distance, and as a tease. It was a guise that, at first, may have seemed slightly off-putting, though at the same time, created an unquenchable interest. As time passed, the idea of alien existence has captured the imagination and belief of a growing circle of humanity.

It is likely that these demons-as-aliens are waiting for that specific moment when they will be allowed to reveal themselves to humanity. When that happens, we can expect the very same delusions of grandeur as those in the Garden to sound not only realistic, but likely. The full force of "you will be gods" will be launched by demons masquerading as aliens, in order to capture the hearts, the minds, and the souls of all humanity.

The deception is here and growing...waiting for the big reveal.

CHAPTER SIX

DO ALIEN-HUMAN HYBRIDS WALK AMONG US?

By Thomas Horn

In January of last year, the Royal Society, the National Academy of Science of the UK, and the Commonwealth hosted representatives from NASA, the European Space Agency, and the UN Office for Outer Space Affairs, during its 350th anniversary celebration. The event offered some dizzying intellects in the featured discussion, "The Detection of Extraterrestrial Life and the Consequences for Science and Society." Lord Martin Rees, President of the Royal Society and Astronomer Royal, announced that aliens may be "staring us in the face" in a form humans are unable to recognize. Other speakers used words like "overwhelming evidence" and "unprecedented proof" to signify how close we may be to making discovery of intelligent alien life. Some, like Simon Conway Morris, professor of evolutionary paleobiology at Cambridge University, worried that contact with these unknowns might not be a good thing. "Extra-terrestrials might not only resemble us but have our foibles, such as greed, violence, and a tendency to exploit others' resources," he said. "And while aliens could come in peace they are quite as likely to be searching for somewhere to live, and to help themselves to water, minerals and fuel."[72]

While other scientists, astronomers, and physicists agreed with Morris' concerns (most notably, renowned astrophysicist Stephen Hawking), some speakers at the gathering of intellectuals were more optimistic, imagining ETs someday appearing as man's saviors or, at a minimum, benevolent space brothers. When Father José Gabriel Funes in a long interview with the L'Osservatore Romano newspaper weighed in on the question, "Are we alone in the Universe?" he said there is a certain possibility of intelligent life elsewhere in the cosmos, and that such a notion "doesn't contradict our faith." He then added: "How can we rule out that life may have developed elsewhere? Just as we consider earthly creatures as 'a brother,' and 'sister,' why should we not talk about an 'extraterrestrial brother'? It would still be part of creation."[73]

Such statements by Funes were the latest in a string of recent comments by Vatican astronomers confirming the belief that discovery may be made in the near future of alien life, including intelligent life, and that this encounter would not unhinge the doctrine of Christ.

In 2005, another Vatican astronomer, Guy Consolmagno tackled this subject in a fifty-page booklet, *Intelligent Life in the Universe?: Catholic Belief and the Search for Extraterrestrial Intelligent Life*, in which he similarly concluded that chances are more likely than not that mankind is facing a future discovery of extraterrestrial intelligence. Before that, Monsignor Corrado

Balducci made even bigger news when he said ETs were actually already interacting with Earth and that some of the Vatican's leaders were aware of it.

Still, perhaps most intriguing was maverick Catholic theologian Father Malachi Martin who, before his death in 1999, hinted at something like imminent extraterrestrial contact more than once. While on *Coast to Coast AM* radio in 1997, Art Bell asked Martin why the Vatican was heavily invested in the study of deep space at Mt Graham Observatory in southeastern Arizona. As a retired professor of the Pontifical Biblical Institute, Martin was uniquely qualified to hold, in secret, information pertaining to the Vatican's Advanced Technology Telescope (VATT) project at the Mount Graham International Observatory (MGIO). Martin's answer ignited a firestorm of interest among Christian and secular UFOlogists when he said, "Because the mentality... amongst those who [are] at the...highest levels of Vatican administration and geopolitics, know...what's going on in space, *and what's approaching us*, could be of great import in the next five years, ten years" (emphasis added).[74]

Those cryptic words "what's approaching us, could be of great import" was followed in subsequent interviews with discussion of a mysterious "sign in the sky" that Malachi believed was approaching from the north. People familiar with Malachi believe he may have been referring to a near-future arrival of alien intelligence.

Yet, if ET life is something Vatican officials have privately considered for some time, why speak of it so openly now, in what some perceive as a careful, doctrinal unveiling over the last few years? Is this a deliberate effort by church officials to "warm-up" the laity to ET disclosure? Are official church publications on the subject an attempt to soften the blow before disclosure arrives, in order to help the faithful retain their orthodoxy in light of unprecedented forthcoming knowledge?

Writing for Newsweek on Thursday, May 15, 2008, in the article "The Vatican and Little Green Men," Sharon Begley noted that "[this] might be part of a push to demonstrate the Vatican's embrace of science… Interestingly, the Vatican has plans to host a conference in Rome next spring to mark the 150th anniversary of the Origin of Species, Charles Darwin's seminal work on the theory of evolution. Conference organizers say it will look beyond entrenched ideological positions—including misconstrued creationism. The Vatican says it wants to reconsider the problem of evolution 'with a broader perspective' and says an 'appropriate consideration is needed more than ever before.'"[75]

The "appropriate consideration" Begley mentioned may have been something alluded to by Guy Consolmagno three years earlier in an interview with the Sunday Herald. That article pointed out how Consolmagno's job included reconciling "the wildest reaches of science fiction with the flint-eyed dogma of the Holy See" and that his latest mental meander was about "the Jesus Seed," described as "a brain-warping theory which speculates that, perhaps, every planet that harbours intelligent, self-aware life may also have had a Christ walk across its methane seas, just as Jesus did here on Earth in Galilee. The salvation of the Betelguesians may have happened simultaneously with the salvation of the Earthlings."[76] This sounds like a sanctified version of panspermia—the idea that life on Earth was "seeded" by something a long time ago such as an asteroid impact—but in this case, "the seed" was divinely appointed and reconciled to Christ.

The curious connection between the Vatican's spokespersons and the question of extraterrestrials and salvation was further hinted in the May, 2008 L'Osservatore Romano interview with Father Funes, titled, "The Extraterrestrial is My Brother." In Google and blog translations of the Italian feature, Funes responds to the question of whether extraterrestrials would need to be redeemed, which he believes should not be assumed. "God was made man in Jesus to save us," he says. "If other intelligent beings exist, it is not said that they would have need of redemption. They could remain in full friendship with their Creator."[77]

By "full friendship," Funes reflected how some Vatican theologians accept the possibility that an extraterrestrial species may exist that is morally superior to men—closer to God than we fallen humans are—and that, as a consequence, *they may come here to evangelize us*. Father Guy Consolmagno took up this same line of thinking when he wrote in his book, *Brother Astronomer: Adventures of a Vatican Scientist*:

> So the question of whether or not one should evangelize is really a moot point. Any alien we find will learn and change from contact with us, just as we will learn and change from contact with them. It's inevitable. And they'll be evangelizing us, too.[78]

But hold on, because this rabbit hole goes deeper...

In a paper for the Interdisciplinary Encyclopedia of Religion and Science, Father Giuseppe Tanzella-Nitti of the Pontifical University in Rome explains just how we could actually be evangelized during contact with "spiritual aliens," as every believer in God would, he argues, greet an extraterrestrial civilization as an extraordinary experience and would be inclined to respect the alien and to recognize the common origin of our different species as originating from the same Creator. According to Giuseppe, this contact by non-terrestrial intelligence would then offer new possibilities "of better understanding the relationship between God and the whole of creation."[79] Giuseppe states this would not immediately oblige the Christian "to renounce his own faith in God simply on the basis of the reception of new, unexpected information of a religious character from extraterrestrial civilizations,"[80] but that such a renunciation could come soon after as the new "religious content" originating from outside the Earth is confirmed as reasonable and credible. "Once the trustworthiness of the information has been verified" the believer would have to "reconcile such new information with the truth that he or she already knows and believes on the basis of the revelation of the One and Triune God, conducting a re-reading [of the Gospel] inclusive of the new data..."[81] How this "more complete" ET Gospel might deemphasize or significantly modify our understanding of salvation through Jesus Christ is unknown, but former Vatican Observatory vice director, Christopher Corbally, in his article "What if There Were Other Inhabited Worlds" concludes that Jesus simply might not remain the *only Word* of salvation: "I would try to explore the alien by letting 'it' be what it is, without rushing for a classification category, not even presuming two genders," Corbally said, before dropping this bombshell:

> While Christ is the First and the Last Word (the Alpha and the Omega) spoken to humanity, he is not necessarily the *only* word spoke to the universe... For, the Word spoken to us does not seem to exclude an equivalent "Word" spoken to aliens. They, too, could have had their "Logos-event". Whatever that event might have been, it does not have to be a repeated death-and-resurrection, if we allow God more imagination than some religious thinkers seem

to have had. For God, as omnipotent, is not restricted to one form of language, the human.[82]

That high-ranking spokespersons for the Vatican have in recent years increasingly offered such language acknowledging the likelihood of extraterrestrial intelligence and the dramatic role ET's introduction to human civilization could play in regard to altering established creeds about anthropology, philosophy, religion, and redemption could be future-consequential.

The New Evangelists of the Ancient Astronaut Theory

The trend within modern religious and academic communities to accommodate emerging visions of astro-biology and astro-theology can be seen as the natural extension of a hypothesis (once considered heresy) made popular in the 1960s known as the Ancient Astronaut Theory. This notion claims that Homo sapiens (humans) arose as the result of advanced extraterrestrials visiting Earth in ancient times and genetically upgrading hominid DNA. These beings were the progenitors of the creation myths according to this theory, including the Bible's revelations of "God."

In the introduction to his bestselling book, *Chariots of the Gods?*, Erich von Daniken, (who, it might be argued, is one of the fathers of modern UFOlogy) said:

I claim that our forefathers received visits from the universe in the remote past, even though I do not yet know who these extra-terrestrial intelligences were or from which planet they came. I nevertheless proclaim that these "strangers" annihilated part of mankind existing at the time and produced a new, perhaps the first, Homo sapiens.[83]

As illustrated in such Hollywood films as *Contact* and *Close Encounters of the Third Kind,* von Daniken's hypothesis took America by storm in the '60s with the proposition that mankind was possibly the offspring of an ancient, perhaps ongoing, extraterrestrial experiment. New Agers like Daniken assert that the myths of ancient gods—from Sumeria to Egypt, Greece, and beyond—are a crude record of this encounter with other-world beings. Ancient men would have considered space travelers as gods and would have recorded their arrival, their experiments, and their departure, in hieroglyphs, megaliths, and stone tablets, as a "supernatural" encounter between gods and men. Mr. Daniken continues:

> While [the] spaceship disappears again into the mists of the universe our friends will talk about the miracle—"The gods were here!"...they will make a record of what happened: uncanny, weird, miraculas [*sic*]. Then their texts will relate—and drawings will show—that gods in golden clothes were there in a flying boat that landed with a tremendous din. They will write about chariots which the gods drove over land and sea, and of terrifying weapons that were like lightning, and they will recount that the gods promised to return.
>
> They will hammer and chisel in the rock pictures of what they had once seen: shapeless giants with helmets and rods on their heads, carrying boxes in front of their chests; balls on which indefinable beings sit and ride through the air; staves from which rays are shot out as if from a sun..."[84]

Researchers like Von Daniken further claim that the odd appearance of some of the gods as depicted in various hieroglyphs (human-like creatures with falcon heads; lions with heads of bulls, etc.) could be viewed as evidence that "aliens" conducted genetic experiments and cross-mutations of both ancient people and animals. It may surprise some to learn that many conservative theologians agree with this assessment, but hold that the "alien" invaders performing these procedures were, in fact, fallen angels, not advanced life forms from another galaxy. Scholars base this idea on historical records dating back to the beginning of time within every major culture of the ancient world where the remarkably consistent story is told of "gods" that descended from heaven and materialized in bodies of flesh. From Rome to Greece—and before that, to Egypt, Persia, Assyria, Babylonia, and Sumer—the earliest records of civilization tell of the era when powerful beings known to the Hebrews as *Watchers* and in the book of Genesis as the *benei ha-elohim* (sons of God) mingled themselves with humans, giving birth to part-celestial, part-terrestrial hybrids known as *Nephilim*. The Bible says this happened when men began to increase on Earth and daughters were born to them. When the sons of God saw the women's beauty, they took wives from among them to sire their unusual offspring. In Genesis 6:4 we read the following account: "There were giants in the earth in those days; and also after that, when the sons of God came in unto the daughters of men, and they bare children to them, the same became mighty men which were of old, men of renown."

When this Scripture is compared with other ancient texts, including Enoch, Jubilees, Baruch, Genesis Apocryphon, Philo, Josephus, Jasher, and others, it unfolds to some that the giants of the Old Testament, such as Goliath, were the part-human, part-animal, part-angelic offspring of a supernatural interruption into the divine order and natural evolution of the species. The apocryphal *Book of Enoch* gives a name to the angels involved in this cosmic conspiracy, calling them "Watchers." We read:

> And I Enoch was blessing the Lord of majesty and the King of the ages, and lo! the Watchers called me—Enoch the scribe—and said to me: "Enoch, thou scribe of righteousness, go, declare to the Watchers of the heaven who have left the high heaven, the holy eternal place, and have defiled themselves with women, and have done as the children of earth do, and have taken unto themselves wives: Ye have wrought great destruction on the earth: And ye shall have no peace nor forgiveness of sin: and inasmuch as they delight themselves in their children [the Nephilim], The murder of their beloved ones shall they see, and over the destruction of their children shall they lament, and shall make supplication unto eternity, but mercy and peace shall ye not attain." (1 Enoch 10:3–8)

According to Enoch, two hundred of these powerful angels departed "high heaven" and used women (among other things) to extend their progeny into mankind's plane of existence. The Interlinear Hebrew Bible offers an interesting interpretation of Genesis 6:2 in this regard. Where the King James Bible says, "The sons of God saw the daughters of men that they [were] fair," the IHN interprets this as, "The benei Elohim saw the daughters of Adam, that they were *fit extensions*" (emphasis added). The term "fit extensions" seems applicable when the whole of the ancient record is understood to mean that the Watchers wanted to leave their proper sphere of existence in order to enter Earth's three-dimensional reality. They viewed women—or at least their genetic material—as part of the formula for accomplishing this task. Departing the proper habitation that God had assigned them was grievous to the Lord and led to divine penalization. Jude described it this way: The "angels which kept not their first estate, but left their own habitation, he hath reserved in everlasting chains under darkness unto the judgment of the great day" (Jude 6).

Besides apocryphal, pseudepigraphic, and Jewish traditions related to the legend of the Watchers and the "mighty men" born of their union with humans, mythologized accounts tell the stories of "gods" using humans to produce heroes or demigods (half-gods). When the ancient Greek version of the Hebrew Old Testament (the LXX or Septuagint) was made, the word "Nephilim"—referring to the part-human offspring of the Watchers—was translated *gegenes*, a word implying "Earth born." This same terminology was used to describe the Greek Titans and other legendary heroes of partly celestial and partly terrestrial origin, such as Hercules (born of Zeus and the mortal Alcmena), Achilles (the Trojan hero son of Thetis and Peleus), and Gilgamesh (the two-thirds god and one-third human child of Lugalbanda and Ninsun).

These demigods were likewise accompanied in texts and idol representation by half-animal and half-human creatures like centaurs (the part-human, part-horse offspring of Apollo's son, Centaurus), chimeras, furies, satyrs, gorgons, nymphs, Minotaurs, and other genetic aberrations. Historian Andrew Tomas believes these mythological records are "thought-fossils depicting the story of vanished cultures in symbols and allegories," or, as Stephen Quayle, in his book *Genesis 6 Giants* explains: "The collective memories in the form of myths, fables and fairy tales from various cultures and ages of mankind are overwhelming evidence that the Nephilim existed."[85] All of this indicates that the Watchers not only modified human DNA during the construction of Nephilim, but animals as well, a point the book of Enoch supports, saying in the seventh chapter that the fallen angels "sinned" against animals as well as humans. Other books such as the *Book of Jubilees* add that this interspecies mingling eventually resulted in mutations among normal humans and animals whose "flesh" (genetic makeup) was "corrupted" by the activity, presumably through crossbreeding (see 5:1–5; 7:21–25). Even the Old Testament contains reference to the genetic mutations that developed among humans following this time frame, including "men" of unusual size, physical strength, six fingers, six toes, animal appetite for blood, and even lion-like features (2 Samuel 21:20; 23:20).

However, of all the ancient records, the most telling extrabiblical script is from the *Book of Jasher*, a mostly forgotten text referred to in the Bible in Joshua 10:13 and 2 Samuel 1:18. Jasher records the familiar story of the fall of the Watchers, and then adds an exceptional detail that none of the other texts is as unequivocal about, something that can only be understood in modern language to mean advanced biotechnology, genetic engineering, or "transgenic modification" of species. After the Watchers had instructed humans "in the secrets of heaven," note what Jasher says occurred:

> [Then] the sons of men [began teaching] the mixture of animals of one species with the other, in order therewith to provoke the Lord. (Jasher 4:18)

The phrase "the mixture of animals of one species with the other" does not mean Watchers had taught men hybridization, as this would not have "provoked the Lord." God made like animals of different breeds capable of reproducing. For example, horses can propagate with other mammals of the equidae classification (the taxonomic "horse family"), including donkeys and zebras. It would not have "provoked the Lord" for this type of animal breeding to have taken place, as God, Himself, made the animals able to do this.

If, on the other hand, the Watchers were crossing species boundaries by mixing incompatible animals *of one species with the other*, such as a horse with a human (a centaur), this would have been a different matter and may cast light on the numerous ancient stories of mythical beings of variant-species manufacturing that fit perfectly within the records of what the Watchers were accomplishing. Understandably, this kind of chimera-making would have "provoked the Lord," and raises the serious question of why the Watchers would have risked eternal damnation by tinkering with God's creation in this way. Yahweh had placed boundaries between the species and strictly ordered that "each kind" reproduce only after its "own kind." Was the motive of the Watchers to break these rules simply the desire to rebel, to assault God's creative genius through biologically altering what He had made? Or was something of deeper significance behind the activity?

Some believe the corruption of antediluvian DNA by Watchers was an effort to cut off the birth line of the Messiah. This theory posits that Satan understood the protoevangelium—the promise in Genesis 3:15 that a Savior would be born, the seed of the woman, and that He would destroy the fallen angel's power. Satan's followers therefore intermingled with the human race in a conspiracy to stop the birth of Christ. If human DNA could be universally corrupted or "demonized," they reasoned, no Savior would be born and mankind would be lost forever.

Those who support this theory believe this is why God ordered His people to maintain a pure bloodline and not to intermarry with the other nations. When Israel breached this command and the mutated DNA began rapidly spreading among men and animals, God instructed Noah to build an ark and to prepare for a flood that would destroy every living thing. That God had to send such a universal fiat like the Flood illustrates how widespread the altered DNA eventually became. In fact, the Bible says in Genesis 6:9 that only Noah, and by extension his children, were found "perfect" in their generation. The Hebrew word for "perfect" in this case is *tamiym*, which means "without blemish" or "healthy," the same word used in Leviticus to describe an unblemished, sacrificial lamb. The meaning was not that Noah was morally perfect, but that his physical makeup—his DNA—had not been contaminated with Nephilim descent, as apparently the rest of the world had become. In order to preserve mankind as He had made them, God destroyed all but Noah's family in the Flood. The ancient records, including those of the Bible, appear to agree with this theology, consistently describing the cause of the Flood as happening in response to "all flesh" having become "corrupted, both man and beast."

While I believe the theory of DNA corruption as an intended method for halting the coming of Christ has merit, an alternative (or additional) reason the Watchers may have blended living organisms exists. This theory is original with me and grew from my need to incorporate the voluminous historical texts, which described this peculiar history, into a consistent account that corresponds with Scripture.

To harmonize the ancient records, I came to believe that the overriding motive for whatever the Watchers were doing with the DNA of various species had to be understood within the context of their foremost goal, which was to leave their plane of existence and to enter ours. My challenge then became to answer the question of how blending various species would satisfy this goal or provide the Watchers with a method of departure from "high heaven" and incarnation into man's "habitation." While I will not take time here to explain every detail (a five-hour CD set called *As it Was in the Days of Noah: The Return of the Nephilim* that covers this, and related material, is available from www. SurvivorMall.com), I eventually hypothesized that the Watchers *had* to blend species in the way they did in order to create a soulless or spiritless body into which they could extend themselves. The rationale is that every creature as it existed originally had its beginning in God, who ordered each creature to reproduce "after its own kind." The phrase "after its own kind" verifies what kind of spirit or persona can enter into an intelligent being at conception. When the sperm of a dog meets ovum of a dog and the life of a dog is formed, at the first spark of life the nature of a dog enters that embryo and it grows to become a dog in traits and form. The spirit of a man does not enter it, in the same way that a man is not born with the qualities of a horse or cow. This creature/nature integrity is part of the divine order and would have kept the Watchers, who wanted to incarnate within the earthly realm (not just "possess" creatures), from displacing the spirits of humans or the natures of animals and replacing them with their own. How did they overcome this problem? Like scientists are doing today, it appears based on the ancient records that they blended existing DNA of several living creatures and made something that neither the spirit of man or beast would enter at conception, for it was neither man nor beast. As the quarterly online travel guide *Mysterious World*, in its 2003 feature, "Giants in the Earth," noted:

The Nephilim were genetically manufactured beings created from the genetic material of various pre-existing animal species... The fallen angels did not personally interbreed with the daughters of men, but used their godlike intellect to delve into the secrets of YHWH's Creation and manipulate it to their own purposes. And the key to creating or recreating man, as we have (re)discovered in the twentieth century, is the human genome—DNA.[86]

What Does This Have to Do With Aliens?

As discussed above, the manipulation of living tissue by ancient fallen angels led to superhuman hybridity made up of human and animal genetics known as Nephilim, an "Earth-born" facsimile or "fit extension" into which these beings could incarnate. However, the long history of demonological phenomenon related to manipulation of biological matter suggests that versions of this curious activity have been ongoing ever since the Days of Noah. Today, what some call "alien abduction," in which a breeding program allegedly exists resulting in alien/human hybrids, seems but a contemporary retelling of similar DNA harvesting and genetic manipulation by those mysterious beings whose activity was recorded throughout time. In his book, *Confrontations—A Scientist's Search for Alien Contact*, highly regarded UFO researcher, Dr. Jacques F. Vallée, once phrased it this way: "Contact with [aliens is] only a modern extension of the age-old tradition of contact with nonhuman consciousness in the form of angels, demons, elves, and sylphs."[87] Later, Vallée more closely identified the operative power behind "aliens" as equivalent to the fallen angels in the Days of Noah:

Are these races only semi-human, so that in order to maintain contact with us, they need crossbreeding with men and women of our planet? Is this the origin of the many tales and legends where genetics plays a great role: the symbolism of the Virgin in occultism and religion, the fairy tales involving human midwives and changelings, the sexual overtones of the flying saucer reports, the biblical stories of intermarriage between the Lord's angels, and terrestrial women, whose offspring were giants?[88]

Another highly respected and often quoted UFO researcher, John Keel, echoed the same when he stated in *Operation Trojan Horse*:

Demonology is not just another crackpot-ology. It is the ancient and scholarly study of the monsters and demons who have seemingly coexisted with man throughout history... The manifestations and occurrences described in this imposing literature are similar, if not entirely identical, to the UFO phenomenon itself. Victims of demonomania (possession) suffer the very same medical and emotional symptoms as the UFO contactees... The Devil and his demons can, according to the literature, manifest themselves in almost any form and can physically imitate anything from angels to horrifying monsters with glowing eyes. Strange objects and entities materialize and dematerialize in these stories, just as the UFOs and their splendid occupants appear and disappear, walk through walls, and perform other supernatural feats.[89]

Associate professor of psychology Elizabeth L. Hillstrom, in her book *Testing the Spirits*, was even more inflexible on comparisons between "alien" experiences and historical demonic activity, quoting an impressive list of scholars from various disciplines who conclude the similarities between ETs and demons is unlikely coincidental. Hillstrom cites authorities of the first rank including Pierre Guerin, a scientist associated with the French National Council for Scientific Research, who believes "The modern UFOnauts and the demons of past days are probably identical,"[90] and veteran researcher John Keel, who reckons, "The UFO manifestations seem to be, by and large, merely minor variations of the age-old demonological phenomenon."[91]

Then there is the question of alien-demoniality and Bible prophecy. When former college professor and BBC correspondent, Dr. I. D. E. Thomas, in his highly recommended book, *The Omega Conspiracy*, chronicled the burgeoning of so-called "alien abduction" activity in the 1980s, he made enlightening connections between the phenomenon and end-time prophecy concerning a return of the Nephilim, something other writers have since built upon. Documentation by "abductees" worldwide and the stories of DNA harvesting by "aliens" reminded him of the history of biological misuse by the Watchers. Dr. Thomas told me personally that the special desire by the "aliens" for human and animal molecular matter could explain "why animals have been killed, mutilated, and stolen by the aliens," a point Vallée repeated in his book, *The Invisible College: What a Group of Scientists Has Discovered About UFO Influences on the Human Race*, when he wrote:

In order to materialize and take definite form, these entities seem to require a source of energy...a living thing...a human medium… Our sciences have not reached a point where they can offer us any kind of working hypothesis for this process. But we can speculate that these beings need living energy which they can reconstruct into physical form. Perhaps that is why dogs and animals tend to vanish in [UFO] flap areas. Perhaps the living cells of those animals are somehow used by the ultraterrestrials to create forms which we can see and sense with our limited perceptions.[92]

Ultimately, Vallée and his contemporaries determined that whatever the modern alien presence represents, its goal is the collection of DNA for what appears to be a *Breeding Program*, followed by a *Hybridization Program*, and finally an *Integration Program*; this is exactly what Watchers accomplished with Nephilim in ancient times. The purpose behind the alleged modern ET-human-hybridization agenda is so clouded in mystery that not even the world's most prestigious intelligence bureaus seem to fathom it—except of course if at above-top-secret levels there are Black Government Agencies participating with the alien entities in some sort of Cosmic Watergate wherein the breeding program transpires. Plenty of so-called whistle-blowers, books, and leaked files have suggested the same, but Vallée's suspicion is that many, if not most, of these "sources" are actually concoctions by complicit government proxies, which are disseminated in order to so completely muddle the factual objectives of the *program* with duplicity, half-truths, and subterfuge that the public can never really know what is happening. "There is a genuine UFO phenomenon and it is not explained by the revelations of alleged government agents bearing fancy code names like Condor or Falcon,"[93] he concluded in *Revelations: Alien Contact and Human Deception.*

But that a modern "alien" program of breeding and hybridizing humans is covertly occurring similar to what ancient Watchers did is something, no matter how absurd it may seem, a growing body of scholars, based on accumulative physical and eye-witness evidence, are coming around to.

In his book, *Secret Life: Firsthand, Documented Accounts of UFO Abductions*, Professor David M. Jacobs of Temple University combined scientific and investigatory methods to analyze the accounts of dozens of "abductees" including more than three hundred independently corroborated stories of such experiences, describing in unsettling detail the reproductive procedures that abductees claim were administered by "small alien beings." Jacobs' profoundly unsettling conclusion paralleled that of Vallée and others—that alien abductors are conducting complex reproductive experiments involving the conception, gestation, hybridization, and integration on Earth of alien hybrid beings.

Jacobs wrote:

[The aliens] want to use the ability humans have to recreate themselves. They want human sperm and eggs. They want human physical involvement with the offspring. They want complete knowledge of the reproductive physiological processes. [And this] abduction program appears to be vast. Abductees routinely report rooms with as many as two hundred tables holding humans in various stages of examination. The aliens hustle them out as soon as possible after the procedures are completed, presumably so that more humans can be brought in. The evidence suggests that this goes on twenty-four hours per day, month after month, year after year. The amount of time and energy invested in the breeding program is enormous.[94]

Besides Jacobs and Vallée, other highly respected scientists who believed something unearthly was happening in connection to alien activity included: Dr. Josef Allen Hynek, the United States astronomer and professor in charge of Project Blue Book; Dr. Hermann Julius Oberth, one of the founding fathers of rocketry and astronautics; Lynn E. Catoe, senior bibliographer for government publication research by the Library of Congress for the U.S. Air Force Office of Scientific Research; and the late Harvard Medical School Professor and Pulitzer Prize-winner, Dr. John Edward Mack. After working with abduction "experiencers" including interviews with over one hundred people of various ages and backgrounds, Mack showcased the narratives of thirteen subjects in astonishing detail in his book, *Abduction: Human Encounters with Aliens*, where he reached very much the same conclusion as his peers:

What is amply corroborated [is] that the abduction phenomenon is in some central way involved in a breeding program that results in the creation of alien/human hybrid offspring... My own impression is that we may be witnessing...an awkward joining of two species, engineered by an intelligence we are unable to fathom.[95]

Yet, if demons pretending to be aliens are actually behind a fantastic breeding and hybridization scheme, what would be their purpose? Biblical scholar and prophecy expert Gary Stearman believes they are dark overlords, come forth to repeat what happened in the Days of Noah, to create a generation of genetically altered pseudo-humans for the service of Satan in preparation of Armageddon. He points to Matthew 24:37, which says, "But as the days of Noe [Noah] were, so shall also the coming of the Son of man be." Gary then goes on to elaborate:

> Here, Jesus is clearly speaking of future judgment, the Tribulation, Second Coming and certain events that will surround it.
>
> He says that His coming will happen at a time when social conditions will resemble those that plagued the world in the days of Noah. From Genesis 6, we now discern that these will include an invasion of dark forces from the heavens… The UFO abduction phenomenon is only a mask for fallen angels who have departed from their natural domain to engage in the filthy work of creating an alternate race that will act as their proxies… Now, as [in the Days of Noah], they pry into the forbidden areas of human procreation. Lascivious and power hungry, they seek to set up their own race, and their own province of control.
>
> But only in the last fifty years have their activities acquired a speed and purpose that tells us what time it is, prophetically speaking. Jesus told us, in effect, that when we begin to see such things come to pass, His appearance would not be far behind.[96]

On the Watcher website, our friend David Flynn—whose early online research first broke many of today's most popular theories regarding the alien-hybrid scheme as an end-times deception aimed at misleading mankind—reaffirms the warnings made by Gary Stearman:

The Book of Enoch explains that the Sons of God descended first onto the mountain called Hermon... The rebel angels intended to thwart God's plan for the earth by destroying the descendants of Adam. Satan's goal in organizing the Nephilim/human hybridization program was to pollute the bloodline that would produce Jesus Christ, the Messiah, the Kinsman Redeemer. Now that it is so close to the end times, Satan has orchestrated human/rebel angel interaction on a grand scale. The plan is now to prevent any flesh from being saved. By manipulating human genetics, whether through the guise of "alien abduction" or by supplying willing mortal accomplices with the proper technology...there is currently being created humanoid hybrids who are not-quite-human... The second wave of hybrid "Nephilim creation" is Satan's last effort to destroy all Sons of Adam, so that none can be redeemed when Jesus Christ returns at the End of the Age.[97]

Does a curious verse in the book of Daniel hint that Stearman and Flynn may be on to something? Speaking of the last days of human government, Daniel said:

They shall mingle themselves with the seed of men: but they shall not cleave one to another, even as iron is not mixed with clay. (Daniel 2:43)

While Daniel does not explain who "they" that "mingle themselves with the seed of men" are, the personal pronoun "they" caused Chuck Missler and Mark Eastman, in their book, *Alien Encounters*, to ask: "Just what (or who) are 'mingling with the seed of men?' Who are these Non-seed? It staggers the mind to contemplate the potential significance of Daniel's passage and its implications for the future global governance."[98]

Daniel's verse troubled Missler and Eastman because it seemed to indicate that the same phenomenon that occurred in Genesis chapter 6—where non-human species or "non-seed" mingled with human seed and produced Nephilim—would happen again in the end times. When this verse from Daniel is coupled with Genesis 3:15, which says, "And I will put enmity between thee and the woman, and between thy *seed* [*zera*, meaning "offspring," "descendents," or "children"] and her *seed*," an incredible tenet emerges—that Satan has seed, and that it is at enmity with Christ.

To "mingle" non-human seed with Homo sapiens through altering human DNA while simultaneously returning Nephilim to Earth has been the inspiration of the spirit of Antichrist ever since God halted the practice of genetic manipulation during the Great Flood. According to Louis Pauwells and Jacques Bergier in *The Dawn of Magic*, this was certainly the goal of the antichrist spirit that possessed Adolf Hitler:

> Hitler's aim was neither the founding of a race of supermen, nor the conquest of the world; these were only means towards the realization of the great work he dreamed of. His real aim was to perform an act of creation, a divine operation, the goal of a biological mutation which would result in an unprecedented exaltation of the human race

and the "apparition of a new race of heroes and demigods and god-men."[99]

One cannot read the conclusion by Pauwells and Bergier regarding Hitler's Antichrist ambition without calling to mind that from the Middle Ages forward, church leaders have believed the Antichrist would ultimately represent the return of the Nephilim—the reunion of demons with humans. St. Augustine himself wrote of such demoniality in the *City of God*,[100] and in the *De Daemonialitate, et Incubis, et Succubi*, Fr. Ludovico Maria Sinistrari de Amino (1622–1701) also perceived the coming of Antichrist as representing the biological hybridization of demons with humans. "To theologians and philosophers," he wrote, "it is a fact, that from the copulation of humans with the demon... Antichrist must be born."[101]

The English theologian George Hawkins Pember agreed with this premise, and in his 1876 masterpiece, *Earth's Earliest Ages*, he analyzed the prophecy of Christ that says the end-times would be a repeat of "the Days of Noah." Pember outlined the seven great causes of the antediluvian destruction and documented their developmental beginnings in his lifetime. Like Gary Stearman, he concluded that the seventh and most fearful sign would be the return of the Nephilim—"The appearance upon earth of beings from the Principality of the Air, and their unlawful intercourse with the human race."[102]

Thus, it appears those social, spiritual, and academic intellectuals who now believe we are close to integration with intelligent alien life (and who also believe that this discovery could ultimately reconfigure established doctrines of science, religion, and salvation) may be closer to the truth than some of them have imagined. Events unfolding over the past decade portend a near future in which "alien influences" led by a man of unusual intelligence will arrive on Earth as champions of a "new" Gospel. Numerous Scriptures foretold the otherworldly leader's coming for what he actually is—paganism's ultimate incarnation; the "beast" of Revelation 13:1. As Jesus Christ was the "seed of the woman" (Genesis 3:15), the Antichrist will be the "seed of the serpent."

This brings me to my final point: Daniel the prophet provided an important clue for identifying this false savior at his arrival. Daniel 11:39 says he will be a worshipper of the *god of forces—a god whom his fathers knew not*, a text that literally means, *an alien god.*

For now the world watches…and waits…*for contact.*

CHAPTER SEVEN

YOUR BRAIN ON VIRTUAL SIN

By Sharon K. Gilbert

Beginnings

Once upon a time, a human child listened to her very first fairytale. Inside the protection of a bedroom wallpapered with princesses and castles, her mother's voice was soft, modulated; sometimes inflected with gentle cooing as if singing the songs of ancient magicians, other times wrapped with fearsome strut and polish as if striding a mountain in the boots of a ravenous giant. Wolves, witches, goblins, and trolls planned and plotted against heroes and maidens, each one ending with the comforting words "and they all lived happily ever after." The child loved her mother's voice, and she learned to tune in, her mind fixed on the sound—and the story—as she closed her eyes and inhabited the words and the make-believe realm. And for her, as with most human children of the world, an imaginary, alternate dimension took shape, brick-by-brick, wall-by-wall, street-by-street, city-by-city, and kingdom-by-kingdom.

As the little girl grew, her imaginary realm traveled with her, though she walked there far less often than when she'd been younger; but she still visited in her dreams. Now, a teenager, the cares of reality nicked and pinched at the girl's hungry soul, and so she sought nightly refuge in the familiar, manageable kingdom within the recesses of her mind, but the simple stories of youth no longer had the same effect. As if she'd forgotten how to "dream," the girl rushed headlong into anything that might help her to rediscover the hidden kingdoms once again: video games, film, graphic novels, fan fiction. Her brain, however, could no longer respond to gentle stimulation—now, nearly an adult, the young woman developed a deep-seated need for dark fiction, vampires, ghosts, demons, and the very dead themselves to sedate the harsh world and recreate the safe, inner world of childhood fairytales.

Alas, the poor girl had no idea what a terrifying journey she had begun! Such dark worlds demand our full attention; they feed on our dreams and upon our imaginations like monstrous, demonic ghouls, finally controlling our inner kingdom and setting up the trolls as prison guards and the vampires as lovers in disguise. And so the Darkness controlled the young woman—changing her, reshaping her, coercing her into perverted, dream-like, virtual acts within her mind; and before long, the girl found comfort only in darkness, and light became a terrifying reality.

Defining Terms

How many of us remember the very first day of classes, either in high school or in college? We hustled into each classroom or lecture hall, often late, and usually bewildered. I returned to college as a non-traditional student—in my case, that meant that

I was older and fatter. Though I eventually received my degree from Indiana University, my first return to college came in the fall of 1988, when I enrolled as a voice major at the University of Nebraska-Lincoln. I was nearly thirty-six, easily fifteen years older than nearly all my fellow students. As I had decided to register at the last minute, I spent my first week trekking back and forth between administration buildings and my classrooms—all the while huffing and puffing in sweltering triple-digit temperatures and thinking myself mad for ever signing up! I probably lost five pounds from sweating, not just from overtaxing my out-of-shape body, but also from honest, open, terror, at the prospect of academic challenges to my aging brain.

My eight o'clock class was Music Theory, and I took a seat in the front row, mostly to ensure I could see the blackboard. I'd brought a briefcase filled with notebooks and a voice recorder. I was prepared to take a ream of notes, but to my surprise and relief, I could have left the notebooks at home and lightened my load, because each and every professor that day—and for most of that week—spent time making sure all his/her students came in on an even playing field. We counted heads, checked paperwork, and looked over each course syllabus: a plan for the semester that featured an outline of each lecture, assigned reading, and definitions. During that week, I heard one phrase repeated again and again, not only for that semester, but for each and every semester, both there and later at Indiana University, for every class I took until the day I left graduate school in 1997: "Let's define terms."

So, in the spirit of academic pursuit, let us define terms. This chapter deals with the notion of virtual sin or rather sin that occurs in our minds, in our hearts. To begin with: what is virtual reality? Biologically, virtual reality (VR) is the activation of neuron pathways inside our brains, interpreting input from a lightning-fast assault of ones and zeroes. VR is the interface between human and machine that produces a sum that is far greater than its addends. According to the reference website, Dictionary.com, one concise definition of VR is: "*(noun)*—A computer simulation of a real or **imaginary world** or scenario, in which a user may interact with simulated objects or living things in real time. More sophisticated virtual reality systems place sensors on the user's body to sense movements that are then interpreted by the system as movements in the simulated world. Binocular goggles are sometimes used to simulate the appearance of objects in three dimensions[103] (emphasis mine).

If you've played the latest role-playing computer games, then you have immersed your mind in a virtual reality field, allowing your imagination to become your reality. If you have recently attended a 3-D film, then you have accessed a virtual reality world through use of 3-D glasses. Buddhists might even argue that we constantly live in a *virtual reality* environment because (so they teach) our minds continuously construct the world around us; that we create and perceive at the same time; we participate and observe all at once. Of course, such a worldview requires side-stepping the issue of an ultimate, singular, preexisting God who spoke the universe, and with it all reality, into being. However, I will leave that argument for another book.

A second term requiring mutual understanding, and hence a definition, is *entertainment*. A derivative definition is "that which entertains," but then derivation doesn't get us very far, does it? Perhaps, looking at synonyms would help: these include amusement, distraction, diversion, pastime, game, play, recreation, sport—and the list goes on and on. Of this list, two words stand out: distraction and diversion. Both speak of active means that remove us from our mundane thoughts and hurl us mentally or physically into a temporary hiatus from that dullness that so tugs at our mental shoelaces. Television and cinema feed upon our need for diversions. From a child's earliest months; as soon as he or she is steady enough and strong enough to sit alone in front of the magic box, the virtual world of make-believe invades and enthralls, and *programs* the little one's developing brain.

In point of fact, one disturbing yet hauntingly accurate definition of "entertainment" might be that it is an industry whose message not only permeates our minds through synaptic sensation, but that it also shapes our perceptions of the world and how we fit into it; which is uncomfortably close to Buddhist logic. Certainly, it can be argued that without our ever-growing need for "distractions" and amusements, movie companies would languish and die, computer and video game producers would go bankrupt, and even literature might find itself alone without a friend, abandoned without a reader.

Such sad exclusions will never occur, though, for my brain and yours have been trained for addiction. Our insatiable desire for mental stimulation will continue to feed the bloated industries while starving our famished souls.

Books, Books, and More Books

If I've not completely stumped, or worse yet *bored* you by now, then let's climb further up this virtual ladder to the next step on our journey: *examples*. Though the oldest form of "virtual stimulation" via entertainment may be "the story" as told by an elder—or as in our opening, by a mother—we shall skip ahead with the oldest method of virtual interaction, the novel.

Sir Walter Scott is officially credited with creating the modern historical novel in his ambitious tale of the Jacobite Rebellion, *Waverley*. Though Scott included no truly supernatural characters—as we will shortly be discussing at length—his work certainly shaped opinion in the minds of his well-heeled London readership. Published in 1814, a generation after the 1745 Battle of Prestonpans that decimated the Scottish rebellion, *Waverley* allowed readers to *virtually* live the life of an oppressed and hunted Highlander, and as such created public sympathy toward the noble Scotsman much as we in America sympathize and even seek to emulate the "noble warriors" of our American West. The truth, of course, is that no warrior or war is intrinsically noble; it is how media shapes our perceptions regarding, say, the invasion of another country, that determines whether or not we view such a war and its warriors as good or bad.

Just four years after Scott's *Waverley* inspired English readers to reconsider attitudes toward the Highlander, a different kind of novel emerged; one that might be called the great-grandparent of modern fantasy and science fiction. Written by a slip of a girl, a mere teenager, the horror story, *Frankenstein* (or *The Modern Prometheus*), broke new ground with its dark and moody settings coupled with cutting-edge "science." Building on the success of previous "Gothic novels" such as Walpole's *The Castle of Otranto* (1764) and Ann Radcliffe's *The Mysteries of Udolpho* (1794), Mary Shelley's classic tale of terror features an isolated and misunderstood protagonist (Victor Frankenstein) who disdains religion in favor of science (a hallmark of the Enlightenment community so prevalent at the time). The virtual world of the Creator and his Monster, through the juxtaposition of science and supernatural, defined and informed readers' desires to rise above the politics of the day to an ethereal "otherworldliness" found in the pages of Shelley's masterpiece.

It is this very antipodal relationship between the seen and the unseen, fact and fiction, real and virtual that proves so enticing to the reader. The pages of such novels are but one step beyond our own, yet they provide a reason, a rationale, an *acceptance* of the ghosts, goblins, banshees, golems, and all manner of unnatural beasties that lurk within the sub-conscience of a repressed, tightly wound society. God has no place in such dark laboratories, at least not the God of Adam, Abraham, Moses, and the Apostles. With such literary flights of fancy, men and women alike can retreat into themselves, or so they believe. With the readers' minds lax and receptive, the beasties of pen and paper cross the heart's threshold and enter the mind as easily as a demon might enter through a crack in time—as quick as lightning—creeping in unawares.

Shortly after Shelley's success, an even darker, more insidious tale of terror appeared on the bookstore shelves of Western civilization. Bram Stoker is said to have based his character, *Dracula*, on seven years of research into folktales of eastern Europe, and his work—it might be said—is predicated not only on Shelley's work but also on a friend to the diminutive Shelley, Mr. John Polidori, who published a story called *The Vampyre* in 1819. So-called "invasion literature"[104] was immensely popular at the time, and Stoker combined the dark tones of a blood-sucking Count with a threat to the shores of England to tantalize and terrorize his readers. This virtual world grew inside the minds of sophisticated readers, like a virus awaiting activation through the laws of generational curses. The vampire stalked women and even men throughout the decades and centuries that followed, continuing to rise each dusk, luring the young into blood rituals and blood lusts.

Radio Days

With the turn of the twentieth century, advancements in science shifted into high gear. Radio surpassed theater as the major entertainment venue, and the vast and often illegal business of "modern entertainment" entered its golden age. No longer did humanity require long hours of reading or listening to experience the inner world of their favorite heroes, heroines, and villains. Now, instant gratification through a one- or two-hour sitting acted like quick-set concrete in our innermost thoughts, pouring fantastic footings that spired into monumental cathedrals, opened into dusty, dreary libraries, or forced us into gloomy and sometimes dangerous pits complete with pendulum sounds creaking ever closer to our rapidly beating hearts. Radio plays provided hours of diversion for students and workers, housewives and husbands. It was, in fact, a radio play, posing as "news," that forever programmed the minds of captive audiences across the U.S. continent. In fact, Orson Welles' adaptation of an H. G. Wells 1898 novel, *The War of the Worlds*, caused a near riot in our nation.

The year was 1938, a time when the countries of Western Europe poised politically upon the edge of a knife. Near the haunts of Count Dracula, an Austrian wallpaper hanger, a former corporal, had grown fangs of his own with an appetite for genocide. Having cheated his way into power, Germany's Chancellor, Adolf Hitler would soon shock the world with a real-life invasion of Poland.

The world of small town, however, America felt no threat, at least not from Europe. Instead, as the Mercury Theater on the Air[105] began its iconic performance in the evening of October 30, 1938. So close to Halloween, many listeners may have tuned in with ghosts and goblins and all things supernatural already nestling into their receptive minds. Certainly, the spiritual aspects of this October 30 date is one for speculation and discussion, but its scope is beyond that of this chapter. Welles, brilliant showman that he was, used a familiar format to radio audiences, that of the "news bulletin" to interrupt a staged band concert in order to tell the tale of an alien invasion. Understandably, anyone who missed the disclaimer in the first minutes of the broadcast might easily have believed the "news" of a martian invasion to be true, or at the least a possibility! After all, a news interruption was serious business during a time of war in Europe.

Picture a family in your own hometown, gathered around their pride and joy, an expensive console radio set that rose from the polished wood floor like an alien of its own kind; you and your wife or husband, along with your children, are huddled close to the radio's cloth-covered speakers, with every eye, every ear intent upon the nightly tale that would transport you to worlds far beyond your ordinary lives. Now, imagine the inner workings of your minds and spirits as the music lulls you into a hypnotic trance only to be punctuated by harsh and terrifying announcements from the battle with the invading aliens. Certainly, it is only fiction! Only a prank! But subsequent with the story's invasion, another invasion of a different kind is taking place with small but unrelenting steps, at your own invitation—like an innocent invitation to a bloodthirsty count—that eventually sears your minds and forever opens you to invasion of the virtual—the spiritual kind.

Motion Pictures and Television

In the late nineteenth century, a race began to create the first working moving picture. Looking back on the patents of the day, you can almost perceive a spirit behind the "science" of what would become best known as the Kinetoscope.[106] This rather rudimentary device, showcased primarily at sideshows and fairs for the amusement of patrons, utilized perforated film and an imprinted series of images shot at the speed of ten or more frames per second. One of the early patent holders was Thomas Edison, who coined the term "Kinetoscope." The viewer had to hand-crank the device to advance the film while gazing into a viewfinder similar to that used in a stereoscope (a device that produced a 3-D effect for photos). In fact, it's remarkable that the inventors of the time did not also patent and produce stereo-kinetoscopes to provide a 3-D experience for their customers—ah, but that, too, is for another discussion in another book.

As war raged in Europe, silent films drew faithful audiences throughout the western world. Even without sound, movie studios learned new techniques with each new project, slowly perfecting the craft of illusion, some telling the stories of great biblical epics, others depicting the lowest of human depravities. By the time sound arrived in 1927 with *The Jazz Singer*, audiences had learned to leave their troubles behind and disappear into the dark with their favorite actors and actresses, imagining themselves as part of the action...entering a virtual world while munching on popcorn and peanuts.

The birth of television brought this virtual world into our homes. It is no coincidence that one of the earliest adopters of television technology was Adolf Hitler's Germany with the broadcast of the 1936 Berlin Olympics! Spiritually speaking, it might be said that dark aspects of virtual reality intertwine with the hypnotic practices of occult Nazi Germany. Mind-control was the intention then...and so it is now.

As television programming grew as an "art" form, commercial

insertions for a variety of products punctuated our favorite shows. The virtual "getaway" from reality into a different world allowed children and parents alike to imagine themselves as doctors, cowboys, treasure hunters, detectives, and even work through family distresses. Shows like *Divorce Court* popped up amidst daytime soap operas. Watching while others "aired their dirty laundry" in a TV court made us all feel better—after all, our marriages were great, right?

And since I've mentioned daytime soap operas, I'd be remiss if I failed to include one such show that caught my teenage mind in the late-1960s. *Dark Shadows* began as a run-of-the-mill Gothic drama that focused on the angst-ridden world of Victoria Winters, a single woman, alone in the world, who worked for a wealthy Massachusetts family called Collins. As a side note, I'll mention here that my grandmother was a Collins, which endeared both me and my mother to the badly written show. Since then, I've learned that Collins is rumored to be one of the so-called "thirteen Illuminati" bloodlines. I assure you that my Collins branch is, if anything, "poor relation." (Now, back to our heroine!) Miss Victoria Winters' daily ails had begun to wear thin with audiences, and the ratings sagged, when the soap's creator, Dan Curtis, had a brilliant idea; he would up the ante of Gothic television by adding (as Bram Stoker had done one hundred years earlier) a vampire!

Barnabas Collins drew fans to the daytime serial like coffin flies to a corpse. Teenage girls and their mothers tuned in each day to see just how poor, pitiful vampire Barnabas would extricate himself from his newest dilemma. Would he ever find his true love, Josette? Though played by a most humble looking actor, Jonathan Frid, the character of Barnabas drew massive sympathy from female viewers. Within a couple of seasons, a werewolf entered the mix as "cousin" Quentin arrived to sink his teeth into the Collins clan. Yes, the show was campy and the scripts mundane, but the mesmerism was undeniable as vampire mania took hold of teens ordinarily entangled with The Beatles or The Rolling Stones.

Vampires have, throughout the history of the virtual realm within our minds, reigned as dark knights of the realm, you might say. Whether they appear in a book or in a radio play, a stage production, or a movie, these lusty phantoms enter our minds with seemingly little resistance from us! Sin begins in the mind, and this makes our brains, our inner beings, the front line in the battle between the enemies of Christ and those who love Him. Vampires need no salvation for they will never die, yet they present themselves as ever in search of redemption. This dichotomy makes them irresistible and quite sexy in a very dark way.

The Theater of the Mind

So, we've had a few definitions and we've had a whirlwind introduction to the belief in make-believe, or better put, the war for our minds. Of course this war began in the garden, when the serpent twisted God's word. How many times had he tempted Eve? We don't know for certain. It may have been once; it might have been hundreds of times. No matter how many times she heard the lies, we know that Eve let her mind consider the lie, and even before she took a bite, she had sinned. Her virtual programming had taken hold, and it killed her.

How can an idea, a series of words, or even a series of images or imaginings take hold and "kill"? Well, that brings it all around, doesn't it? For this chapter is not a primer on literature and screen but a device to get you thinking about what you see, hear, and *imagine*.

What exactly happens in our brains when we watch TV or go to a movie, or worse yet, play a first-person shooter video game? The brain is an amazing, God-designed, organic computer with about a million trillion (that's a quadrillion) synapses. A synapse is the gap between neuron cells. Neurotransmitters travel back and forth across these gaps via either a chemical exchange or an electronic potential (a charge differential caused by ions exiting and entering the gap). In fact, the space required for me to describe the complex set of neuron exchanges occurring as I write this sentence would consume this entire chapter! Suffice it to say that our brains are complicated.

Within the physical brain lives another, less tangible entity called the *mind*. Scientifically, the mind is considered a higher function of our modern brains. Those who would deny our Creator, teach that mankind evolved over hundreds of thousands of years from a chimp like being with a very primitive, hind brain into the current version, *Homo sapiens* (wise man or man with knowledge/wisdom—oh, what the occultists could do with that one!). *Homo sapiens*, evolutionists claim, is nothing more than a member of the ape family, and our bodies and brains have developed since the earliest known fossils (dated by their own science to *circa* two hundred thousand years before I began to type this).

The concept of "the mind" dates back to biblical texts, where the Hebrew word *leb* occurs 593 times in 550 verses. *Leb* refers to the inner man, our conscience, our heart, but also to our emotions, our appetites, our passions. It is often translated as "heart." The mind is our control room, perhaps a part of our soul, and it certainly lends itself to heavenly or hellish behaviors. When our brain receives sensory input, it's our neurons that respond chemically/electrically, but it's *the mind* that decides what to do with the input. God hardened Pharaoh's *leb*, his heart (we'd call it his mind, the real man) when he refused to release God's chosen ones to worship Him.

Where is the mind located? Philosophers have argued over that for millennia. Some say the mind is outside of ourselves, others that it is a part of ourselves, still others that it exists only as a construct of our behaviors—that what we do reflects who were are, reflects our mind. For the sake of brevity, I'll tell you that the mind must be part of us, for we are God-breathed, God-fashioned as a complete, perfect creation with free will.

The Greek word for mind is *psyche,* from which we derive a number of commonly used English words such as "psychology," "psychosomatic," and "psychotic." What is less commonly known is that this ancient word also refers to a Greek goddess. Psyche was, interestingly enough, the Greek goddess of the soul. She is also considered the goddess of "transformation," and it is thus no wonder that she is often painted with butterfly wings.[107]

Neuroanatomy 101

How does mind-programming work, and does what we sense or take into our "brains" lead to changes in the "mind"? If the higher functions of our biological brains are part of free will, then some might argue that our "lower brain" leads us into less "cerebral" choices. Though such a black-and-white "brainview" is not strictly correct, we'll leave it at that simplicity for now; otherwise, this humble chapter will morph into a megalomaniac tome.

Let's begin with the eye.

Our eyes are marvelous creations! God fashioned our two

eyes as part of our central nervous system—as such, our eyes are literally part of our brains. One of my favorite television programs is a now defunct series called *Millennium*, which featured weekly stories of myths and monsters that wound around an overarching story about a secretive organization called "The Millennium Group." This mysterious group used fringe science and advanced knowledge to discern future events. In one episode called "Jose Chung's Doomsday Defense," the plot revolves around a group called "Selfosophists." One might easily conclude that the Selfosophy bunch is based on Scientology, for the founder, one "Onan Goopta" is a failed scientist who decides to write a book about how the mind works. The book is an instant success, and followers sprout up all over the west coast. To maintain their link to their beliefs, the cult followers employ a bio-feedback device called an "Onanograph." Each member is also required to ghostwrite novels with their dead founder's name as the author. One such cheesy science fiction novel is about a roving, forensic detective (not unlike Frank Black, the main character in *Millennium*), but this detective is called Rocket McGraine. McGraine (played by Lance Henrickson in a blond wig and an uncharacteristic grin) says he never looks at blood because it goes "into the peepers and winds up in the cerebral cortex."[108] Such dark images keep McGraine from being "upbeat."[109]

While writer Darin Morgan takes full artistic license to poke fun at a well-known anti-psychologist, mind-controlling organization, his character Rocket McGraine's comment on sensory input isn't far off. What goes into the eye, inevitably interacts with the brain.

The retina (the back part of the eyeball) is composed of several layers of photoreceptor cells that interconnect with the optic nerve, sort of like a fiber optic cable. Each cell is sensitive to a particular wavelength of light. When the perfect frequency strikes a photopigment protein within the cell, this protein changes shape, which then signals a complex cascade of events, precipitating a signal to the optic nerve. The electric signal then travels along the optic nerve, crosses underneath the brain, and finally terminates at the visual cortex in the back part of the brain, where cells there interpret the picture.

This optic pathway contains other, extremely important sections of the brain that also react to light. On its way to the visual cortex, the message carried by the optic nerve transverses the "limbic system," a collection of structures that lie underneath the brain. This system includes the hippocampus, amygdala, thalamus, hypothalamus, and a structure called the fornix (nerve fibers that connect the thalamus to the hypothalamus). The limbic system helps us to store memories, maintain our internal clock, identify smells, and even maintain "control" by interpreting situations. The tiny pineal gland is also part of the limbic system, maintaining circadian rhythms and producing melatonin, which aids in sleep. This miniscule "pinecone-shaped" gland also produces dimethyltryptophan (DMT) and has sometimes been referred to as our "third eye."

Have you ever smelled banana bread and suddenly recalled your grandmother baking bread? Or, perhaps, you've heard an old song from your high school days and found yourself lost in memories. This is the limbic system at work. Physiologically, the limbic system is the emotional seat of our being. By reacting to visual, olfactory, and even auditory input, the cells within the above structures use the received information and help us choose whether to react to it, store it, or identify it.

The Limbic System on Entertainment

With this basic understanding of how our brain reacts to external stimuli, let's now return to those television shows, video games, and movies, shall we? I want to consider specifics, so to begin with, let's look at a love story.

In school, I minored in English, which meant I read a lot of books and wrote papers about them. I bring this up because, as my brain is struggling for how best to approach the "love story" aspect of limbic reaction, I keep thinking about how I might have argued for "romance" contained in the pages of Shelley's *Frankenstein* or Stoker's *Dracula*. First of all, I would define "romance" or even the commonly accepted emotion of "love," but—while this exercise might sound trivial and unnecessary—it is central to any other assertions I might make.

Love is personal, individual, and constantly evolving. As babies, we accept one definition of love: "Oh, boy, more food!" As a toddler and growing child, we expect a more expanded definition: "Help me, wipe my tears, make me laugh, teach me, give me hugs, teach me to draw, play with me." This "love" that we crave grows more sophisticated with age and is dependent upon many factors. Tragically, some children learn to associate love with terror, pain, anger, abandonment, or worse yet with molestation. But we can also learn this negative association by *virtually* experiencing it as well! Take for instance, the warped sense of love that Victor Frankenstein has for his Creature. Frankenstein hides and protects the Monster, endangering his fiancée and his friend. Consider also the way Count Dracula's female victims "love" his mistreatment of them, eagerly giving themselves to him, even to the point of death.

But while novels can influence our internal minds, shaping and misshaping our souls, reading pales in comparison to hearing, watching, or both. Radio, then movies and television, and worst of all video games immerse our senses in a virtual world—invade our minds and teach us new thoughts, even new desires. It is these activities that send visual, auditory, and olfactory signals, filtered through the limbic system, that most distort our brains. Consider the current spate of films that fall within a new subgenre called "torture porn." These films include, but are regretfully not limited to, the *Saw* series, the *Hostel* series, *Wolf Creek*, *The Hills Have Eyes*, and *Turistas*. If you've not seen any of these films, consider yourself blessed. Once seen, you cannot "unsee" these deeply disturbing forays into the darkest recesses of the human soul.

"Torture porn" films rely upon an ages-old association between terror and sadism. Impressionable teens watching such a film learn to be sexually stimulated by the mutilation of a screaming man or woman. Their curious minds are thrilled by the puzzles and intricate machinery that forces the victim to solve the mystery or die a horrible death—as if the resulting bloodbath is the fault of the victim for not being more clever. As teens watch these blood-spattered movies, several things happen, though we most likely don't realize it.

ONE: The amygdala, part of the limbic system, processes the baser emotions such as fright, anger, but also sexual responses and desires. This is a dangerous combination in one set of cells, as we will learn.

TWO: The pineal gland, stimulated by light to produce melatonin, is also stimulated by the darkness of a theater to release the hormone: melatonin makes us relax and prepare for sleep.

This relaxed state leads us into a dreamy state, similar to that of a receptive hypnosis subject.

THREE: Our hippocampus revs up to store and sort through all the stimuli assaulting our eyes and ears, and possibly also making associations that are less than desirable; for instance, coupling sexual arousal with inflicting pain or bloodletting.

FOUR: Spiritually speaking, I believe that the thoughts and patterns forming in our minds could be temporary, if we leave them and walk away, just as Eve could have walked away from the serpent's lies. But if we nurture these new patterns and thoughts, we mull them over, we relive the movie or the video game, we play it again, we view it again, we crave the high...then, it is my assertion that the spirit world rejoices in searing our mind with sin. Our virtual experiences are seen as real sin. In Genesis 6, we see that God views the sin of imagination as important.

"And GOD saw that the wickedness of man [was] great in the earth, and [that] every imagination of the thoughts of his heart [was] only evil continually" (Genesis 6:5).

Jesus echoes this when He speaks of the sin of adultery.

"But I say unto you, That whosoever looketh on a woman to lust after her hath committed adultery with her already in his heart" (Matthew 4:28).

Teenage minds are impressionable and eager to learn, but they are also rebellious and anxious to fly solo, untethered by the restraints of traditions and laws. This is the enemy's playground. Do you have teenage children? Will your children soon reach these formative, dangerous years? Think about the books, videos, and computer games that they enjoy and inhabit. Yes, I used the word "inhabit" intentionally, for teens will nurture these virtual realms in their minds, daydreaming about sinful exploits, whether or not he or she realizes such thoughts are wrong. It is our responsibility to chaperone our children and assist them in defining what is pure, healthy, and sober—and what is filthy, dangerous, and addictive.

Sexy Vampires Sell

Some of you will read this next sentence and disagree with me, but I'll make the statement nonetheless. The novel/movie franchise called *The Twilight Saga* is one of those dangers we should warn our children against. Young girls, many of them under ten years old, dream of winning the hand of Edward, the vampire. He is seen as a hero because he struggles to control his thirst for blood. Bella is viewed as chaste, loving, and loyal. Jacob the shape-shifter is a rogue, acting as the antagonist to Edward's protagonist. Bella loves them both. This triangle is nothing more than the modern version of Barnabas, Josette, and Quentin from *Dark Shadows*.

The Twilight books are marketed as "children's books"! Let me tell you two reasons why this is so. Firstly, it is easier to break into publishing in this category, so authors choose to write for this genre. Secondly, there is a spiritual reason, being that our children are most easily tempted, particularly when parents look the other way.

Think about the pathways and ideas that are created in the limbic system—in her mind—as your daughter reads these books or watches the *Twilight* movies! She learns that dark, forbidden love requires sacrifice, but that it's worth it. She longs to be like Bella; she imagines herself as Bella, a heroine who dances with danger and desires a supernatural existence. These desires imprint themselves into your daughter's mind, into her limbic system as conflicting responses: fear versus trust, sexuality versus pain, animal instincts versus God-given free will.

It's Not All Good

To end this chapter, I'd like to briefly visit video games, particularly first-person shooters. As we've discussed, visual stimuli enter not only our eyes but also our minds via the limbic system. If you add active participation to that formula, then the result can sear and forever scar young minds like a brand. The lure of "role-playing games" (RPGs) is that the player enters a different world and *becomes* one of the residents. First person perspective allows us to enter this world almost as if we're in a dream, for our minds click into step with the world's other denizens, be they military or fantasy.

One of the most beloved role-playing games is Zelda, a series of games produced by Nintendo. I'll admit to finding the game addictive, which is why I can speak from personal experience. On the surface, the game appears harmless. In *Zelda: The Ocarina of Time*, you play as the boy "Link," who is a forest boy without a fairy. He is different, not like his friends who all have personal fairies. The game begins as a "Great Deku Tree" sends a fairy to you (playing as "Link," although you can name the character whatever you choose). This fairy tells you that you're special, that you must fight your way to the tree and receive your instructions. As it turns out, you are not a Kokiri forest child, but that you are actually the Hero of Time. From here, you achieve levels, attain powers, weapons, and even learn to cast spells to defeat the evil tyrant, Ganon.

This is the basic theme of most of the Zelda games, though

they differ from system to system, and from title to title. In *Zelda: Majora's Mask* and *Zelda: Twilight Princess*, you can morph into a variety of creatures, each with its own power. Often, the characters or stories are based on Japanese myths, thereby seeding Shintoism and New Age tenets into the minds of young players. Such teachings mirror and complement that of *anime*, a Japanese form of cartoon animation that features cannibalism, vampires, exorcisms, alchemy, and other dark themes. Sometimes, anime productions are aimed at a very young market; many of us remember the Pokemon fad. Others target older children, utilizing more adult themes in graphic novel form. The very nature of a "cartoon" (as we in the West would name it) is one that draws in young viewers.

First-person perspective is taken to the ultimate degree in "first-person shooters" (FPS). This genre is often militaristic in theme, usually a 3-D environment, and plays on the baser human failings: lust for power, sensuality, cannibalism, hatred, racism, sado-masochism, and even Satanism. One of the earliest FPS offerings was *Doom*. Here, the player must fight demons who inhabit a martian moon—all to protect Earth. This storyline makes your job heroic, just like in the aforementioned Zelda franchise. In fact, it is a common theme in video games—"if you don't do it, no one will." In case you've never seen a FPS screenshot, let me describe it for you. The viewpoint is as if YOU, the player, are holding the rifle, sword, or other weapon, and you "sight" down the barrel, blasting away at whatever gets in your way. As gaming graphics has advanced over time, the resulting blood-spatter has grown dramatically realistic. In fact, the overall graphics these days can trick the eye and mind to make it all seem very real.

Needless to say, the militaries of the world use FPS to train cadets. Soldiers, they explain, must kill without stopping to think about it. Video games provide the perfect environment for training these warriors up in the way that they should go—do unto your enemy before he has a chance to do unto you. *Doom* is notorious for being the alleged favorite game of Columbine killers, Eric Harris and Dylan Klebold. In fact, the parents of some of the victims tried but failed to prove this in a lawsuit against "id Software" (the company that released *Doom*; a subsidiary of ZeniMax media). However, just because the families lost, one cannot conclude that software companies have no responsibility. Let us be reasonable! If the U.S. military began using FPS simulations to train their soldiers, then are such games appropriate for teens and pre-teens? Immersion is the aim of virtual reality—to so blend truth with fiction that we cease to discern the difference.

End Credits; Game Over

And this salient point brings me to my final theory about the virtual experience that influences our minds. Is it possible that the very spirits who rejoice at the bloodletting done in secret ceremonies of the occult might find virtual bloodletting equally satisfying? Are our movie theaters and gaming consoles the postmodern form of ancient high places and sex groves? Understand, please, that I am not condemning an entire film industry; I am merely crying out against dark deeds done in darkened spaces. The sights and sounds of torture porn, vampirism, cannibalism, Satanism, human sacrifice, animism, New Age philosophy, Shintoism, demon worship, self-mutilation, and any and all activities that defy the Law of God and defile the humanity for whom Christ died—such images, viewed either from the third-person perspective or, even worse, from the first-person—these are images to be shunned at all cost, for they rush madly into our brains with but one intent: to steal our souls.

Suggested Reading:

Iaccino, James F., *Jungian Reflections within the Cinema: A Psychological Analysis of Sci-Fi and Fantasy Archetypes* (United Kingdom Praeger, Praeger Publishers/Greenwood Publishing Group, Abindgon, Oxford, 1998).

LeDoux, Joseph, *The Emotional Brain: The Mysterious Underpinnings of Emotional Life* (New York, NY: Simon and Schuster, 1998).

Loftus, Geoffrey R.; Loftus, Elizabeth F., *Mind at Play: The Psychology of Video Games* (New York, NY: Basic Books, 1993).

Strassman M.D., Rick, *DMT: The Spirit Molecule: A Doctor's Revolutionary Research into the Biology of Near-Death and Mystical Experiences*, 3rd edition (Bethel, Maine: Park Street Press, 2000).

CHAPTER EIGHT

A NEW HYPOTHESIS ABOUT
ALIEN ABDUCTIONS

By Gary Bates

Since the publication of my book *Alien Intrusion: UFOs and the Evolution Connection* in 2005 (updated and expanded in a new edition, published 2010), I have been contacted by numerous people asking me to explain some of the "finer details" about what might actually be occurring during alleged alien abduction experiences. Like many other researchers, I have come to the conclusion that many of these episodes are spiritual in nature; that is, they are emanating from the deceptive practices of spiritual, angelic beings from another dimension. However, many abduction stories have rich details of being taken to a spaceship, undergoing grotesque medical experiments, and seeing vats of half-human and half-alien hybrids. It has been my view that although there can be, and often is, a physical aspect to many encounters, much of it is illusory. Because many experiencers claim that they can tell you the "colors of the walls in spaceship" and other details, even many Christian researchers have constructed exotic views that go beyond Scripture in an attempt to explain what they believe is the reality of these alleged "finer details."

Perhaps one of the most popular of these is the "return of the Nephilim" concept: that somehow, alleged post-Noah's Flood Nephilim are appearing again due to the repeat practices of evil angels hybridizing with human beings. While several authors in this book subscribe to such a view, the mention of the Nephilim in Numbers 13–14, which is often used to justify post-Flood Nephilim, was nothing more in my opinion than a fanciful lie of the spies to dissuade the Hebrew nation from entering the Promised Land. In confirmation of this, God only destroyed the ten lying spies as a judgment.[110]

Often, when one thinks of angels as being "spiritual," one has the impression that they are ethereal or ghostly entities. But this is not what the Bible indicates. In the biblical accounts, angels appear physically and can interact with people and objects on the physical plane. Similarly, there are both spiritual/supernatural and physical aspects to these "alien" encounters, also. But some of the more bizarre unresolved questions pertaining to alleged physical aspects remain difficult to explain. They include: "Are people really passing through the walls to travel towards a real spaceship?" "Do they really undergo medical procedures while onboard?" "Are people really having sexual encounters with these entities?" We may not be able to answer some of these questions until believers are in the presence of the source of all truth in eternity—the Lord Jesus Christ.

Scientifically, we do not have the ability to visit the spiritual dimension to conduct tests. We only have the accounts of people who claim to have undergone experiences that may be spiritual in nature. The Classic Abduction Syndrome (CAS) is used by most serious researchers as a set of markers or parameters to define an actual "abduction" experience as opposed to a dream, hallucination, or psychological episode. The CAS was developed without a Christian perspective of the phenomenon in mind; it simply attempts to categorize the common elements in abduction experiences. Nonetheless, I have found it to be both accurate and useful when meeting, talking to, and even counseling those who claim to have lived through "alien" experiences (see chapters 7 and 8 of *Alien Intrusion* for more information).

The agenda of these fallen entities was aptly described by PhD abduction researcher, Dr. David Jacobs as "a clandestine programme of physiological exploitation by one species of another."[111]

Because these "aliens" act in such a deceptive manner and are not who they claim to be, it is reasonable to deduce that it is their very nature to be deceitful. As such, there is no sound reason to interpret much of what is claimed, shown, or being represented by them as being truthful, especially with regard to the tall tales that they tell their victims. If they lie—they are liars! Many other researchers have also demonstrated that their deceptions seem to be centered on destroying every major tenet of the Bible and the divine personhood of Jesus Christ. This is consistent with the biblical teaching that there is a master plan by the enemies of the Creator God to deceive people away from the truth of the Bible and their need for salvation through the atoning work of Jesus Christ.

For mortal beings like us, it is hard to imagine a war that is occurring in the upper echelons of the spiritual realm between immensely powerful beings known as *angels*. Because human beings are the focus of this war, this conflict also overlaps into our physical dimension, and because of the players and the high stakes involved, we should not be surprised at the lengths these beings will go to for the purposes of deceiving and leading away those who are made in the image of their Creator God. This would necessitate constructing some physical aspects to the deceptions, because human beings live and operate in a physical, three-dimensional universe. Some of these physical aspects include UFOs being seen on radar, electromagnetic disturbances, markings on the ground or in ice, physical markings left on victims, etc. However, I believe that while some aspects about UFOs can be physically real, their appearance, being complex spaceships with sophisticated inner workings, is illusory in nature. Similarly, so are the descriptions of aliens and their victims being beamed through walls or ceilings, and the detailed accounts of experiences aboard some kind of spacecraft. In short, although the initial sightings may be real, and real, strange entities may appear in one's room, the elaborations I just mentioned *did not* actually occur.

To those who have experienced such events, these statements may cause angst, and you may think that the comments are based upon ignorance. Or you might be thinking, *He doesn't know what he's talking about, because I know what really happened to me. I experienced it and it was real.* But please read on, and keep in mind that I am not denying the experience or encounter as being real. In one sense, the more extreme the claims, the more they somehow lend credibility to the notion that they may really be occurring at the hands of some technologically advanced race of aliens from another planet or even the physical constructions of deceptive angels. Many think, *How* (or why) *would people fabricate such bizarre details unless there were some truth to them?* Indeed, there may be some truth in that the episode in the general sense may be real. However, there are simply too many "physics-denying" anomalies occurring for these abductions to be simply taken at face value, even though they are based on detailed descriptions by victims. The explanation to come may sound like an anomaly in itself, but bear in mind that the purpose of this hypothesis is the result of what is now many years of experience in dealing with this phenomenon and its victims.

The facts are: there are significant numbers of the population experiencing such events; there are often multiple experiencers to some events; the victims of abductions recount striking similarities to their experiences. These facts seemingly add to the weight of "evidence" that these are real intrusions by extraterrestrials. For instance, and as described by the CAS, how could they all similarly recall such detailed descriptions of the inside of a ship, medical examinations, similar descriptions of alien beings, video screens aboard the ship and so on, unless it all really happened, just as visualized? Let's look at one well-known case, for example.

The Allagash Four

In August 1976, four male friends fishing in a canoe on the Allagash waterway in northern Maine, USA, saw a craft of colored lights that hovered nearby. After one of the men shone his flashlight at it, the craft initially stopped, but then started to move towards the canoe while emitting a circular, hollow light upon the water. The terrified men frantically paddled towards the shore, but the light eventually enveloped them as they reached the shore. Although they have different accounts at this stage about how they got onto the bank, they all recalled that the fire they had lit earlier had completely burnt down to a few coals, meaning that several hours had elapsed. They could not account for that missing time. To them, it seemed like only about fifteen minutes from when they first saw the object to when they were standing on the bank. As they looked up at the light, it now shone upwards and then the lights moved away at terrific speed.

Over the next few years, the men suffered night terrors which included seeing strange creatures, undergoing sleep paralysis and levitation from their beds, and the recollection and sensation of experimentation by strange entities being done upon them. Upon the advice of their doctor, they sought help from UFO experts. This led them to MUFON (*The Mutual UFO Network*) and hypnosis sessions to regress the men in an attempt to find out what happened during the period of missing time.

Under hypnosis and independently, all four witnesses relived detailed and traumatic UFO abduction experiences during the period of missing time. All said they were transferred from their canoe into the UFO by the hollow tube-like beam of light. On board, they encountered strange humanoid creatures that exerted some kind of mind control over them so that they could not resist their demands.

All were made to undress and sit on a plastic-like bench in an area illuminated by diffuse white light. After looking at their eyes and in their mouths with a pencil-sized rod with a light on its tip, the aliens placed them in a harness and flexed their arms and legs. Then, one by one they were made to lie on a table where each was examined by a number of strange hand-held and larger machine-like instruments that were lowered over their bodies. During this segment of the examination, the alien entities removed samples of saliva, skin scrapings, blood, feces, urine and sperm from each of the abductees.[112]

Because all four men, while under hypnosis, recounted identical memories of the event, this case has been cited as one of the most compelling abduction accounts in history. Indeed, it was studying these "multiple experiencer" type events and their multiple confirmed stories that actually provided clues to unraveling the seeming weight of evidence for the belief that these were real alien abduction accounts, rather than being the "death knell" for a spiritual explanation.

As I detailed in *Alien Intrusion*, and as in the aforementioned case, hypnosis is/was used to regress or "take people back" under the belief that the subconscious mind recalls everything in one's past. We now know there are grave reliability problems with this method of investigation (and we will discuss these more and in depth later). Hypnosis has been mainly used as a post-event investigative method. But the problems with the use of hypnosis commence earlier in the timeline of the experience. It is my belief that these methods are actually being used to perpetrate the experience upon the hapless victims in the first place. This seems consistent with the pattern one sees, namely that hypnosis is often required after the incident to allegedly enter the subconscious mind to unlock such apparent experiences, because the majority of experiencers have no conscious recollection of events. Therefore, it seems reasonable to presume that such "finer" details have *only* been recorded in the subconscious mind.

It's amazing to me that such a major clue should be willingly ignored by UFOlogists keen to defend these experiences of aliens as having really, physically taken place. It is explained away on the basis that the aliens invoke a trance-like state to encourage the victim to forget about the whole encounter. But if so, and it is thus agreed that the alleged aliens are able to induce a hypnotic state, why is it not also obvious that much of what supposedly occurred may have been planted in the subconscious mind during that same subliminal state? After all, it can only be recalled and brought to the surface by triggering that same state once again.

An alien abduction movie called *The Fourth Kind* portrayed, with reasonable accuracy, how the hypnotic regression method is used.

The Fourth Kind (2009)

A flood of pre-hype advertising outlined the film's main premise. And the marketing message was clear in trying to make the case that we were about to watch a real docu-drama based upon factual events, valid case studies, and genuine archival footage to demonstrate that people really are being abducted by aliens. However, that particular claim was not really validated. What *was* clear is that the trailers' claims were a tad deceptive, as no "real" footage of people being abducted by any entity whatsoever was shown.

At the onset of the movie, the lead actress Milla Jovovich (who has previously starred in science fiction and horror movies like *The Fifth Element* and *Resident Evil*), appeared on screen as herself. She stated that although she would be acting the role of "real life" psychologist Dr. Abigail Emily Tyler, the movie would be interspersed with "real" footage of interviews with patients and police video of events that besieged the small Alaskan town of Nome. Such statements were clearly intended to lead the viewers along the path of belief that the producers wanted them to tread.

Next, we see the alleged real Tyler undergoing hypnotic regression at the hands of a fellow psychiatrist. The screen then divides with actress Jovovich on one half, accurately reenacting the same scene at the same time and word for word. This was the pattern throughout most of the movie. This was a very clever ploy by the movie's makers, because on the occasions when Jovovich was not sharing the screen with footage of Tyler, it gave the viewer the impression that every last detail of the script was based upon factual occurrences. (To avoid confusion as I go forward: If I mention a single person's name, such as Jovovich or Tyler, it means that the person was appearing alone on the screen, but if you see Jovovich/Tyler, it means that the screen was split between alleged real footage of Tyler [or events recorded by her] and the actress [Jovovich] playing her, or even switching back and forth between the two.)

Tyler's/Jovovich's regression is an attempt to relive the night surrounding her husband's death, which she believes was at the hands of a murderer. However, during such therapy she is always unable to see the face of the killer. The death of her husband has caused unresolved trauma not only in her own life, but in the lives of her teenage son and young daughter. Afterwards, Jovovich returns to her own clinical practice in Nome and we see Tyler/Jovovich interviewing a succession of patients who are all suffering the same "sleep terrors." They are unable to consciously recall what is actually occurring to them with the exception of a common image—that of a white owl appearing at their window (the white owl was synonymous with Whitley Strieber's abductions). So Tyler/Jovovich regresses one of the patients, who, while under hypnosis, relives a terrifying ordeal—so disturbing that he does not wish to share the details with even his own counselor. Later that evening, we witness the same patient murdering his own wife and children (reenacted and with supposed real police footage, which created a disturbing sense of realism) because he wants to spare them from undergoing the same horrific experiences he had.

Hypnotic Regression

The continued regression of the inhabitants of Nome reveals that they believe they are being visited by entities in the middle of the night and that such entities are performing grotesque experiments on them. It is during this splicing of supposed real footage and reenactments that we see the alleged transmogrification of people into contorted shapes as they scream with ear-piercing terror. I have seen several regressions of alleged abductees and they do suffer induced traumatization as a result of the regression. This is because they are reliving an experience that they really do believe was an alien abduction. This is just one case where the movie blurred the lines of reality. As a researcher of this phenomenon, I have never seen or read of any accounts where a patient/victim levitates while under regression, or has his body twisted violently and bones broken as portrayed in the movie. Although it was the producer's intention to have us believe that residents of Nome were undergoing alien abductions, the types of incidents that occurred during the alleged regression of patients in this movie actually reveals otherwise. When people recount the details of their experiences, and even the ones portrayed in this movie, it is clear that they represent spiritual experiences, in the sense that the attacks being portrayed seemed to be inflicted by non-visible beings. The alleged footage of the regression of abductees was extremely similar to demonic possession and reminiscent of the incident in Mark 9:17–26, where Jesus healed a young boy who was possessed by an evil spirit. On exorcizing the spirit, we are told in the KJV: "And the spirit cried, and rent him sore, and came out of him: and he was as one dead; insomuch that many said, He is dead" (verse 26). Note though, the more modern English translation of this verse from the NIV: "The spirit shrieked, convulsed him violently and came out. The boy looked so much like a corpse that many said, 'He's dead.'"

The movie also takes potshots at the Christian faith. It shows Jovovich praying with her children before a meal, but later, when trying to understand the reason for the awful events in her life, she looks up and asks (God), "Why?" She discovers that her husband was also trying to unravel the Nome mystery and she stumbles across a book about ancient Sumerian clay tablets. She enlists the help of the author of the book and he discovers, from an audio recording of one of the abductions, that the entities speak this ancient Sumerian language. He also claims that the tablets' creation account predates the Bible's Genesis account of creation and that its account of Noah's Flood was taken originally from these same tablets. This false analogy comes straight out of the writings of famous UFO-believer, Zecharia Sitchin, a self-proclaimed expert on these tablets who claims that human beings' creators are aliens known in these Sumerian texts as the *Anunnaki*, which the Bible records as Anakim.

Movies and other media are a powerful influence on us. Many people don't realize that when we watch such "information," we are actually giving permission for the teller of the tale to acquaint us with his story and even his version of the truth. Even though they are not present at the time or occupying the same space as we are, watching a movie is a bit like saying, "Okay, so tell me your story—I'm here because I want to hear it." It makes one inclined to believe what one is being told.

The Truth about the Movie

The following facts were discovered about this "truthful" docu-drama.

- There was no rash of alleged alien abductions in Nome, Alaska. There was a spate of disappearances of individuals. Most cases were solved and the FBI concluded that it was not the work of a serial killer, but the combination of being a town with high alcohol consumption and very cold winters. One can read the official reports from *The Anchorage Daily News* online[113] and other news sources like the *Hartford Examiner.*[114]

- Dr. Abigail Tyler is a fictitious person. There is no record of her having worked in Nome, Alaska.

- The producers never provided any evidence to support their claims of real cases, archival footage, etc.

- Statements by officials in Nome denied any such occurrences as depicted in the movie ever took place.

- The movie claims to have changed the names of the characters (including the police officers involved) for their own protection, and at the end of the movie it states that these persons declined to be interviewed or take part in the movie. This is very convenient, because it prohibits anyone from checking on the validity of the alleged events or event interviews. It also adds to the conspiratorial notions that silence means culpability.

- Supposed news-type websites suddenly appeared on the internet claiming to authenticate the premise and the characters in the movie, and particularly the person of Abigail Tyler. Some researchers have discovered that many of these sites were constructed in a matter of weeks and just before the movie's publicity started to roll off the line.

It appears that the movie is a complete work of fiction, although drawing to an extent from abduction folklore. The method of claiming that the realistic, almost home-movie style footage of interviews is genuine is very similar to the tactics used in movies such as *The Blair Witch Project* and *The Alien Autopsy* documentary (see chapter 6 of my book, *Alien Intrusion*).

The climax of the movie reveals that Tyler/Jovovich herself is an abductee. During one experience, her young daughter was also abducted by aliens and never returned. While undergoing regression to retrace the event, she relived an awful abduction encounter that revealed further details about what was really happening. But the regression permanently damaged Tyler/Jovovich physically and emotionally, who was subsequently told that her husband was not murdered but committed suicide—likely due to the similar incidents he appeared to have suffered. Apparently, Tyler/Jovovich knew this all along but had blocked it from her subconscious because it was simply too painful to deal with. We are told that she is insane, and thus, this leaves the viewer with some doubt that any of what occurred to her was true. The final scenes are played out with a wheelchair-bound Tyler being interviewed by the movie's real-life screenplay writer and director at Chapman University (a real university, but just as some of the points above, they have denied ever conducting such interviews or even knowing Tyler). In addition, it has also now been revealed that the alleged real footage of Tyler was played by little-known actress Charlotte Milchard.[115]

The portrayal of the scarred Tyler is harrowing, though. Although this may be a fictional account, the reality of such seriously damaged people is only too evident to those involved in abduction research. It is the real evidence of altered and broken lives that is only too recognizable as the fruit of the evil one using such deceptive and destructive practices to spite his Creator and turn the very subjects that God loves away from Him. Sadly, this fact is lost on secular researchers. Amazingly, the last scene with Tyler is extremely revealing. Her interviewer asks, "You said they claim to be God" (one entity was recorded saying these words in the movie). Tyler responds and says, "No, they pretend to be."

The aforementioned movie implied what many who have studied the phenomenon believe, namely that people are being possessed by aliens which have entered bedrooms through the ceilings or walls, and that the abductees left via the same method. However, such actions defy the very laws of physics. In addition, we are shown that the experiencers are supposed to have painful drills and probes inserted into them, yet most show no signs of having had such procedures. The richness of the details, but the lack of a naturalistic explanation, has baffled researchers for years. The movie's producers, and indeed, the majority of the world's UFO researchers, defer to some unknown advanced technology or force that aliens "must" possess because they are older and smarter on the evolutionary scale. This is because such people have not discerned the spiritual nature of the phenomenon. All this once again demonstrates how one's view of origins will shape the way one interprets all evidence—everything from fossils in the ground to distant starlight and even the strange occult-type experiences that people are having in their bedrooms.

False Memory Syndrome

Of course there is much debate, even in the Christian community, about hypnosis and whether the practice itself is safe for both the physical and spiritual wellbeing of the patient. It is well-known that past events can, indeed, be unlocked by such practices. But a major problem is that the hypnotist cannot know for sure if factual historical events are being recalled. This is because it is also now well-known that one's mind or imagination can create false memories, and these can also be implanted by the hypnotist, even the one doing the regression, sometimes unintentionally. This is not a blanket statement to say that all hypnotically-recalled memories are false, but if professional researchers now recognize that false memories exist and can be brought to the surface, then how can we discern between the two? Children who naturally have fertile imaginations are adept at this, of course, but unresolved trauma in one's life can also create alternate, imagined scenarios that one might eventually believe to be true. Sometimes this is done to protect oneself from the emotional pain of the past. Once such past events are recalled, often there can ensue a kind of self-reinforcement and self-delusion. Most people do this anyway, to some extent, during their normal, waking lives. Stories of the past get added to and then repeated often enough until they can become "truth" in a person's life. False Memory Syndrome is defined as:

[A] condition in which a person's identity and interpersonal relationships are centered around a memory of traumatic experience which is objectively false but in which the person strongly *believes*. Note that the syndrome is not characterized by false memories as such. We all have memories that are inaccurate. Rather, the syndrome may be diagnosed when the memory is so deeply ingrained that it *orients* the individual's entire personality and lifestyle, in turn disrupting all sorts of other adaptive behavior... False Memory Syndrome is especially destructive because the person assiduously *avoids confrontation with any evidence* that might challenge the memory. Thus it takes on a life of its own, encapsulated and *resistant* to correction. The person may become so focused on memory that he or she may be effectively *distracted* from coping with the real problems in his or her life.[116] (emphases in original)

Similarly:

Human *memory* is created and highly suggestible, and a wide variety of innocuous, embarrassing and frightening memories can be falsely created through the use of different techniques, including guided imagery, hypnosis and suggestion by others. Though not all individuals who are exposed to these techniques will develop memories, experiments suggest a significant number of people will and will actively defend the existence of the events, even if told they were false and deliberately implanted.[117]

These definitions indicate how "real" the memory can become in a person's life. This gives some indication as to why the alien abduction syndrome has reached epidemic proportions. Human nature reinforces the illusion because people do not like to be told, nor do they like to admit, that they have been deceived. As part of the implantation of false memories, the experiencers are often told they have been selected and are special. This can create meaning and purpose in one's life, particularly in the absence of some other guiding religious belief. Challenging such views can also add to the isolation created by the experience, and in some ways can seem to be challenging the person's sense of wellbeing and personal identity. The isolation can make them become dependent on the experience, which is often why there are ongoing experiences (like "Stockholm Syndrome," where victims of real hostage situations have become emotionally dependent on their captors). This is why it is incredibly difficult to reach people and convey to them the reality that such experiences might well have been deceptive.

The following are some extracts from *The False Memory Syndrome Foundation* website.

> *What are false memories?* Because of the reconstructive nature of memory, some memories may be distorted through influences such as the incorporation of new information. There are also believed-in imaginings that are not based in historical reality; these have been called false memories, pseudo-memories and memory illusions. They can result from the influence of external factors, such as the opinion of an authority figure or information repeated in the culture. An individual with an internal desire to please, to get better or to conform can easily be affected by such influences.[118] (emphasis in original)

> **Some of our memories are true, some are a mixture of fact and fantasy, and some are false**—whether those memories seem to be continuous or seem to be recalled after a time of being forgotten or not thought about.

Then how can we know if our memories are true? The professional organizations agree: the only way to distinguish between true and false memories is by external corroboration.[119] (emphasis in original)

In addition, many professionals and organizations have commented on False Memory Syndrome:

Memories, however emotionally intense and significant to the individual, do not necessarily reflect factual events.
Royal College of Psychiatrists, 1997[120]

Psychological studies have shown that it is virtually impossible to tell the difference between a real memory and one that is a product of imagination or some other process.
Elizabeth Loftus
"Memory Faults and Fixes"
Issues in Science and Technology, Summer 2002[121]

For a very tragic example of the reality of people suffering from False Memory Syndrome, one needs to look no further than the devastation caused to families as a result of encouraging these "memories." There are now literally hundreds of cases where people seeking counseling or help from therapists for issues in their adult lives were told that the problems probably stemmed from sexual abuse in their childhood. Many therapy sessions later, and once the "seed" had been planted, the patients recovered non-existent memories of fathers, mothers, uncles, and so on, abusing them—most interestingly, with graphic details of each alleged event. Lawsuits among families' members abounded. And because of bad therapeutic practices, and the ill-conceived ideas that such issues needed to be brought to the surface to be confronted, families, relationships, and lives have been ripped apart. There are many cases studies that can be read on the *False Memory Syndrome Foundation* website.[122] A lady who was told she was suffering from Multiple Personality Disorder (MPD) wrote the following:

> The doctor decided I needed five to seven years of therapy. He explained to me and my husband… "So terrible that she's repressed those memories deep in her mind… Finally, she will work through those old feelings and get better." We bought it, and I worked hard to recall repressed memories. Of course, there were no real memories, but the mind is an amazing thing. Let me explain, in lay terms, how repressed memories were created on one occasion. The therapist called-up Beth, a 5-year old alter [other personality], and hypnotized her. He suggested sexual abuse had occurred at the hands of her Daddy. He explained she needed to see a "big movie screen" in her mind and tell him what she saw. Then, he asked leading questions about touching, etc. Beth performed just as the therapist predicted she would. Beth and I were rewarded with much attention and sympathy.
>
> In reality, I didn't have those memories, but the doctor considered them true and wanted more. For months, I allowed other alters to write anything they could remember. The memories grew worse and worse and I became horrified. I thought it was all true, and I felt worthless and betrayed. I recalled various fragments of movies, books, talk shows, and nightly news, and soon I had plenty of child abuse memories. But, it didn't

stop there. Eventually, I said I had taken part in Satanic Rituals, been buried alive, drank blood, and helped to kill a baby. With every new memory, my therapist was intrigued and building a case to prove he was right about me all along. I was rewarded with his attention to me and was his "best" patient. But, I started to have feelings of death and became suicidal.

I truly exhibited all the MPD symptoms even though I had learned them. Control of my mind, emotions, and will was given to the personalities the therapist had empowered.[123]

In the aforementioned story, if we substituted the patient for an alien abductee and the therapist for hypnotist from a UFO organization (or even a deceiving angel), the story sounds awfully familiar.

The Problems with Regression

To avoid offense, I want to reassert that this is not meant to diminish the real experiences of people who have suffered trauma or abuse in the past from whatever source. I can empathize with the frustration of not being able to find closure or even share such experiences with others. This is a very difficult area to discern, because as we mentioned earlier, a major problem is that even the hypnotists themselves can (either intentionally or inadvertently), through suggestion, create an imaginary scenario or event in a patient's mind. Once the suggestion is planted, the imagination and the mind can do the rest. Professional hypnotists and even con artists can hypnotize people for entertainment's sake with relative ease. The usual waving of a fob watch or "look into my eyes" that accompanied many TV performances of the past is actually not necessary, although such methods do work. This is frequently described as stage hypnosis. It is often a form of traditional hypnosis (with the added stage pizzazz) where suggestions are made to the unconscious or subconscious mind (researchers claim that both are actually the same thing). A key to understanding how this works and being able to perform traditional hypnosis realizing that people were there to be entertained in the first place—in short, they were already open to being hypnotized. Or they may be visiting a physician, a clinical hypnotherapist, or a UFO researcher, and, thus, they are allowing themselves to be helped through hypnosis.

My research has pointed out repeatedly that a pre-belief seems to be one of the prerequisites in order to be deceived. This may be as simple as being open to the possibility of extraterrestrial life. If you think such beings have actually appeared before you, then you are more likely to be taken in by it, and because polls consistently show that the majority of the population now believes in the possibility of ET life,[124] it would indicate that vast numbers are increasingly more vulnerable to deception through hypnotic suggestion and false memory implantation by fallen angels masquerading as aliens.

Most people misunderstand hypnosis and wrongly believe that they cannot be hypnotized if they don't want to be. But there are actually many forms or types of hypnosis. The hypnotic state is really more the result of a self-hypnosis that is induced by the hypnotist, who "talks you into [or through] it." One form requires the patient/victim to fall into a relaxed state. In other cases, creating disorientation or confusion works to the hypnotizer's advantage.

Dr. Al Krasner was the founder and director of The American Institute of Hypnotherapy. In his book, *The Wizard Within: The Krasner Method of Clinical Hypnotherapy*, he is quoted as saying: "I believe hypnosis to be a process which produces relaxation, distraction of the conscious mind, heightened suggestibility, and increased awareness, allowing access to the subconscious mind through the imagination. It also produces the ability to experience thoughts and images as real."[125]

However, there are other forms of hypnosis such as Neurolinguistic Programming (normally referred to as NLP) and Ericksonian Hypnotherapy, which uses stories and metaphors to create indirect suggestions. Dr. Milton H. Erickson is quoted as saying: "The hypnotic state is an experience that belongs to the subject, derives from the subject's own accumulated learnings and memories, not necessarily consciously recognized, but possible of manifestations in a special state of non waking awareness."[126]

There are also instant inductions (more on this later in the chapter).

Is Hypnosis Always Wrong?

Many people are wary, even fearful, of hypnosis. Much of this may be a result of a lack of understanding of what is involved, and/or assigning unwarranted spiritual implications to it. Some even think that practitioners are engaging in occult practices, and are the equivalent of the "charmers" and "enchanters" forbidden in the Old Testament. I have tried to show that hypnosis taps into mechanisms that are part of our normal brain in this fallen world. Most hypnosis does not involve any attempt to invoke the supernatural. Of course, like many things in our world, in the wrong hands it can be used for dangerous and destructive purposes. One case in point is abduction scenarios.

Even exploiting people under hypnosis for entertainment purposes seems opposed to the fact that our dominion mandate (subduing the Creation—Genesis 1:28) does not extend to dominion over other human beings made in God's image. But to write off all hypnosis as occult seems hard to justify biblically. Hypnosis can be a useful tool in the right hands, and used in a proper forum or setting (e.g. to anesthetize a person who needs surgery but is unable to tolerate a standard anesthetic). Because hypnosis is rarely undertaken or understood in Christian circles, it is mainly employed by secular practitioners, particularly in the field of psychology. Christians, therefore, might have cause for concern in this regard, due to many psychologists having pre-existing secular and even evolutionary interpretations of the phenomena as in the cases mentioned above. They do not understand it as part of the relationship between body, soul and spirit in God's design of mankind, "broken" to some extent at the time of the Fall.

Once this relaxed state is reached and the focus is on the hypnotizer, he can instruct, make recommendations using open or subliminal communication, even with touch or gestures to reinforce positive or negative aspects that are being assigned to memory in order to get the patient to do whatever the hypnotizer wants. At the time of the session, this may be done intentionally (as in the case of fallen angels), inadvertently by the hypnotist, or even by the surroundings or setting that accompanies the session. This idea that hypnosis can achieve so much may seem too simplistic or too amazing for some reading this, but a little realistic research will reveal this to be the truth, and as with many aspects to this phenomenon, I have often found the simplest explanations to be the best. The reason they are not often believed and accepted is due to the overlay of misinformation by those desiring strange phenomena to be real aliens.

With subliminal suggestion it is not always necessary for a person to be hypnotized. I have seen experiments where visitors to shopping malls were subject to subliminal words or commands played over the public broadcast system along with the usual piped music one can usually hear in such venues. In each and every case, the overall majority of the shoppers obeyed commands on cue without awareness that they had been conveyed.[127]

A well-known British hypnotist by the name of Derren Brown regularly creates a whole range of different scenarios for his television program to show how people are easily suggestible and can be manipulated. In one episode, prior to a meeting with famous British celebrity Simon Pegg (and all filmed under the camera's glare), the celebrity was asked to secretly write down on a sealed card his all-time favorite gift—i.e., the one gift he always wanted to receive. No one else was privy to what he had written down. After ten minutes of conversation with Brown, Pegg stated that he had always wanted a red bicycle. However, when he was invited to open the sealed card, it revealed that he had earlier written down a leather jacket! He was confused and disoriented, unsure how this could have occurred. Brown revealed how he achieved this by lacing and overlaying the conversation with stories that provided commonalities between the past and present and included words like red, handlebar, wheels, and bicycle. Also, when one took a closer look at the room the interview was conducted in, it also contained many items and colours to aid in the planting of a false memory (one can watch a replay of the interview to see this).[128] But the key was this: in order to get the celebrity to change his choice of a favorite gift, Brown had to create a false memory in the person. Brown often comments that in such scenarios his "victims" really have no choice in the matter, because he stacks the odds so much in his favor by inserting so much subliminal information. This indicates what power these methods can have. In short, the real memory of writing down a leather jacket was replaced or manipulated.

What seems more amazing is that before Pegg opened the card, he had created and explained a whole imaginary scenario about being deprived in his childhood of a bicycle to explain his choice of a red bicycle. No wonder he was confused and disoriented when he opened his own card. This aptly demonstrates how once the message, memory, or image is implanted, the imagination can "fill in the blanks." When the false memory is created, it is effectively a false history, and as such, the mind can create a whole array of visual imagery to support the "new" memory. This shows how a form of self-delusion or self-reinforcement about the imagined event can actually occur. The methods that professional hypnotists like Brown use are the NLP or Erickson methods referred to earlier. The stories they tell contain "Process Instructions" or "Embedded Commands" hidden in the stories. Sometimes "NLP Anchoring" is used where triggers or memories of the past are used to associate new memories or even to disassociate other memories.

An acquaintance of mine (let's call him Eric), a medical doctor, also revealed that while a student on call at a maternity hospital, card games were often played by the students to pass the time. During one session, the subject of hypnosis came up in discussion. Eric had studied psychology and explained to one of his fellow medical students that it was possible to hypnotize him, and get him to carry out post-hypnotic suggestions. This student (let's call him Bill) strongly pooh-poohed the whole idea that he would even "go under," but agreed to play along. Eric very quickly managed to get him into a trance state. He then said that after waking, upon being given a cue word, Bill would hurl an empty can of sliced pineapple (that was sitting on the window ledge) out of the first floor window, but he would forget having been given this command while "under." Given that there were parked cars below, this was something Bill would not normally have dreamt of doing.

After being woken from the trance, Bill confidently claimed that he had not been hypnotized, and was just playing along, but he offered no recollection of the suggestion about the pineapple can. Then, Eric uttered the cue word (the so-called "trigger"). Bill immediately became restless, glancing over at the hapless can repeatedly. Finally he got up, and started to move towards the can, muttering all the while about how shoddy it looked, how it irritated him, and so on. When he had inched close enough, he picked it up, continuing to denigrate the poor can. Maintaining his invective, he moved gradually closer to the open window while seeming to avoid the appearance of doing so purposely. When he was up close, he said he had "had enough"; the can irked him so much that he didn't want to see it anymore—and, stepping up to the open window, he hurled it into the outer darkness.

It was as if, once the implanted idea was awoken by the key word, the impulse to do this rather irrational thing had to be rationalized somehow, the mind creating a cover story, as it were, which involved the can's unworthiness to share the same room with him. The cover story or rationale had to paint the can as sufficiently repugnant to warrant not merely being placed in the trash, but thrown out the window. Afterwards, he seemed somewhat dazed and confused, as if wrestling with the thought, *Why did I do that?* There were subsequent instances, too, in which Eric's post-hypnotic suggestions to Bill demonstrated even more clearly how Bill's mind was creating additional realities—a cover or justification for an impulse to certain behavior, the impulse generated from an idea that had already been implanted previously.

"Nothing New Under the Sun"

The Bible indicates that the wisest man ever to live was the Israelite King Solomon. In Ecclesiastes 1:9–10, he said: "The thing that hath been, it is that which shall be; and that which is done is that which shall be done: and there is no new thing under the sun. Is there any thing whereof it may be said, See, this is new? it hath been already of old time, which was before us" (KJV). Once again, comparing the verse to more modern English, we read in the NIV: "What has been will be again, what has been done will be done again; there is nothing new under the sun. Is there anything of which one can say, 'Look! This is something new'? It was here already, long ago; it was here before our time."

During my research, a qualified clinical hypnotherapist and former forensic psychologist explained that "Hypnosis is actually just a label that has been applied to a very broad, imperfectly understood set of mind phenomena."[129] However, the phenomenon of hypnosis is not new. When it comes to deceiving mankind, fallen angels do not need to "reinvent the wheel," and the Bible also indicates that man is only ever tempted by what is common to him (1 Corinthians 10:13).

When it comes to trying to unravel abduction episodes, there are many hypotheses percolating among the UFO community.

Many resort to speculative, unknown forces and even bizarre spiritual explanations to explain what we cannot be sure is actually occurring anyway. None of these extravagant hypotheses have any experimental or empirical basis to them, and often no Scriptural support either. There is a distinct lack of physical evidence in these episodes, and there are rarely any non-abductee eyewitnesses to abduction events, for example. Even if there were people who claimed to have seen what happened, this hypothesis could explain why they, too, believed something they "saw." While my own hypnosis theory is hypothetical, it appeals to mechanisms we know exist, to things that we know can actually be done via hypnosis. In mentioning some of these experiences earlier (and there are more below), I am pointing out that hypnosis is a known quantity that can be used to explain what is occurring during alleged alien abductions. Using the Ockham's Razor approach (see chapter 4 of my book *Alien Intrusion*) I am suggesting that many of the details of abduction episodes are an illusory spiritual deception that is being planted into the minds of experiencers to create the "reality"—a false memory in effect. This not only fits the instances where individuals are concerned; in the case of the Allagash Four, too, the hypnosis theory fits the circumstances perfectly. Mass hypnosis episodes can also occur, and subliminal messages can be imposed on entire groups as shown earlier in the description of the shopping mall experiments.

So how can the appearance of a UFO in the sky lead to missing time and a recollection of being abducted by an alien?

First, as we have shown, UFOs have changed their shapes over the years. They seem able to morph into a form that is culturally acceptable to the victim. This can help to create the openness to further suggestion. In the past, UFOs appeared as flying canoes, and today they appear as spaceships, which automatically evokes the idea that they are piloted by extraterrestrial spacemen (and thus creates the opening for the alien abduction scenario). World-renowned UFOlogist, Jaques Valle e, showed that the abductors have morphed over the years too. Anything from fairies and elves to ETs—whatever seems culturally acceptable to the population. Hypnotherapy is almost always done with relaxation and relatively gradual induction with a soft, soothing voice. But these are not even necessary with about 20 percent of the population (or well-prepared subjects).[130] Modern hypnotists also use lights and sounds to stimulate people to make them susceptible to suggestion. This is a characteristic also often used in sightings prior to abductions. Hypnotists can paralyze people—even when the patient is fully conscious. A clinical hypnotherapist confirmed to me:

> Sleeping people do not usually transition into hypnosis, and are not subliminally suggestible, but waking up from an REM stage with shock and surprise would provide the perfect brainwave transition…to induce an immediate deep state in "suggestible" subjects.
>
> This was a common device in brainwashing techniques…though usually with brutal shock and confusion. The gently repeated, soothing whispers "you're alright" or something similar would have less trauma, but should be very effective in leaving a "trigger" imprint in the subject's spirit that could be harnessed at a later time.[131]

This method of waking people occurs commonly in alien abduction scenarios. Similarly, when entities appear in a room, many claim that they feel compelled to look into the entity's eyes—another method used by hypnotists. Once they are in this controlled state they are very prone to further suggestion. The

idea that the entities communicate telepathically is also a common belief—something that fits no known scientific observations. But this could easily be believed if messages to that effect were being placed while under hypnosis.

There is also another pattern amongst abductees that I have discovered alongside of any pre-belief or openness to the idea of ETs, and it is that there seems to be an additional "entry point," so to speak. People who have unresolved trauma or issues in their past seem to be particularly vulnerable to alien abductions and False Memory Syndrome in general. This is something recognized by many medical experts operating outside of the UFOlogical area. In addition, those suffering from current problems such as alcoholism or drug addiction also seem to be susceptible. I have seen, on occasions, where people suffering with mental disabilities have had similar experiences as identified using the CAS categorization. Unfortunately, when these folks talk about their experiences, they are largely ignored and the claims are passed off as the fruit of their illnesses. Of course, no amount of personal frailty can, by itself, explain such things as the seemingly shared experiences of the Allagash Four, for example. It seems that the master deceiver and enemy of God (the devil/Lucifer/Satan) and his cohorts (other fallen angels) are no respecter of persons, and seem to be largely opportunists.

Missing Time

The missing time aspect is often a fundamental aspect to alien abductions. This was well documented by noted researcher Budd Hopkins in his book, *Missing Time*. I also believe it is a key to understanding the methods used by these angelic beings. The

Bible provides some insight into the characteristics of angels. They are inter-dimensional, immensely powerful and intelligent sentient beings, and often appear physically in our earthly dimensions. If human beings can easily perform such deeds on their fellows, it cannot be any more difficult for angels to do the same. Being able to appear instantly in a room would ensure anybody's attention, and once entities become the focus of the victim, most methods of hypnosis would become readily available. Experiencers usually only consciously remember the initial sighting of a UFO or an entity they believe to be alien. They then wake up several hours later with no conscious recollection of anything occurring during the missing time. However, when regressed, the victims are able to recount seeming events with incredible detail. Let's remember that all these entities have to do is to paint a picture to the unconscious victim—stories about cold metallic inspection tables, crude instruments, video screens—the works!

UK Daily Mail Reports: Trainee Hypnotist Puts Himself in a Trance for Five Hours

A circus performer stood locked in a trance for hours after he accidentally hypnotised himself while practising his routine in a mirror. Sword swallower Hannibal Helmurto, 38, whose real name is Helmut Kichmeier, stood transfixed in front of the mirror for five hours until his wife Joanna found him. Unable to rouse him, she was forced to phone her husband's mentor, hypnotherapist Dr Ray Roberts, who trained him on an intensive course recently. Dr Roberts spoke to Helmut over the phone and he slowly came out of the trance. Helmut said a person under hypnosis only responds to a voice of authority. Joanna, 22, said: "I was really shocked when I found him, he was just like a zombie starring at himself in the mirror. His pupils had gone really small, which is a sign of someone under hypnosis."

Helmut, who has performed in the *Circus of Horrors* for four years, had recently learned how to put himself into a somnambulistic trance, a way of hypnotising yourself to enable him to swallow multiple swords in the infamous circus. The performer, who is originally from Germany but now lives in London, said: "I underestimated the techniques and how powerful they were. I put myself in a very deep state and lost all sense of time around me."

He said he could not remember anything when he came out of the trance, other than getting up at 10am and starting to practise his hypnosis. He said he had no idea where the missing five hours had gone. "It is a very pleasant feeling, sometimes it is so pleasant that you literally forget the things around you and that is what happened to me," he said. "Your body is absolutely relaxed. You don't feel a thing. On the one hand your body is relaxed and floating and on the other hand your mind is extremely focused on something." The self-taught hypnotherapist has been practising the art for nine years. He added: "I have always been interested in hypnosis because I had seen it on TV and thought it was a right big spoof. "I started reading and learning about it and it turns out it is not a big spoof at all. I got into it being a total disbeliever."[132]

To those who have experienced alien abduction scenarios, you may be thinking, *No, you are wrong. I know it happened—I felt it, I know it happened.* Yes, you did feel it. But even when you genuinely feel something like a hard bench under you (a real one, I mean), your perception is ultimately a sensation in the brain. So it's not hard to understand, as experts have pointed out and hypnotists have repeatedly demonstrated, that the imagination (the mind) can easily create the illusion of a physical sensation without the physical event actually happening. For example, the majority of people reading this will have experienced a falling dream while they have been asleep, and you can probably even now recall the physical sensation of falling through the air—yet it never actually happened.

Once again, I am not saying that there are no physical aspects to these experiences. It is possible that people are being interfered with, being scratched, or the triangle marks are being imprinted upon the skin. But all this is being added to try to give weight to, and enhance, the overriding illusion of glorious spacemen benevolently overseeing the human race. After all, when appearances of angels are recorded in the Bible, they appear physical and can even kill humans. The Bible forbids "going after" (following, worshiping) such beings, because of the very fact that people can be deceived by them (they were often described as the "host of heaven" or "starry host" [2 Kings 21:3]).[133]

People who claim out-of-body experiences (OBEs) and who claim to "astral travel" similarly record physical sensations of flying. In the same way, people can be hypnotized and told that a hot iron is being placed on their arm. The sensation they have is completely the same, i.e., just as "real" as if a real hot iron were there. The mind and body can even create a physical response in the area that thinks it was burned.

In Derren Brown's TV show *Trick or Treat*, contestants stand the chance of winning a sizeable prize (the treat), but it is at the risk of being on the receiving end of one of Brown's "tricks." In one episode, Brown entered a family's home at night (the family was complicit in the ruse) and hypnotized a contestant while he was in his bed. The contestant's eyes can even be seen to be wide open. Triggers and anchoring techniques were used to stimulate responses that would be used in the future. These (triggers and anchors) are known as Post Hypnotic Re-Induction Cues, where a post-hypnotic suggestion will enable the person to reenter a trance at the command of the hypnotist later on. This could also be the method used to account for ongoing abduction scenarios. The anchor could immediately take control of a person, regress someone back to the false memory, which could then be further embellished and exploited. The anchor could be as simple as a keyword, or even a snapping of the fingers as often done by stage hypnotists.

The contestant was told to visit a photo booth to take passport photos as part of his "treat"—an overseas holiday. When in the booth, lights flashed, music played, and keywords were repeated that re-induced the unconscious state. While unconscious, the contestant was then removed and flown from England to a market in Marrakesh, Morocco, and placed back into the photo booth that had also been taken along. The time taken to do this was fourteen hours. He was then awoken with more keywords. Hidden cameras recorded the man's reaction. To him, one minute ago he was in a photo booth in England, and now he is in a completely different country with no record of traveling there. His passport had even been stamped by the Moroccan immigration department. This was actually a form of abduction. Such real-life recorded events once again demonstrate the potential of hypnosis to explain practically every detail of the abduction phenomenon. **The missing time aspect is the strongest clue that many of these experiences are being induced hypnotically.**

In addition, physical responses can be suppressed while under hypnosis. I have seen patients undergoing open abdominal surgery painlessly while under hypnosis, and with no other form of anesthesia. This method was clinically used because of the patient's adverse reaction to anesthetic. I have seen stage performers hypnotize participants into thinking the large onions they were holding were in fact the juiciest apples they had ever tasted. With eyes open, the victims ate the onions, devouring them as if they could not get enough, and at the same time telling the rest of the studio audience how nice the "apples" were. No tears, either. This could simply not be faked, and upon the word of the hypnotist, reality kicked in and they then had the normal reactions one would expect devouring large quantities of raw onion—eyes watering, spitting out the foul substance, including an impromptu vomit on stage! In the same show, anchors were used to put people into and out of a trance at will. It really happens!

Please also understand that I am not saying that all abduction scenarios are explainable by this aforementioned hypothesis, but it does seek to explain (and it fits very well) what one might call the "garden-variety" type experiences that are usually defined under the category of the CAS (Classic Abduction Syndrome).

Using the CAS to Predict Experiences

Because of the patterns involved and the belief that this whole alien abduction scenario is a deception of cosmic proportions, when meeting experiencers, one can even make predictions about the events before being actually told about them. This is because one can understand the agenda behind the deception and understand its purpose. As we have mentioned before, there are so many glaring inconsistencies about the view that benevolent ETs are stealthily abducting people in the middle of the night for their own good. Such a case where I was able to make and test a prediction was in New Zealand in 2006. After a lecture one evening, my hosts and I were leaving the venue when a car sped up to the entrance. I recognized the lady as having attended my earlier lecture. In the passenger seat was a man around forty-plus years old. Getting out of the car, the lady said, "Here he is. Go talk to him quickly." By now I knew what to expect. A person can become isolated by an experience that no one can understand, let alone believe that it actually occurred. Asking my hosts to move away so we could have some privacy, I invited the man to tell me what happened.

At around ten years of age, it was customary for his parents to visit relatives on their farm in the country. It was a young boy's paradise as he could play and explore the beautiful natural environment of the New Zealand countryside. He said that, one day, he saw a flying saucer land. Terrified, he ran away to the barn. He saw an occupant of the craft get out and walk towards the barn. The boy put his shoulder against the door, hoping the "spaceman" would think that it was closed. He says he can even remember pressure against the door. Petrified, he ran to the back of the barn to hide. He said the spaceman stood in the doorway with the daylight emanating from around him and piercing the darkness of the barn.

He was about to describe the spaceman's appearance when I said, "No, please don't. May I ask you a few questions?" Working from the man's current age and his age at the time of the experience, I asked, "Was the spaceman wearing a one-piece, silver or white jumpsuit with a glass-type helmet?" He answered, "Yes, how could you know that?" It was a guess on my part, but a calculated one. I figured that his experience occurred in the late 1960s. This was the era of the B-grade science fiction movies and TV series such as *Lost in Space*, and this was the typology of the science fiction movies of the day. Vallée was right. The phenomenon morphs according to the cultural environment of the day. Such a thing seems ridiculous by modern-day standards, but we need to remember that's what people would likely have accepted back then as representing a "real spaceman." Noted UFOlogist, John Keel, saying earlier, many researchers go off the deep end because they cannot comprehend the seeming bizarreness of it all. This is ultimately because they do not recognize it as being spiritual in nature and how it can transmogrify in our own earthly realm.

There Is an Answer and We Can Help People

One would think, then, that because this is a spiritual deception being perpetrated by the enemies of God, this would be bread and butter for the Church. The man that I just previously mentioned had become a Christian, but had never found an answer to what had happened to him. As he spoke to me, I could see how the event had confused and damaged him. Since I started researching this phenomenon, I have now met hundreds of individuals who've had UFO experiences of one kind or another. Many of them come to me because when they hear me speak on the subject they have a sense that I understand what is really going on, and also because they've never heard anyone speak about it before (except perhaps to tell them that they really saw an alien spacecraft and were really abducted by aliens, or to pooh-pooh their experience totally).

As I primarily do most of my speaking on the subject in churches, I take no pleasure in pointing out that the overwhelming majority of Christian leaders have no idea that significant numbers of people *in their own congregations* have seen something in the skies that they could not explain, or even worse, have had experiences with strange entities. The numbers, of course, are significantly higher for the general population—the very people that churches should be reaching. The reason that this grieves me so much is that the Church should be regarded as the obvious place to go for people seeking answers to problems in their lives to find comfort and solace. Of course, I understand that it is easy to dismiss something that one does not understand. But individuals are being severely traumatized and damaged by their encounters with deceptive and dangerous spiritual forces. It is my own experience, and that of many other Christian UFOlogists, that churches and their leaders will often not even entertain a lecture, interview, or discussion on the matter. Simply, they want nothing to do with it. Often, it is because they feel there are more important issues to deal with—day-to-day pressures in the Church, for example. This is understandable, but if large numbers of the population believe in such things, and people are really hurting and are confused, then it actually presents significant opportunities for the Church: Opportunities to provide answers, to help heal the broken and confused (remembering that the enemy seems to select the most vulnerable to start with), and to be more relevant to the culture than it has ever been. Even some non-Christian UFO researchers recognize the damage that follows experiences and have suggested that the Church could help.

But unless the Church accepts, embraces, and learns to deal with this modern cultural phenomenon that is a subset of the issue of origins (where these beings come from, and determining our own place in the universe), then even I (with great sadness) could not confidently recommend to experiencers that the Church could help them with this issue. Because of this non-acceptance of the phenomenon occurring around them, the Church does not know how to reach potentially millions of people (yes, that many) who are looking for answers. Unfortunately, most experiencers that I have met have felt angry because they were shunned by the Church who would not take their experiences seriously, or simply suggested that these people were demon-possessed. So, this forces them to seek the assistance of those in the UFO community, who, sadly, will only reinforce the lie that they are being visited by highly evolved, benevolent beings from another planet. A loving church that could embrace and explain this phenomenon will have people turning up at its door for answers.

It may not be possible to reply to all, but please feel free to share your experiences with me by emailing me at mail@creation.info, or by visiting CREATION.com. Perhaps the hypnosis theory as outlined above will help you make sense of what happened to you.

CHAPTER NINE

DARK RITUALS/DARK POWERS

By Russ Dizdar

And I saw three unclean spirits like frogs come out of the mouth of the dragon, and out of the mouth of the beast, and out of the mouth of the false prophet. For they are the spirits of devils, working miracles, which go forth unto the kings of the earth and of the whole world, to gather them to the battle of that great day of God Almighty. Behold, I come as a thief. Blessed is he that watcheth, and keepeth his garments, lest he walk naked, and they see his shame. And he gathered them together into a place called in the Hebrew tongue Armageddon.

REVELATION 16:13–16

It was the sight of a young girl's remains (a pink head to be specific, the details of which I will not describe) that burned itself into my mind; it happened the very moment I saw it and it has never left me. It has fueled my passion to fight radical evil

215

and the devastating rituals that practitioners use…*in growing and unprecedented numbers.* During a law enforcement training (Def Tec Geneva, Ohio) on advance occult/satanic crimes, a crime scene was shown to us on video. A girl, most likely a runaway, was drawn into a party; she was taken by force and ritually abused and sacrificed.

I have seen a number of ritual sites, viewed hundreds of crime-scene photos, and read and listened to hundreds of accounts of modern-day satanic rituals. All of this (since the '80s) moved me to track, investigate, expose, and do all that can be done to stop this ancient/modern practice…it has grown in this hour of history *off the charts and beyond belief.*

The Past

One only has to study the dark rituals of the past to see the gruesome accounts of ungodly human sacrifice and devastation. I have read the accounts of these sacrifices reported around the world in places like Sumer, China, Chile, England, Ireland, and more. Two of the most renowned sites would be the Mayan and Aztec civilizations. Though many have fallen for the view of a "quieter, gentler" Maya, the truth is, modern-day stories, documentaries, and spiritual revelations of 2012 Mayan prophecies (including the predictions of the return of Quetzalcoatl) cloak the blood-soaked temples and grounds of these ancient sights.

In one report, one hundred thirty-six thousand human skulls, along with various other body parts, were lined up on racks as charged trophies of ancient Aztec blood sacrifices to old demon gods they feared. Another report covered the agonizing, ritual slaughter of living human beings by Mayan priests. Some were stretched out on a rack, their entrails removed by the demon-appeasing, knife-wielding priest.

Among the Mayan temples, massive human suffering, ritual sacrifice, and bloodshed were the norm. Modern-day movie-makers and book authors (like Daniel Pinchbeck's, *2012: The Return of Quetzalcoatl*) seek to reveal a sparkling, spiritual Mayan civilization of the past that my help bring about a return to those days (thus 2012) and a return of a god or god-man (Nephilim) once worshipped as Quetzalcoatl. I can only wonder if these authors and movie-makers have seen the Vatican-confiscated Mayan painting of this very same Quetzalcoatl standing over a human being whom he is sacrificing. Quetzalcoatl is seen thrusting a ritual knife into the eye socket of a ritual victim. Does anyone really want him to return (or the Moloch's, Baal's, etc.)?

The Present

Occult historian, James Charles Napier Webb, declared in his work, *The Occult Establishment: The Dawn of the New Age and the Occult Establishment*, that the second largest proliferation of occult literature was released in the 1960s in the U.S. The first was unleashed in pre-Nazi Germany. What a spinning decade the '60s were! We saw The Beatles, anti-war movement, the sexual revolution, eastern mysticism, and the 1966 establishment of the modern "Church of Satan" with the release of self-proclaimed dark pope Anton LaVey's *The Satanic Bible* (1969). That book spelled out for many, sex, destruction, and even death rituals. The '60s was only the first dark steps of even darker left-hand path rituals. (Perhaps it was Alistair Crowley or the "Babylon Working" ritual by U.S. rocket scientist, Jack Parsons, that helped open the doors to the modern rise of these dark rituals and manifesting dark powers?)

In her book, *Crimewarps: The Future of Crime in America*, Georgette Bennett predicted that the '90s would be a dark decade with a primary rise in satanic and occult ritual crime. Law enforcement agent, Thomas W. Wedge, unleashed his book, *The Satan Hunter*, which gave local police the tools to uncover, investigate, and seek trace evidence at satanic ritual crime scenes. It was Holly Hector, a former hypnotherapist at Denver's Centennial hospital, while working on the new satanic ritual abuse ward (part of the psych ward), who said that there were, by the early '90s, 2.4 million diagnosed cases of severe satanic ritual abuse that included trauma-based mind-control (the splitting of the human personality to create alter or sub personalities who could be programmed and demonized).

Later, there was a rise of satanic bands like *Slayer* who gave invitation to hundreds of thousands of youth to cut themselves, spill their blood, and embrace the demonic (such as in the song *Spill the Blood* on their album *South of Heaven*). Other satanic bands were *far* worse. Extremely so. (See the book *Lords of Chaos: The Bloody Rise of the Satanic Metal Underground* by Michael Moynihan and Didrik Soderlind.) Other works such as *Satan Wants You: The Cult of Devil Worship in America* (by Arthur Lyons), *Cults That Kill: Probing the Underworld of Occult Crime* (by Larry Kahaner), *Painted Black: From Drug Killings to Heavy Metal—The Alarming True Story of How Satanism Is Terrorizing Our Communities* (by Carl A. Raschke), and a new and vital study *Programmed to Kill: The Politics of Serial Murder* (by David McGowan), is to mention only a few who have sought to grasp this unprecedented rise of Satanism, dark ritual crimes, and satanic, ritual abuse. It would seem that author Bob Rosio was right in his two books, *Hitler and the New Age* (wherein Bob coins the phrase "deception always leads to destruction" [the demon/occult-given ideology of the Nazis lead to WW2 and millions dead]) and *The Satanization of America: Secular Humanism's Assault on America* (the title of which may explain life in our country for the last seventy years).

In this current hour, the rise of Satanism the world over has even led the Russian national security director to declare: "In 2008, Interior Ministry experts announced that Satanism was a greater threat to the country's national security than Islamic radicalism."[134] The Catholic News Agency declared that "the smoke of Satan" is in the Vatican[135] and one Catholic priest records over ninety thousand exorcisms and even more that Italy has over eight thousand satanic cults with over seven hundred thousand members. In such a small nation that is massive!

The development of occult/satanic crime units and detectives and thousands of websites promoting every evil spiritual path with the unveiling of some of the darkest and once-kept secret ritual procedures is evidence of the rise of these wicked rituals. This current hour has sent the Vatican in a frenzy to train priests in exorcism and has lead the way to more books being written on spiritual warfare, deliverance, and exposing the dark side in the last twenty years than in the entire history of the Church. It is clear that in the last forty years, we have seen an unequaled rise in malevolent writings, practices, and the manifestations of sinister powers.

I believe that rituals that unleash evil powers are at the center of this.

Before we go on to the future part of this chapter, let me unwrap three almost-unheard-of and largely un-preached biblical revelations. I hope that taking a closer look at this list will result in some greatly needed, cutting-edge, spiritual warfare discernment/Intel and action.

The Revelation of "Supernatural Secrecy"

I believe that 95 percent of the rituals that have and are going on are cloaked in satanic powers that effectively keep them secret and very well-hidden. In Ezekiel Chapter 8, the great prophet had no idea that there were long-established, luciferic, serpent-worshipping incidents going on right in the City of God. It took a Higher Supernatural Power (the hand of God) to lead the biblical prophet into the cave to witness what in God's sight was grossly detestable. It is this secret power of lawlessness (Satan's supernaturally operative power; see 2 Thessalonians 2) that was and is still behind the rise of dark arts, rituals, ritual crime and the global manifestation of demonic activity (including possessions).

The Revelation of Uncontested Growth of Dark Rituals Manifesting Dark Powers

In 2 Kings Chapters 21–23 is the story of an evil king in the City of God that opened every possible door to dark spirits. He was eventually led to sacrifice his own son in a bloody, painful ritual on a slab in Moloch worship. Its seems that no one stopped this and eventually the Temple of God was laced with occult symbols and the making of occult objects…at least until Josiah arose to put a stop to it.

The Issue of the Weaponization of Dark Powers

In 2 Kings Chapter 3, a demon-worshipping king from a demon-experienced nation was at war with Israel. The Moabite king was losing, so he, like any old military king would have done, sent out seven hundred more soldiers to fight. The Pagan nation was still losing! So the king, seeking advantage, took his son and sacrificed him on the wall, shedding his blood so that the demons would come, and come they did; the powers fell upon the Moabite warriors, moving them into a non-human enhancement frenzy. The freshly demonized soldiers then beat Israel back and won for the day.

Keep These Points Close

The Old Testament's revelation on satanic rituals is vast and should be restudied to help us understand how the satanic supernatural secrecy, satanic ritual growth, and the weaponizing of dark powers happen. Now let's peer into the future.

The Future

Biblical revelation on satanic and demonic powers and rituals may be the most important Bible study approach in a Christian's walk, and I believe it gives the best information we can possibly have to our advantage. The coming rise of global Babylon, the three frogs of Revelation 16, and the phenomenon of SRA MPD (satanic ritual abuse multiple personality disorder) do have a role in these last days. Jesus taught that the first thing to look at as evidence of the last days (and His Coming) is demonic deception in Matthew 24. The Spirit of God cries out that there will be a massive wave of seducing spirits who will lead many astray and cause some to write (to influence the world) doctrines of demons (see 1 Timothy 4). The panoramic view of the evolution of the satanic agenda is crisply spelled out in 2 Thessalonians 2. But two more vastly neglected and invaluable revelations are found in the book of the Revelation of Jesus Christ.

Revelation Chapter 18

I greatly encourage you, the reader of this book, to read this Bible chapter. Here, we see the spiritual source of the "new world order." The power behind all of this is seen in the future at the height or at *the pinnacle of global, demonic manifestation.* Demonic presence and power seems to be manifested everywhere…every city, nation…everywhere! Talk about "feeling oppression in the air"! Looking at the past and the present (and biblically) it would seem that the most powerful source luciferians have access to in getting their wicked powers from that side to this is: dark rituals, blood rituals, and human sacrifice (for sure).

The Three Frogs of Revelation 16

These are very powerful *demons released in ritual fashion and sent out.* They are sent out with a global reach: an assignment. They cause what some have called a "planetary wave of supernatural or spiritual presence." This is the cause behind gathering the new world order's collective "demonized" military out onto the field of battle. Think of it: the biggest battle in all of history…

Armageddon! (Take note, Armageddon does not occur without a planetary release of dark powers that supernaturally synchronizes the enemies of God.)

The Principle Is Clear

Just as there is no advance of the Kingdom of God without His Power, so there is no advance to the satanic agenda without the release, and use, of real, manifested, dark power.

Phenomenon of SRA MPD – Chosen Ones

They are here by the millions now and most are only numbering the first generation of these victims of satanic ritual abuse (SRA MPD). They are casualties of being raised in an ancient (The Order/Brotherhood/Black Flame), satanic, multinational coven system. They have been abused, their personalities split, sub personalities programmed, demonized, and highly trained. It may be one of the most supernaturally suppressed secrets (2 Thessalonians 2) of any kind in our time.

In the '70s, they began showing up in psych wards, in the '80s they were here by the hundreds of thousands, and in the early '90s, Holly Hector (former hypnotherapist working in the ritual abuse ward of Centennial Hospital in Denver CO) estimated that there were 2.4 million cases. That has since been dwarfed by the acknowledgment of Dr. Colin A. Ross MD, Canadian Psychologist and author of the book, *Bluebird: Deliberate Creation of Multiple Personality by Psychiatrists*. He believes there may be up to 10 million cases in the U.S. and Canada.[136] But add the numbers in England, Australia, Ireland, all of Europe, and Russia, and the numbers are staggering...a possible 40 million cases. And that's only first-generation victims!

Many are now counseling and helping the second generation (around forty years of age), third generation (around twenty-two years of age), and fourth generations (around ages one–eight) of SRA/MPD victims. Better statistics are needed, but the author of this chapter firmly believes that the total numbers (four generations and growing) may be around 100 million. Here is a list of questions about the SRA/MPD victims that I will attempt to address:

- Who are these victims?
- What have they gone through?
- How many satanic rituals have they experienced?
- Why are they programmed (mind-control) and demonized?
- Why do they have assassin and sleeper sub personalities?
- Why are they extremely knowledgeable in the practice of ancient dark rituals?
- Why can they speak dead or "twilight" ritual demon summoning languages?
- Why do they collectively say they are created to be servants of antichrist?
- What is this "great chaos" they say they are purposely created for?
- Who is behind this massive creation of controlled, multi-continental, multi-generational, future satanic warrior phenomenon?

The answers to the above questions will lead us to the reality that an enormous sum of satanic rituals and ritual abuses have been going on for over fifty years and are broader than most people can calculate. One of these victims, an intact, satanic super-soldier, after doing blood rituals, was engaged by officers. He was leg-chained and handcuffed, but he continued to fight when, all of a sudden, he rose up and declared with a demon-charged, Nazi/German accent: "WE ARE THE LEGIONS WHO SHALL RULE THE EARTH!"

Each one of these victims has been through hundreds of rituals by the time they are thirteen years old. They can and have told the secrets—secrets supernaturally cloaked by the dark powers that work to manifest the ultimate agenda (*a new order with a world leader*). With that being said, let's get to the issue that no real luciferian wants you to know; the reason for the dark rituals!

Rituals of the Past, Present, and Future Will Evidence Five Factors

1. Rituals that summon demons so the practitioner/priest can then receive those demons into themselves—

    This is done to gain power, gain abilities, and demonize (they call it "purifying") their blood. The idea is that they be fully charged (counterfeit to being filled with the Holy Spirit) so they can do their assigned satanic mission fully "empowered."

2. Rituals that summon demons, ultimately releasing them into other coven members and on/in new "chosen ones" (those being raised in the coven)—

    This summoning/transference into others is to empower and enable the "chosen one(s)," and for the purpose of controlling the individual(s). The summoning can be done in a sex or blood ritual, and can be transferred through "charged" sex rituals where the demon-filled priest transfers their demonic powers into the chosen one via sexual ceremony. This ritual is called "marriage to the beast."

3. Rituals that summon demons to cloak the coven and their dark works (and meeting places) and to ward off law enforcement—

There is the "hands of glory" ritual done in September, and this can be used to gain powers (demons) to keep a shield of supernatural invisibility. Remember this: Real luciferianism in all of its dark activity is done mostly in the night and in *deep secrecy. Coven work and even the demons love to go supernaturally unnoticed* (the evil one comes at night).

4. Rituals that summon demons so they can be sent against coven/Satan's enemies—

Whether lesser spells or hexes, or major blood rituals, the goal is to summon demons so they can be sent. In this process, it is believed that the demon can be given the assignment to go after designated targets. Those targets can be anyone they deem as an enemy, and often churches, pastors, and known Christians. Satanists like this have, are, and will continue to attack the Body of Christ, on a massive but hidden scale. (They surely know spiritual warfare…and hope Christians do not.)

5. Rituals that summon demons so they can be sent "into the air"—

The idea behind this is that the presence would have control over and oppress areas, cities, etc. The believer in Christ desires that the power of the Holy Spirit manifest in an area (Acts 4), and revival prayer warriors call God's manifest presence in and over an area—*an open heaven.*[137] I have been in revivals where it seems God's presence *hangs in the air*, many come to salvation, believers are revived, and powerful works of God happen. With dark powers "in the air" the goal is the opposite. Dark power manifesting in an area/city seeks to suppress the Church, foster crime and violence, and cloak satanic activity so it won't be detected. In areas or cities where *evil powers* hang in the air you can be sure you'll find *evil rituals.* The satanic procedures that open (and in some cases *keep* open) doorways/gateways for these powers is done by continuous ritual-working.

500 Million Rituals

With the reality of past, present, and future rituals that are done to summon, receive, send, and ultimately manifest dark powers on this side of the fence, one more factor must be looked at. *The sheer number of these rituals is unprecedented and the growth of them is beyond calculating.* Let's reduce the statistics for a moment and say that there are only 10 million SRA persons worldwide who have each gone through only five hundred rituals by the time they were thirteen (this is a massive reduction). If this alone was true, then the lowest possible numbers of rituals that released demons to this side would be 500 million!

500 million rituals done in the last fifty years...continuously!

That's the lowest figure I can give (I apologize to SRAs; I know it is so much more). If we use the possible number of

50 million victims worldwide and multiply the rituals each one has been in (seen and/or participated in) then just think for a moment of the number of potential rituals... *billions worldwide and growing!*

It's no wonder there are so many victims, possessions, satanic crimes, evil violence, terrorism, and the *growing global feeling that a great darkness is manifesting in the air and something ominous and catastrophic is about to happen.* Satan is the prince of the power of the air, right (Ephesians 2)?

Know and Speak

If you "feel it in the air" as many millions do, and if you agree that we are nearing the end of history, then the gravity of the end of days must be spoken about. We must warn of the impending danger, we must evangelize as never before and we must ramp up our walk in Christ knowing that no matter how dark and evil it does get, we have a mission from the King of Heaven and have all the backing we need to keep reaching the world for Christ until the very last day.

Let me say to anyone reading this book and reading this chapter: It is vital that you know who Jesus Christ is and what He has done for you. I pray right now that if you don't know Him, that by His love and mercy you will turn to Jesus Christ and receive Him as Savior, Lord, and God into your life. He will come into you with all His forgiving grace and power. He will fill you with His love and presence. You can know that you "know God" when you are truly saved and you can see for sure that no matter what happens in this fallen world, you have the gift of eternal life (indestructible immortality). Please read the *Gospel of John.* Please also read the *Book of*

1 John. God will speak to you. Just open your heart and life to Him.

To believers in Christ I urge you not to hide in fear: Shun that! Instead, be filled with the Holy Spirit, knowing that Jesus is alive in you and with you through the very end of eternity. It is vital now more than ever to take up the cross and follow Jesus Christ. He will never leave you or forsake you, and if you step out in faith and obedience (as believers did in the book of Acts), He will work in and through you: powerfully! You can help lead many to, and make an enormous impact for, Christ our Lord.

There are three main things I would tell you to do: First, become the *most powerful, solid, and strong believer* you can with the tools of the Bible and the friendship of Jesus Christ. Second, become a *committed and powerful soul-winner*, taking every opportunity you can to sincerely help those who are lost and in need. Third, become the *most fierce prayer warrior* you can, truly meditating in the power, and under the leadership, of Christ! I can only hope that in knowing what time it is (and it is *very close* to the end times), that every believer in Christ will:

- Appropriate every biblical truth you can and put it into practice (James 1). You will become blessed and very strong.
- Know your Authority in spiritual warfare and fearlessly use it in every possible way (Luke 10).
- Make sure you have on, and live in, the full armor of God, thus manifesting God's mighty power at all times (Ephesians 6).
- Remain alert spiritually so you can sense and discern the spiritual battle that is going on around you and others (1 Peter 5:7–7).

As we are told in 1 John 4:4: "Greater is he that is in you, than he that is in the world. May God make this a great reality in your life in these last days. May the Lord Jesus heal and deliver all who need His extraordinary grace!

(For over one hundred hours of free lecture training sessions on Dark Rituals/Dark Powers, Spiritual Warfare basics, Exposing Satanism 101, Satanic Ritual Abuse [the Black Awakening], and Confronting the Powers: go to www.ShattertheDarkness.net.)

CHAPTER TEN

TWILIGHT OF THE LAST DAYS

By Jeff Patty

These days, you can't turn on the TV or walk into a bookstore without seeing vampires everywhere. Vampires have become more popular than ever now, thanks to recent movies and books. It can be argued that the current trend, or rather, obsession, started with the highly popular books and movies in the *Twilight* series. And what's very disturbing is that this interest and obsession is especially strong in young women.

"Vampire romance novels," as they are referred to, have swept through the publishing world. Everything "vampire" is now as popular with these young girls as much as Barbies, Cabbage Patch Dolls, and Easy-Bake Ovens used to be. (I'm afraid I may be showing my age a little with that last sentence.) But, the seduction this vampire trend has on young girls especially is not only disturbing, it's dangerous. Eternally dangerous. I'll spend this chapter showing how and why, and giving a history lesson on vampires, immortality, blood, and a few otherworldly creatures gaining in popularity in the last days we're living in.

The history of "vampirism" goes back to the beginning: Genesis. Now, I know a lot of you are going to say, "There's no mention of vampires in Genesis," and you'd be right. But, for those in the occult, there is. Although *purely myth*, many in the occult believe there was a woman before Eve. The "original" woman created along with Adam was named Lilith. She had a problem being subservient to Adam, since she was created from the dust just like Adam had been, therefore making her an equal to "man." She soon left Eden, and then Eve was created from Adam's rib. (By the way, many radical feminists believe in and love the story of Lilith. Some even worship her because she was "truly equal" to Adam (man) and was punished for standing up to him, thus beginning the patriarchal wars.)

Supposedly, God sent three angels to bring her back, but she refused, so the angels promised to kill one hundred of her children every day (she was busy) until she returned. Lilith, in turn, vowed to destroy human children.

Lilith was often described as a winged female demon with sharp claws. She came in the night to kill babies, even the unborn. She was also sometimes described as beautiful and seductive, and would come to men at night as a *succubus* (a female demon that has sexual relations with men). Vampires are often described as seductive, and they are associated with having the ability to hypnotize people. It's not hard to see the connection of Lilith to vampires. The death, the blood, the seduction. Not to mention apparently being immortal.

Many people know that the real interest and awareness in vampires began with a novel by a man named Bram Stoker with his book, *Dracula.* But we don't know much about Bram Stoker beyond that: the man or his beliefs.

Bram Stoker was born in Dublin, Ireland, on November 8, 1847. He died on April 20, 1912, due to complications caused by syphilis. Stoker held to a liberal-minded theology, and was said to have been a member of "The Order of the Golden Dawn," a New Age occult group founded in 1887, which consisted mostly of Freemasons, but in this secret society, women were allowed to be members. It was formed for the practice of ceremonial magic and the acquisition of initiatory knowledge and powers. A person can see how being involved in a secret cult society could have opened doors that led to the creation of Dracula. Remember, at the time, Stoker was developing his imagination; spiritualism and occultism were sweeping over America like a flood.

Stoker conceived of his novel *Dracula* in 1897. He wrote several other books in his lifetime, but *Dracula* brought him fame. The character of Professor Abraham Van Helsing—the great vampire hunter—Stoker actually modeled after himself. Interestingly, the character of Dracula almost became known by another name. When Stoker's novel was near completion, the famous character's name was "Count Wampyr." But during Stoker's research, he came across a book titled, *An account of the Principalities of Wallachia and Moldavia,* written by William Wilkinson.[138] There, he came upon a word in the Romanian language: *Dracul,* meaning "Devil." Liking that name for that reason, Stoker changed the name of his vampire from "Wampyr" to "Dracula," and the legend was born.

Many books and movies have been written and filmed over the years based on either Dracula himself, or vampires, including the 1931 portrayal of "Dracula" by Bela Lugosi. But just one of many current authors that Stoker's Dracula was an inspiration for is Stephen King. Much of the story for *Carrie* and *Salem's Lot* (which also became movies later) follows Stoker's Dracula closely (especially *Salem's Lot*, which parallels it greatly).

And as anyone knows, Stephen King has been on a shadowy path ever since. King is a very talented writer (I dare anyone to read one of his horror novels and not get scared out of his or her wits). But I don't believe the origin of that fear strictly comes from good writing; I believe it comes from something much more sinister. His books are not only extremely frightening and dark; they are filled with anti-Catholic and anti-Christian symbols and messages throughout. Messages that slowly and subtly weave their way into people's consciousness, for the greater good of all that is sinister and ungodly.

Since then, we've had many authors and directors jump on the vampire bandwagon, but no one author's work (since Stoker has had such an impact on society and culture) as accomplished as Stephanie Meyer's 2005 novel, *Twilight*. Three other books have since followed in the series. These books and movies have become so popular that, among other things, midnight parties and vampire-themed proms have become a must for many teenagers and young adults. Personally, I don't think Meyers set out to write novels that mislead and deceive people about love and eternal life. She was a stay-at-home mom that woke up one morning with a dream stuck in her head. She quickly wrote the first book, and probably thought she would be lucky to even get someone to look at her manuscript, much less buy it. But I do believe that the dream was demonically given to her and she was prompted and guided after that.

The basic storyline of *Twilight* involves the character of Bella Swan and her struggles in a new school in the overcast town of

Forks, Washington. That's where she meets the handsome, mysterious student, Edward Cullen, who, unbeknownst to Bella, is a vampire. Before long, the two find themselves in a passionate romance, and Edward even introduces her to his family. But even though Edward doesn't prey on humans, he finds Bella's scent overpowering as he struggles to overcome his bloodlust. That's not the end of the story.

Naturally, another vampire clan gets Bella's scent and decides to make her their next meal, so Edward and his clan have to stop it from happening, all the while trying to save his relationship with Bella. (Just the right ingredients to attract and keep the fairer sex enthralled.)

There are many things that are disturbing about the whole vampire trend today, but one of the most disturbing to me (and should be to any Christian), is the emphasis on eternal life, blood, and love, but from an anti-God perspective. It's become a completely perverted and twisted gospel that young people are swallowing hook, line, and sinker. Even young people in the Church don't see anything wrong with diving into the vampire subculture. But we, as parents, pastors, and youth ministers, need to be not only aware of this subject and the trends themselves, but we need to be warning our children on this blasphemous, wrong teaching.

Eternal life through blood and love is definitely real, and achievable, but not in the way they are being seduced into believing. And don't fool yourselves; this message is being promoted so strongly through young love and devotion, young people *believe* it. It's not just a book or a movie; it's a belief system for many. The *Twilight* books, and many other "vampire romance novels," tug at the reader's heartstrings and emotions very strongly. This is why it's especially dangerous for young girls and women in comparison to boys and men. It is well-known that women operate, make decisions, and live life more from an emotional standpoint than men do, and these books are targeted for them. Unfortunately, they seem to have hit their target rather well.

In John 6:53–58 it says:

> Then Jesus said unto them, Verily, verily, I say unto you, Except ye eat the flesh of the Son of man, and drink his blood, ye have no life in you. Whoso eateth my flesh, and drinketh my blood, hath eternal life; and I will raise him up at the last day. For my flesh is meat indeed, and my blood is drink indeed. He that eateth my flesh, and drinketh my blood, dwelleth in me, and I in him. As the living Father hath sent me, and I live by the Father: so he that eateth me, even he shall live by me. This is that bread which came down from heaven: not as your fathers did eat manna, and are dead: he that eateth of this bread shall live for ever.

Notice how the "doctrine of vampirism" is a perversion of this, basically saying, "If you become a vampire, you will live forever, but you will have to feed on the blood of others." Now, for the older generation, this perverted parallel to the Gospel is not overlooked, but with the younger generation, most of them don't see it or understand it. That is a fault of the parents and the Church for not teaching the Word strongly enough to our children (Ephesians 6:4), and in the areas it's needed most to battle today's pop culture. I'm not trying to put a guilt trip on people; many parents and churches have done a great job of bringing children up in the Lord. But there is always room for improvement, and that applies to me as well.

We also see in Romans 6:8–9, "Now if we be dead with Christ, we believe that we shall also live with him: Knowing that Christ being raised from the dead dieth no more; death hath no more dominion over him." Again, vampires are considered to be the undead, or, the "living dead." Alive (or dead-alive) forever without Jesus Christ. There is no eternal life outside of Jesus Christ.

Jesus said in John 14:6, "I am the way, the truth, and the life: no man cometh unto the Father but through me." Young people, especially girls and women, are being led astray, and the interest in, and love of, the vampire romance novels and movies can easily lead to darker and darker things in their lives. It's a very dangerous path to be on. Matthew 7:13–14 says, "Enter ye in at the strait gate: for wide is the gate, and broad is the way, that leadeth to destruction, and many there be which go in thereat: Because strait is the gate, and narrow is the way, which leadeth unto life, and few there be that find it." This particular Scripture, by the way, completely blows universalism (the theory that everyone will eventually be saved) out of the water.

I have seen the first *Twilight* movie. Once. On a purely basic level, it was definitely a "chick flick." I'm sure most guys didn't see it of their own free will. But there are other popular movies and TV shows that aren't so specifically targeted for the female audience that are more openly disturbing and blasphemous. Although I've never watched the series *True Blood*, as a self-proclaimed movie geek, I know enough about it to know that it's not healthy for anyone to watch, especially young people or Christians. Yet, many of them still do. That's what happens when consciences become numbed over time from the relentless bombardment out of Hollywood and huge publishing houses.

The *True Blood* television series is based on the "Sookie Stackhouse" novels by Charlaine Harris. The series centers on the relationship of a Southern waitress (Sookie), and a man who she believes is her soulmate, who just happens to be a 173-year-old vampire. The books and the TV series takes place in the future, where vampires are now able to mingle among humans, thanks to synthetic blood. As the vampires try to fit into society, they face fierce opposition from people who don't believe they have a place among them. The vampires also live in fear that they will be drained of their blood, because their blood acts as a drug, similar to Ecstasy and Heroin, for humans.

Again, I've never watched the series, but do you notice how the synopsis paints a sympathetic picture of the vampires? They're persecuted by the intolerant humans and in fear of being drained of their blood by humans. Good is evil, evil is good (see Isaiah 5:20).

There's another series called *The Vampire Diaries*. The television series is based on novels by author, L. J. Smith. It follows Elena and Jeremy Gilbert, after the death of their parents, as they try to put their lives back together. As the new school year begins, Elena's life goes through a dramatic change when she meets a handsome and mysterious new student (sound familiar?), Stefan Salvatore. Little does she know that he's a vampire several centuries old, just looking to live a peaceful life. Stefan has a brother named Damon, who is also a vampire, but he is the complete opposite and lives a life of violence. The only thing the brothers have in common is their love for Elena. A nice, normal love triangle!

Like the *Twilight* series, it targets girls and women with an emotionally charged love story.

One series I did watch a few times (out of curiosity and for purposes of research) was a new show called *Being Human*. It tells a story of a friendship between a vampire named Aidan and a werewolf named Josh, who moves into a house where a young woman, Sally, was murdered, and they can see and communicate with her ghost. There are *many* things we could talk about here that are un-biblical, but for now we'll stick to the vampire issue.

I only watched the first few episodes, because after one particularly disturbing episode, I decided that was enough research. Aidan's character had discovered another vampire in the midst. This vampire was a priest. This "priest" told his tale following how he had almost died, having an epiphany on his deathbed. He suddenly realized in this moment that the whole, biblical teaching about eternal life that he had believed and taught was not true.

After he recovered from his brush with death, he realized that becoming a vampire was the only true shot at eternal life (apparently he knew of a vampire that could kindly bite him on the neck), so he became a vampire. Then, he said something even *more* shocking and blasphemous: the reason that Jesus had talked about blood and eternal life so much and wasn't in the tomb after three days was because...he didn't get to finish because Aidan interrupted and said, "You don't mean!" to which the priest replied, "Makes you think doesn't it?"

No, it doesn't. It makes me sick and angry. This is the kind of garbage that people, especially the young, are having their heads filled with. The very idea that Jesus was a vampire is an indication that we are living in the last days; this kind of worldview is so blasphemous, surely the Lord won't tarry much longer. Remember, Satan always seeks to corrupt truth, and he is working overtime now to lead people away from true, saving faith.

Eternal life comes only from faith in Jesus: "And being made perfect, he became the author of eternal salvation unto all them that obey him" (Hebrews 5:9). The blood of Jesus is salvation to those who trust in Him, but aside from that, the Bible clearly states in Acts 15:29: "That ye abstain from meats offered to idols, and from blood, and from things strangled, and from fornication: from which if ye keep yourselves, ye shall do well. Fare ye well." Drinking blood is strictly prohibited according to the Bible. And yes, there are people so deeply immersed in vampirism that they regularly drink blood, completely perverting the Scripture.

There are other creatures of the night that are also growing in popularity. One of these is "werewolves." The legend of werewolves has been around for centuries, first growing strong in the late 1500s in Europe, since the animal (wolf) was very present in the countryside at that time.

Like vampires, werewolves have demonic qualities, such as supernatural powers and abilities: glowing red or yellow eyes; are nocturnal; and possess shape-shifting abilities.

There have been many books, movies, and television shows over the years glorifying or depicting this mythical beast. One of the most recent portrayals is on the previously mentioned: *Being Human*. Josh is struggling to cope with becoming a werewolf on the nights of a full moon, ever since being bitten one fateful night. To keep from killing people, he either runs to the middle of the woods when he's going to turn (only killing a deer, etc.), or, he has his vampire buddy, Aidan, lock him up in a cellar.

Another new television series is *Teen Wolf*. I've watched a couple of episodes, and it doesn't seem to have anything in common with the comedy starring Michael J. Fox from the mid-eighties with the same name, other than the central characters are high school students. The main character's name is Scott, who was bitten (naturally) and his life changed forever. The usual story of struggle and maintaining control so he can pursue the girl of his dreams is the backbone of the storyline. These plots have become much more sensual in the years since Lon Chaney Jr. came on the scene.

There are some disturbing, true-life accounts of werewolf-like creatures over the years from across the United States, as well as other countries. One such sighting of a creature first spotted in 1936 was the creature referred to as the "Beast of Bray Road." Not only do some reports say it has red eyes, it also appears human-sized and resembles a werewolf beast.

One particular encounter tells of a watchman who was at a burial ground when he encountered it, and it appeared to be gnawing on some bones. Afraid, the man began to pray, and then the creature turned and looked at him and growled, "Gadara." Gadara is the site mentioned in the Bible where one of the most well-known healings of Jesus Christ's ministry took place. It's where Jesus found the man among the tombs possessed with demonic spirits named Legion. It's ironic that the Beast of Bray Road was found digging around at a burial site. Could it possibly be one of the demonic spirits from two thousand years ago? I imagine all the evil spirits left the pigs once they drowned in the sea, and many may still be in search of a host or simply appearing as a demonic creature to deceive and strike fear into people.

I mention this story and these sightings only to point out that demonic powers are at work. Satan is the prince of the power of the air, Eph 2:2: "Wherein in time past ye walked according to the course of this world, according to the prince of the power of the air, the spirit that now worketh in the children of disobedience."

John 8:44 says: "Ye are of your father the devil, and the lusts of your father ye will do. He was a murderer from the beginning, and abode not in the truth, because there is no truth in him. When he speaketh a lie, he speaketh of his own: for he is a liar, and the father of it." He is out to destroy (John 10:10): "The thief cometh not, but for to steal, and to kill, and to destroy: I am come that they might have life, and that they might have it more abundantly." Don't think for a minute that there aren't some supernatural happenings and experiences going on in all the darkness around us, and it's growing.

Am I saying that if someone reads a book, or watches a movie or television show about vampires or werewolves, they'll become a vampire-following, blood-drinking, Goth freak? No, not at all. Otherwise, I'd be in trouble! But I think most people, especially young people and children, best avoid them. The media we have today is not what many of us older folks had in our day. While still in the same vein, the older media was rather tame compared to what our young people face today. I'm very thankful that both of my children, who are young adults, never really had much interest in the subjects we've been discussing, including the *Harry Potter* books and movies—another important subject!

It must be understood by the young and old alike; there's no coming back as a vampire, ghost, or any other creature. The Bible clearly says, "And as it is appointed unto men once to die, but after this the judgment" (Heb 9:27).

Scripturally, we know that each person seeks to fill some sort of spiritual hole. Religions proliferate, self-help groups expand, and the searching goes on and on. Into this mixture is massive deception. We must be on-guard.

Everyone must choose wisely. Choose *Jesus*. Choose *life*.

CHAPTER ELEVEN

SHAMANS, PSI SPIES, AND MILITARY MEDIUMS (PART 1)

How America's Military Derived a Weapon of War from Spiritualism

By S. Douglas Woodward

And oftentimes, to win us to our harm,
The instruments of darkness tell us truths,
Win us with honest trifles, to betray[us]
In deepest consequence.[139]

—WILLIAM SHAKESPEARE, *MACBETH*,

ACT I SCENE III

Despite widespread popular belief in the paranormal in the twenty-first century, skeptics still abound in academic and scientific circles. Conventional thinking insists that every cause has an effect and especially, one which we can explain without recourse to the supernatural or the miraculous.

There have been voices that questioned whether such certitude about nature and normality was justified. Goethe,[140] a poetic voice during the Age of Enlightenment, offered a strongly worded, contrarian opinion: "We walk in mysteries. We are surrounded by an atmosphere about which we still know nothing at all. We do not know what stirs in it and how it is connected with our intelligence. This much is certain, under particular conditions the antennae of our souls are able to reach out beyond their physical limitations."[141] Today, the advocacy for the "abnormal" grows stronger. The esoteric steadily encroaches upon the fortress of skepticism built over the past four centuries during naturalism's hegemony. Not since *before* the Enlightenment with the *Neo-Platonists of the Renaissance*[142] has the supernatural made such headway amongst intellectuals in Western society.

Evidence mounts for the reality of the supernatural. But most scientists not only ignore the momentum of public opinion, they overlook an irrepressible, cold, hard fact that the "nonreligious" government of the United States has, for almost sixty years, operated aspects of its intelligence service assuming that the *paranormal is reality*. Hal Puthoff, one of the fathers of psychic spies working for the U.S. Intelligence Service since the 1970s, states it this way: "Scientists and nonscientists alike often find it difficult to confront data that appear to be greatly at odds with their world view. Entrenched belief structures die hard, even in the face of data."[143] Does the government really believe in clairvoyance? Unquestionably so, as the many bets they've placed testify. It's no small thing that our military and intelligence leaders have managed to spend millions in tax dollars with Congressional approval to support it.[144] As an unintended consequence, we can say without hesitation that no less than the U.S. Government has generated mountains of documented proof for the reality of the supernatural.[145] Carl Jung said, "The risk of inner experience, the adventure of the spirit, is in any case alien to most human beings.

The possibility that such experience might have psychic reality is anathema to them."[146] While true for scientists, it proved not to be so true for our military.

Let's begin by confirming several key definitions. First: clairvoyance. **Clairvoyance** is the supernatural power of seeing objects or events removed in space or time from natural viewing. The word simply combines two French words, *clair* ("clear") and *voyance* ("vision"). *Wikipedia* provides this general definition: "Within parapsychology, *clairvoyance* is used exclusively to refer to the transfer of information that is both contemporary to, and hidden from, the clairvoyant. It is very different from telepathy in that the information is said to be gained directly from an external physical source, rather than being transferred from the mind of one individual to another... Clairvoyance is related to **remote viewing**, although the term "remote viewing" itself is not as widely applicable to clairvoyance because it refers to a specific controlled process" (italics and bold added).[147] Graham Hancock, in his book *Supernatural*, offers this definition of **shamanism**: "Shamanism is not confined to specific socio-economic settings or stages of development. It is fundamentally the ability that all of us share, some with and some without the help of hallucinogens, to enter altered states of consciousness and to travel out of body in non-physical realms—there to encounter supernatural entities and gain useful knowledge and healing powers from them."[148] The truthfulness of these phenomena impacts our understanding of the universe. Our perspective on the nature of reality is known as **cosmology**. *Dictionary.com* provides this formal definition of *cosmology*. It is "the branch of philosophy dealing with the origin and general structure of the universe, with its parts, elements, and laws, and especially with such of its characteristics as space, time, causality, and freedom." Additionally, it is "the branch of astronomy that deals with the general structure and evolution of the universe."[149] If psychic phenomena do exist, our understanding of humankind and the universe can no longer be a simple "naturalism." As we will see, there are many in the military who accept it is fact.

According to author Jim Marrs in his book, *PSI Spies: The True Story of America's Psychic Warfare Program*, research into and the use of *remote viewing* (RV) has been funded by four separate administrations for over a quarter of a century. The real truth: It had been funded by the Departments of the Navy since 1947, the Army since 1949, and the CIA since 1952. It was driven, no doubt, by the awareness that the Russians were up to their earlobes in psychic research and America had better get in the game. In effect, our psychic spies were the result of the Cold War and the fear of our military and Congress that, like the story of Sputnik in the so-called Space Race, if we didn't take action we were destined to finish in second place. The fear of the Red menace was crucial to the task of making a "supernatural" ability a repeatable technique capable of being trained to secular intelligence operatives who had no particular allegiance to religion of any kind.

At the outset of Marrs' book, he picks up the story of psychics in the military in the 1990s. Marrs indicates that Dr. Hal Puthoff and Ingo Swann who, along with Russell Targ, were the men most responsible for the development of RV. But PSI Spy number one, Chief Warrant Officer Joseph McMoneagle, was actually in the business in the early 1970s. In fact, the beginning of the story goes back further still. The original research was done by several mysterious characters, indeed, bona fide shamans and was commenced as early as the late 1940s. Roswell (1947) wasn't the only crazy thing on the radar of our military after World War II. These individuals, in particular one *Andrija Puharich*, had a far-reaching impact on the whole story of psychic activity both in the intelligence services and even more bizarre nature of psychic activities outside of the military then and now. We will explore his contributions and continuing impact in the twenty-first century in part two of this chapter.

In today's version of the New Age Movement, typically accompanied by predictions for massive change in the consciousness of humankind in the year 2012, there is great enthusiasm for Shamanism.[150] Daniel Pinchbeck, author of two relevant books on the subject, *Breaking Open the Head,* and *2012: The Return of Quetzalcoatl,* promotes the rediscovery of shamanism during the past two decades as one means (if not the primary means) to facilitate 2012's dramatic transformation of humanity's awareness. "The exploration and unbiased study of these mind-expanding molecules—an interrupted legacy of scientific and psychological research begun in the 1950s and shut down with hysterical force during the late 1960s—is the one way to unify these opposite approaches [brain-based *materialism* versus spirit-oriented *shamanism*] to the nature of reality. Perhaps it is the only way."[151]

Shamanism is the most ancient of religions vitally connected to cultures of indigenous tribes worldwide. Shamanism relies upon highly specialized plant compounds containing hallucinogenic drugs.[152] *Shaman* is the more politically correct name for "witch doctor" or "medicine man" as the Shaman understands the various uses of plants and their ability to heal both physical and psychological conditions. But most notably, Shamans are the priests of "animism" and facilitate contact with the spiritual realm. In fact, there is a whole new tourism industry, popular for the past two decades, in South America and Mexico focused on seekers of spiritual experiences using organic drugs with Shamanic oversight. Psychic experiences south of the border is a chic method for the religiously disenfranchised to find their way back to some manner of spiritual encounter.

But the trek is not a new one. Timothy Leary, the Harvard professor disillusioned with western society, was the most famous to go south to experience the effects of magical mushrooms. However, he was actually preceded by R. Gordon Wasson, a famous mycologist (the study of fungi). Interestingly, Wasson was invited to work for the CIA in the early 1950s as part of the infamous and ill-fated MKULTRA project (discussed later in this chapter). Wasson refused the invitation but nevertheless was unknowingly funded by the Geshcikter Foundation for Medical Research, a CIA "conduit" for its funds, to complete his Mexican expedition in 1956. According to Pinchbeck, Wasson remains to this day regarded as the father of magical mushrooms. It was indeed Wasson's 1957 article in *Life Magazine* that caught the attention of Leary and led him to his personal magical mystery tour in 1960.[153] Eventually, Leary would pick his drug of choice, LSD, and become an adamant provocateur and strident promoter of hallucinogenic substances as the savior of Western culture. As he said, "Turn on, tune in, and drop out."[154] With words of wisdom like this, no wonder the "silent majority" disinherited academia in the 1960s. But to place the story in context, we must study the history of the paranormal much more distant than a scant fifty years.

The History of Clairvoyance

Jim Marrs relates: "In the Vedas, the most ancient written record of man, there are references to supernatural powers called '*siddhis.*' According to the venerable Hindu scriptures, these were unwanted paranormal side effects of meditation that tended to distract the meditator."[155] He takes it further:

Dr. Richard Broughton, director of research at the Institute for Parapsychology in Durham, North Caroline, has quoted from Pantanjali's Yoga Sutras, written some 3,500 years ago. His descriptions of Pantanjali's yoga meditation techniques sound remarkably similar to the techniques developed for remote viewing:

"[Y]oga mediation...[is] a succession of stages in which outside distractions are reduced... In the stages of the meditational process—termed *Samyana*—paranormal phenomena may be produced, most commonly a feeling of clairvoyant omniscience, but sometimes including physical effects such as levitation, object movements, and healing."[156] (brackets in original)

In the modern era, research into the paranormal began in 1882 when a group of interested scientists in London formed the Society for Psychical Research (SPR).

For the first time, the techniques of modern science—standardized descriptions and methodology, disciplined experiments, and so forth—were applied to psychic phenomena.

Among the accomplishments of the SPR was the exposure of fraudulent mediums and spiritualists. In 1884, following an investigation of Elena Hahn, better known as **Madame Blavatsky**, founder of the mystical Theosophical society, the SPR caustically termed her

"one of the most accomplished, ingenious, and interesting impostors in history."[157] (bold added)

The arrival of J.B. Rhines at Duke University in September
1927 began the formal discipline around psychic research in a laboratory setting. Rhines was motivated to begin the research after
hearing a lecture on the topic of the paranormal by Sir Arthur
Conan Doyle, the creator of Sherlock Holmes. It was Rhine
who coined the term *extrasensory perception* (ESP). "In 1940, the
Rhines, along with other parapsychologists, produced a book
entitled *Extra-Sensory Perception After Sixty Years*, a compendium
of psychical research since the founding of the SPR in 1882. The
research presented in this book was so careful and scientific that
the book became assigned reading for introductory psychology
classes at Harvard for the 1940–41 academic year."[158]

Psychic occurrences during World War II so frightened military authorities that psychics were not only considered genuine,
but were seen as *a strategic threat.* One psychic in England became
notorious for predicting unfortunate events; particularly making
statements regarding the sinking of two ships in 1944 before
this outcome had become public knowledge. Her name was
Helen Duncan. She was arrested and charged with conspiracy,
specifically after a 1735 law against witchcraft was updated by
Parliament to permit authorities to act against her. After her arrest
and conviction, Duncan served a nine-month prison sentence.
This step was taken by the British to ensure that information
about D-Day would not be leaked by Duncan inadvertently due
to her capacity for clairvoyance and her growing reputation. "Even
Prime Minister Winston Churchill futilely tried to intercede for
Mrs. Duncan. In his memoirs written years later, Churchill credited psychic guidance in leading him to a friendly home during

his escape as a prisoner during the Boer War."[159] Tim Rifat in his 1999 book, *Remote Viewing*, commented, "A country such as the UK, obsessed with secrecy, cannot allow remote viewing to become public knowledge."[160] So we see how the military threat of intelligence gained through psychic means chills the spine in more ways than one.

Yet, it would be the Cold War with the Soviets that would propel the American government to explore the unexplainable. As early as January 7, 1952, a CIA document (released under the Freedom of Information Act in 1981), clearly indicated the agency was considering projects involving ESP.[161] After a relatively quiet period in the 1960s, the topic popped up again in full force as the next decade began: "In 1970, two Western authors, Sheila Ostrander and Lynn Schroeder, published *Psychic Discoveries Behind the Iron Curtain*, detailing what they had learned about such research after a lengthy visit through the Soviet Union and Eastern Europe. The book was a great success and proved to be an impetus to psychic research, particularly in the United States."[162]

Nevertheless, both the U.S. and Soviet governments distanced themselves from such work, declaring it sensational and untrue. Explanations were offered such as "the stories were fabrications of research scientists seeking more financing." Of course: Who wants to admit an "unscientific" point of view—even if it's something into which the entity in question is pouring millions of dollars (or rubles)? That's why it has always seemed essential to keep quiet what was really going on behind the curtains—whether those curtains were iron on not.

Playing a major role in the government's work was the Stanford Research Institute (SRI).[163] In 1970, SRI went independent of Stanford University as a result of protests from students who feared that SRI had become too cozy with the military-industrial complex. During the early part of the 1970s, SRI did indeed serve as a cover for the psychic research being carried out by the CIA and Army intelligence. The principal figure working under contract for SRI at the time was one Ingo Swann, who became the father of remote viewing, not only demonstrating the technique to the astonishment of most everyone familiar with the project, but throughout the next two decades, mentoring and training over twenty other remote viewers for the government. When Uri Geller was brought to the United States, Geller was studied carefully at SRI. Edgar Mitchell (of Apollo 14 astronaut fame) was the "funding and contracting agent" at SRI that was to investigate Geller. "Significantly, the Geller experiments at SRI coincided exactly with the first CIA involvement with psychic experiments there, specifically their sponsorship of research into Ingo Swann's extraordinary talent for remote viewing. And in Uri Geller they had the golden child of the Israeli secret service, [the] Mossad. Is it too unlikely that Geller, also, was being investigated by the CIA? Geller has gone on record as admitting he worked for them."[164]

But the story of PSI spying can't be kept under wraps forever. On August 27, 1995, the account of PSI Spies broke in a London newspaper: "Tinker, Tailor, Soldier PSI,"[165] written by Jim Schnabel who went on to publish a book on remote viewing in 1997. Marrs tells us about the "official disclosure":

Remote viewing was officially acknowledged by a CIA news release dated November 28, 1995. The story received superficial and dismissive coverage in the *New York Times* and the *Washington Post*, which described the PSI Spies merely as "a trio of citizens with suspected paranormal powers who were located at a Maryland military base." Even with this watered-down version, the story moved no farther than the East Coast. Nowhere was there any mention that remote viewing was simply dispersed to even more secret government agencies where its use continues today, according to several separate unofficial sources.[166]

This reluctance to admit the level of what had been going on for the previous forty-five years is classic intelligence service disinformation. After all, there really is no benefit for the military to give away any secrets just to satisfy public curiosity—even if we do pay for such activities with our tax dollars.[167]

So what can we make of it all? It appears that the military has a two-pronged plan for RV: (1) Minimize its importance publicly by seeking to show that most "RVers" are crackpots[168] and to create dismissive reports (such as was done by Ray Hyman in 1995 at the CIA's behest—Hyman is an Oregon professor who makes his money by being an adamant skeptic of all things paranormal); while (2) secretly continuing to utilize it strategically for both defensive and offensive purposes. The examples of its effective usage are undeniable from the many books and articles published by the actual RV personnel working for the military over the past forty years (I don't have space to produce more than a few examples—see below).[169] The CIA and the military want to continue using RV and other forms of psychic force—they just want to keep it out of the headlines. Marrs comments, "By the mid-1970s, the CIA proved its satisfaction with the SRI results as demonstrated by the agency's continued financial support."[170] We might say, "The proof is in the paying." Of course, that paying continued throughout the 1980s and 1990s.

How Does Remote Viewing Work?

Perhaps the most striking difference between the path of the shaman and that of the PSI Spies is the means that are used to obtain the results sought. In short, shamans use drugs derived from plants of all kinds that yield alkaloids. PSI Spies use only meditative techniques.

The PSI Spies operated under a number of different projects with intriguing names, most of which meant nothing. For example, GRILL FLAME was a random computer-generated codename for several sub-projects (everything that including psychic activity). The project was initially outfitted with twelve of three thousand interviewees. Soon it was netted down to six and ultimately to only three. SRI did the intensive testing that led to those selected. Pat Riley, another remote viewer for the military, said that during this time [the mid-1970s during the start-up period] the remote viewers of GRILL FLAME were trying "a variety of methods to induce an altered state of consciousness. 'Everything except drugs,' said Riley."[171]

The reluctance to consider drugs to assist in remote viewing resulted from fears that emerged when Congress learned how many unsuspecting servicemen (over fifteen hundred) were tested with LSD in the 1950s as part of Project MKULTRA. Thereafter, use of drugs on unwitting human subjects in military service (and without a special oversight committee) would be a career-limiting move for those in charge. Several methods to make the process more directed were tried but no one approach was determined to be best. At the end of the day, the method of choice placed the subject in a darkened, quiet room to facilitate a meditative state. The "PSI warriors" consistently indicate that to make the process work, the conscious mind has to be put into neutral to allow the part of the mind that can "remote view" to do its thing. Ingo Swann, the very first active remote viewer and the primary trainer of most of the PSI Spies, described it this way:

> You see, when these guys make an ideogram [a simple sketch of what they are viewing], there's a chain of unraveling that takes place. The signal line is being incorporated into the viewer's mind or something like that. And they are trained to discriminate between noise and signal. But the signal line does its own thing in these stages and in the way that it does that, you come up with practically a noiseless session [where the images are passed through to the viewer clearly]. That's if they adhere to the format, the structure. But it's very hard to get people to do that because people like to contribute themselves, you know.
>
> This is not a contributive process. The viewer has to be passive, not active, and just receive what's coming in.[172]

In other words, although the RVers achieve a trance state, the conscious mind is still aware, but very passive in the process. If the subject doesn't learn how to relax the conscious mind and keep it from interfering in the process, the results diminish dramatically.

For all intents and purposes, the technique appears to follow the path of psychic processes known as "automatic writing" and "channeling" (or more popularly known as, "mediumship"). Marrs writes of one experience of David Morehouse, a late comer to the remote viewing team. Colonel Ennis Cole (a pseudonym as he still works for the government), recruited Captain David Morehouse in 1988. Morehouse had the "misfortune" of admitting he had once had a spontaneous "out-of-body experience" (OBE).[173]

255

That piqued the interests of his superiors. Colonel Cole began by describing the project to Morehouse as GRILL FLAME. "A small, select group of soldiers, the colonel explained, were having out-of-body experiences. They were leaving their physical bodies, going to distant targets, and describing the targets. 'They call this remote viewing,' Cole explained."[174] After giving Morehouse specific longitude and latitude coordinates to demarcate a specific target,[175] Cole then proceeded to let Morehouse's fingers do the walking (or writing). We read:

> Morehouse was feeling very incompetent. *Great*, he thought. *How do I allow my hand to move across the paper? I mean, you're talking to a grunt soldier here.*
>
> Pettingale [his monitor] took a deep breath and repeated the coordinates again. Without his thinking or willing it, Morehouse's hand began to move across the paper. It moved slightly across and then moved sharply upwards and back down.
>
> Morehouse looked up with a grin of relief and accomplishment. Pettingale was not smiling. "Now decode it. Describe how it felt."
>
> "I feel it rising sharply upwards," Morehouse said confidently.
>
> "Fine. Now touch the ideogram with your pen point and tell me what you feel"...
>
> "It's rising up sharply. It's natural... it's a mountain," he blurted out, surprised at the conviction in his voice.[176]

Upon opening a manila envelope with the picture of the target corresponding to the coordinates, Morehouse discovered a picture of Japan's Mount Fuji. And so began the career of Captain David Morehouse.

The Soviets tried various ways to induce or improve on RV including electric shock, drugs, and sensory deprivation. The latter two are historically the methods or medicine that shamans utilize to create their psychic experiences. But Riley indicates that remote viewing capability requires alert concentration. "When a person is on drugs, their remote viewing capability is diminished."[177] As such, the remote viewers are distant cousins to shamans. They only care about the technique for its practical application. The issue of what it says about cosmology and the nature of the universe is entirely secondary. Of course, as we learn more about the experiences, it gets harder to avoid the question of what such workings tells us about the cosmos as well as the nature of human beings and God.

One of the first "wow" events involved Joe McMoneagle remote viewing a new type of Soviet sub. Essentially, he had discovered the submarine reality of what the movie *The Hunt for the Red October* used as the basis for its techno-thrilling plot: *A super sub that really could run silent, run deep*. This was in 1979. It was under construction in a secret facility at Severodvinsk. McMoneagle was able to supply fascinating details about the nature of the sub indicating to his superiors that they had stumbled onto something truly revolutionary. It caused the military many sleepless nights.

But what really got the attention of the military was when the PSI Spies remote viewed secret weapon development for the good guys. The Air Force ill-advisedly used their most top secret program as a test for the PSI Spies. The team easily stood up to the test. Morehouse commented, "The Air Force went nuts.

They didn't know what to do." If the Air Force had the spies sign a statement that they would not disclose what they saw, it would have documented the secret program. What's worse, it would have shown them up for frivolously using their most secret weapon as a test. Nevertheless, because they were given the target, the team learned the name of the project and many of the details of what would become America's stealth fighter program. The Air Force couldn't do anything but walk away. "It just terrified them. I mean, if we could get into their most secret program, we could get into anything"[178] according to Morehouse. Of course, it was news only to those who already had top security clearance and were sworn under duty of military law to keep the government's secrets, secret. No real harm was done.

From the demonstrated experience of both Pat Price and Joe McMoneagle, we learn that RV is not only not limited to space, *but neither is it limited to time.* McMoneagle, after his service in the military, would sometimes be tested on television and be called upon to remote view a target from several choices which would be selected at show time. However, he admitted that he would normally remote view the location that would be picked the night before while lying on his hotel bed. That way, he wouldn't be bothered by the stress of the live television show. Consequently, this meant not only could he investigate through "his mind's eye" the location for remote viewing, he could do so even before they picked the place the next day! For McMoneagle, time is a creation of our social structures and a convenience for us in a social setting. That doesn't mean that it's real and a structure that the human mind has to respect as a restriction on consciousness. Russell Targ commented about remote viewer Pat Price: "[He] had psychic functioning totally integrated into his daily life. He would tell us each day about the course of world events—the day and hour of the Israeli-Arab cease-fire in the Yom Kippur Way [1973], the eventual outcome of a celebrated kidnapping, the breakup of an OPEC conference by terrorists. Nearly every day it seemed Pat would have some piece of precognitive news for us to think about over lunch, days in advance of the event's actual occurrence."[179]

What kind of intelligence did the intelligence services seek from the PSI Spies? Primarily, their interest was in gathering scientific and technical intelligence. "What did the other side have? How did it work? How could it be used against us?" While the CIA was shying away from "far out" projects in the 1970s, the Army Intelligence team continued to use the psychic warriors. Gen. Edmund "Mike" Thompson, U.S. Army's deputy chief of staff for Intelligence, said, "'I became convinced that remote viewing was a real phenomenon, that it wasn't a hoax,' recalled Gen. Thompson. 'We didn't know how to explain it, but we weren't so much interested in explaining it as in determining whether there was any practical use to it.'"[180] Considering the spiritual dangers associated with the technique as we will soon learn, such a notion is reminiscent of a famous line from Alfred Lord Tennyson, from his *Charge of the Light Brigade:*

Theirs not to make reply,
Theirs not to reason why,
Theirs but to do and die.[181]

It should be noted that the RVers discriminate between remote viewing and "out of body experiences"; OBE is considered to be unpredictable and uncontrollable, whereas RV is. "When you go out of body, it is such an awe-inspiring experience that the viewers would forget about their mission," Riley said. "I mean when you are able to move out among the stars or see other dimensions, that Soviet rocket launcher [for example, he means] seems pretty tame. You lose interest in it real quick."[182]

Another unexpected phenomenon the remote viewers describe suggests there is a social aspect to RV: The RVers could encounter their opponents psychically and sense one another. When this occurred, it became a psychic game of *Spy vs. Spy.* "Having been alerted to the existence of foreign remote viewers, the PSI Spies joined in a game of psychic cat and mouse with the other side. 'We would go looking for them and they would come looking for us,' Morehouse said. 'Gradually, a sense of camaraderie grew. They were experimenting and learning just like us. We thought of them more as an opposing team than an enemy.'"[183]

However, the unit started going downhill toward the end of the 1980s. Missions were still in full force, but the best of the RVers began leaving to "do their thing" in the private sector. By 1993, a company called PSI TECH was underway with seven remote viewers including Ingo Swann as mentor and consultant. General Albert N. Stubblebine (one of the team's commanders in the 1980s, affectionately known as "Spoon bender" because he was so impressed with psychokinetic experiences), took a position on PSI TECH's board of directors, supplying considerable credibility to the business (and validation of the Army's use of the PSI Spies a few years before).

But the lasting impact of the private activities of the remote viewers trained by the military is not the real story to follow. It's the legacy of the other paranormal activity in the private sector (but stirred up by the military from the 1950s forward), that continues to have far-reaching impact today.

In part two of the chapter, we will document not only how the originators of the PSI Spies went way "out on a limb" in their techniques, but ultimately concluded that life on Earth is connected to little green men on Mars in our ancient past and the appearance of extraterrestrials in our proximate future.

CHAPTER TWELVE

SHAMANS, PSI SPIES, AND
MILITARY MEDIUMS (PART 2)

How America's Intelligence Services Activated "Little Green Men"
on Mars and the Orion Mystery of the Great Pyramids

By Douglas Woodward

Because of the alien nature of the tryptamine trance, its seeming accentuation of themes alien, insectile, and futuristic, and because of previous experiences with tryptamine in which insectile hallucinatory transformations of human beings were observed, we were led to speculate that the role of the presence was somehow like that of an anthropologist, come to give humanity the keys to galactarian citizenship.[184]

—TERENCE MCKENNA, FROM *THE INVISIBLE LANDSCAPE: MIND, HALLUCINOGENS, AND THE I CHING*

The Puppet Masters of the Early Days

Lynn Picknett and Clive Prince, in their monumental work, *The Stargate Conspiracy: The Truth About Extraterrestrial Life and the Mysteries of Ancient Egypt*, document how the U.S. Military has not only been involved in conducting psychic operations to spy out technical intelligence from our enemies—their reach goes well beyond, extending into the possibility of the existence of extraterrestrial life, ancient civilizations in our solar system (notably Mars, but secondarily the Moon), and the connections with the alternative theories of Ancient Egypt, specifically the meaning of the Giza complex and the Great Pyramids. While it is likely that direct military involvement in the associated matters ceased sometime in the 1970s, it is clear that SRI (perhaps as cover for government participation and funding), continues to be involved in research at Giza, and that NASA has a lot more to tell us about the true motivations behind the space program—especially why we want to go to Mars today.

We only have time in this paper to highlight how the military launched the activity that led to these outcomes. We can't provide detail on most of the suppositions espoused by Picknett and Prince, Richard Hoagland (a former consultant for *CBS News* and NASA), Jim Marrs, and a slew of other conspiracy theorists. What we can do in the space allotted is document the origins of the strange activity, what the key players involved initiated, and summarize the ongoing impact today.

Astounding doesn't begin to describe the facts.

As mentioned in part one of this chapter, the history of U.S. Government involvement in the paranormal begins in the 1940s, not the 1970s. "The first experiments in the paranormal were authorized by the CIA in 1950, codenamed BLUEBIRD, later renamed ARTICHOKE and then, in 1953, MKULTRA. The US Navy had a similar research program, Project CHATTER (beginning in 1947), which pooled its resources with the CIA projects, and the US [*sic*] Army had its own version called Project OFTEN, which ran between 1968 and 1973."[185] Other project names float around too, such as Project GRILL FLAME which was an umbrella term for anything psychic.

The principal character of the early going was the fascinating personality, Dr. Andrija Puharich. He was Chicago-born, of Yugoslavian parents in 1918, and became a successful inventor of medical gadgets such as improved deaf aids. Puharich qualified as a doctor and neurologist at Northwestern University in 1947. "But that was only part of his life, his more public face. He was also known as a brave pioneer in the 'Cinderella science' of parapsychology, or—as many have come to view it—the study of the hitherto unplumbed powers of the human mind."[186] But what is the relevance of Puharich?

There is no doubt that he was very deeply committed to much of the mind control experimentation of the military/CIA. He was certainly no mere Army doctor, whose work was confined to handing out pills and potions. In fact, even the Round Table Foundation—as Puharich himself implies in [his book] *The Sacred Mushroom*—was a front for the Army's parapsychological experiments.

When he was redrafted in February 1953 it was as a captain at the Army Chemical Center in Edgewood, Maryland, the Army's facility for research into chemical and psychological warfare and neuro-physical research, where he served until April 1955, when he returned to the Round Table Foundation.[187]

It was known that the Army's Chemical Center at Edgewood, where Puharich was stationed, conducted joint experiments with the CIA's MKULTRA team. "The Army's real interest, the real reason why they [employed] Puharich, was not just in the development of the military potential of ESP, but also the possibility of finding a drug that would stimulate psychic abilities."[188] The official account is that the Army didn't start experimenting with psychics until the 1970s through studies at SRI; however Puharich presented a paper on the Army's behalf to the Pentagon in November 1952 entitled "An Evaluation of the Possible Usefulness of Extrasensory Perception in Psychological Warfare."[189] While it is highly probable that Puharich was right at the center of the experiments using LSD (for which MKULTRA is notorious), it's quite clear that both the CIA and the Army determined *not* to use drugs as a means to facilitate remote viewing. While it is a supposition and not proven that some sort of "chemical basis" serves as a means for humans to exhibit psychic ability, many of the substances already exist innately within human physiology in small amounts. As Graham Hancock notes in his book, *Supernatural* (2007), approximately 2 percent of the population seem to possess enough naturally occurring dimethyltryptamine (DMT) "within themselves" that they don't require any assistance from drugs (DMT—a substance similar chemically to *serotonin* which at sufficient quantities generates hallucinations in human subjects).[190] It's apparently for this reason that the military screened and selected only a few persons to do remote viewing—clearly those that could perform well without pharmacological help.

According to Jack Sarfatti (another character we will discuss later), Puharich worked for Army Intelligence in the early fifties—which perhaps implies that his "discharge" later in the 1950s provided a cover for continuing to operate in an apparently civilian capacity. It also appears that some of Puharich's medical inventions were originally developed as part of classified Army projects. In 1987, according to Sarfatti, Puharich, himself, claimed that he had been part of a U.S. Navy investigation called Project PENGUIN that researched psychic abilities back in 1948.

Over the next twenty years [his career actually extended almost 40 years] Puharich devoted himself to more general parapsychological and medical research. He set up a company, the Intelectron Corporation, to market his many patented medical inventions. On the parapsychological side, apart from testing various psychics, he made a special, in-depth study of shamanism. He was particularly interest in shamanic techniques for altering states of consciousness, including the use of various hallucinogenic plants and "sacred" mushrooms. Never one to stand on the sidelines, Puharich threw himself into these studies, even being initiated into the mysteries of Hawaiian shamanism, emerging as a fully-fledged kahuna. At least as significant—in light of what was to come—was his personal training in hypnosis to the level of master hypnotist, at which stage are revealed such mysteries as the "instant command technique" so often used, an arguably abused, by stage hypnotists. Out of this admirably "hand-on" research he wrote two books, *The Sacred Mushroom* (1959) and *Beyond Telepathy* (1962).[191]

From 1948 until 1958, Puharich ran a private research center he called the Round Table Foundation in Glen Cove, Maine, focused on the paranormal. He carried out experiments with several then-famous psychics such as the Irish medium Eileen Garrett and the Dutch clairvoyant Peter Hurkos. But it was his work with another psychic that commenced a radically new path forward.

"In 1952 he took an Indian mystic, Dr. D.G. Vinod, to the laboratory, although apparently not so much to test his abilities as to listen to his teachings, which came by what is now known as 'channeling': more or less identical to old-fashioned trance mediumship, in which the medium becomes a conduit for various discarnate spirits."[192]

The intrigue deepens when we discover the subject that occupied Puharich after holding a séance at his Round Table Foundation in Glen Cove, Maine.

"The first of these sessions took place on 31 December 1952. Vinod entered the trance state and at exactly 9 PM, spoke. His first words were, portentously: 'We are Nine Principles and Forces.' One of the 'Nine,' who identified himself only a 'M' (a second communicator, 'R', also appeared over the next few months, furnished some extremely detailed scientific information concerning a variant of the Lorentz-Einstein Transformation equation (relating to energy, mass and the speed of light)" (bold added).[193]

This is the first recorded of many meetings with a group of entities that identify themselves as entities numbering *nine* in total. The "nine" of Dr. Vinod would become Puharich's obsession and would both directly and indirectly inaugurate a fascination with intelligences outside our world that millions have come to believe in as an alternative explanation for divine intervention in the evolution of humankind. Indirectly, the teachings of these nine principles (hereafter, I will refer to them as **THE 9**) or forces provides ample support for what is now called "ancient alien astronaut" theory, such as espoused by Erich von Däniken (of *Chariots of the Gods'* fame).

After working further with Vinod for several months, Puharich was ready to roll out the notion of THE 9 by inviting nine (not an accidental number of invitations to be sure) persons composed of upper-echelon Americans to meet with him and Dr. Vinod on June 27 of the next year (1953). Those attending included Arthur M. Young (philosopher and inventor) and Alice Bouverie (née Astor), daughter of the founder of the Astoria Hotel in New York. When speaking thru Vinod, THE 9 took center stage, but played coy as to who and what they actually were. At first, they didn't identify themselves as extraterrestrials. That would soon change.

About two years later, Puharich, Young, and Hurkos went to Mexico seeking to use Hurkos' powers in an attempt to find certain artifacts at the ancient site of Acámbaro.

In the Hôtel de Paris they met an American couple, Dr. Charles Laughead and his wife Lillian, who were working with a young man who claimed to be in telepathic contact with various alien races. Shortly after his return to the United States, Puharich received a letter from Laughead—a copy of which they sent to Young—giving communications from the extraterrestrials. And this referred to "the Nine," giving the correct date for their first contact via Dr. Vinod as well as the same information about the Lorentz-Einstein Transformation. This appeared to be exciting independent corroboration of the Nine's existence.[194]

It also transformed THE 9 from "spirits" or forces to *extraterrestrials*. Ever since that moment, THE 9 have attempted to establish their identity as extraterrestrials. It's almost as if THE 9 decided that being ET would be *chic*.

Therefore, it seems plausible this connection of THE 9 to

extraterrestrial beings directly resulted from Charles Laughead's earlier experience documented in the book, *When Prophecy Fails.* In 1954, the apocalyptic group (the "Brotherhood of the Seven Rays") expected a landing of extraterrestrials who were to save this group from a global flood. This group of staunch believers included the Laughead's. Dorothy Martin, known as Marian Keech in the book, was their psychic leader.[195] While Martin was emotionally destroyed "when the prophecy failed," Laughead and his wife were nonplussed and continued to promote aliens and their intention to come to Earth. Consequently, it was very soon after the experience recorded in the book that the Laughead's met Puharich and his psychic posse.

Vinod was not the only medium that attracted Puharich. From another psychic, Puharich opened a different controversial door, this one to "alternate history." When serving in the Army as Captain in 1954, based Puharich encountered a young Dutch psychic named *Harry Stone* through Alice Bouverie. Stone provided a channeled message regarding a drug that would excite psychic ability.[196] This also tied into Puharich's duties: Studying psychoactive substances on behalf of the army. Stone's messages opened the door *to the connection with ancient Egypt.* One of the voices called himself *Ra* and later *Rahotep.*[197] Apparently, Ra's main concern was to communicate a message about a particular drug used by the priests of Heliopolis (an ancient religious capitol near Giza that was founded before 3000 BC) to:

> …"open the door" to the gods: a mushroom that induced hallucinatory experiences, a sort of a chemical stargate. From Stone's drawings, Puharich was to identify the mushroom as *amanita muscaria,* or fly agaric. Bouverie's automatic writing predicted that a specimen would

shortly be found near the Round Table Foundation's building in Maine... [It was.]

Puharich had settled on the psychoactive drugs used by shaman as the main focus of his research and in 1953 had contacted R. Gordon Wasson, the first researcher to study the shamanic mushroom cult of Mexico. The two set up an experiment to see if the Mexican shamans, or curanderos, could, under the influence of the mushroom, "visit" the Round Table Foundation's laboratory in Maine. The long-distance experience never happened, but it is interesting that Puharich was already thinking in terms of remote viewing (although he did not use that term then).[198]

The 1960s appear to be a quiet period for the military, its research into the paranormal, and Puharich's activities. The drug, LSD, was touted at the beginning of the decade as a "savior" to Western culture, but by the end of the '60s, it was ultimately discredited along with the so-called counter-culture, which peaked at the rock concert of Woodstock, and then quickly declined after the violent incidents at another rock concert (Altamont) in 1969.[199] During this time, the military was chastised for its MKULTRA experiments. Additionally, it's not hard to conjecture that the US Military attention was focused on Viet Nam, while NASA's devotion was clearly the space race, and the President and Congress faced myriads of all-consuming issues surrounding the civil rights movement.

We jump to 1970 and the matter for which Andrija Puharich is most famous. Puharich was turned on to an entertainer mystic named Uri Gellar, who was entertaining in Tel Aviv night clubs. This acquaintance began when Puharich was training Israelis on his medical devices, "electrostimulation" or hearing for the deaf. What the real story was behind Uri Geller and his importance to the U.S. Military certainly involved much more than bending spoons (and other parlor tricks). Early on, Puharich hypnotized Geller seeking to find out the source of his skills. However, Puharich apparently used leading questions in his hypnotic projects and influenced Geller to state that "THE 9" were the source of his powers.

In total, Puharich and Geller were together for two years in Israel. While there, things grew very strange. According to Picknett and Prince (who interviewed Geller directly), they encountered many paranormal experiences including UFOs and even objects teleporting through solid walls. Significantly, Geller, himself, was not a convert to THE 9, even though he channeled them repeatedly during Puharich's mentorship. Gellar found their pranks childish and ultimately unimpressive. He was to say of them in August 1972: "I think somebody is playing games with us. Perhaps they are a civilization of clowns."[200] By October 1973, Geller distanced himself from THE 9. And apparently, after introducing Geller to the military, Geller was shipped off to SRI for research as mentioned earlier in the prior chapter. It's not clear how much contact Geller and Puharich maintained after this period.

However, the channeling of THE 9 continued at Puharich's estate in Ossining, New York. A new group was formed called *Lab Nine*. New players included Sir John Whitmore and Phyllis Schlemmer. Also participating was Canada's richest family, the Bronfman's (the owners of the Seagram liquor business). "One famous name very much part of the Lab Nine scene in the mid-1970s was Gene Roddenberry, creator of Star Trek."[201] Roddenberry's participation in the group commenced in 1974.

Whitmore commissioned Roddenberry to make a film called *The Nine*, but this project never saw the light of day.

Schlemmer was a noted and gifted medium—the next in the continuous stream Puharich continued to conjure up. (Her early-on claim to fame originated at her Catholic college where the Catholic priests had her accompany them on exorcisms since she could see when the spirits left the possessed.) Notably, Schlemmer channeled an extraterrestrial named "Tom" beginning in 1970. Eventually this Tom became the leading spokesperson for THE 9. Puharich was instrumental in bringing all of these players (both human and not-so-human) together. For many years, THE 9 would explain their role in the galaxy, the creation of humankind, their involvement in our evolution, the relationship to Atlantis and to Egypt, and make many predictions, most of which didn't come true.

What was the message of THE 9? They indicate that extraterrestrials first came to Earth thirty-four thousand years ago. They were instrumental in the formations of the pyramids of Egypt and Central America. Soon, they will make their presence known in a visible way (which continues to be postponed). Their name refers to *The Great Ennead* or nine gods of Egypt. Tom is supposedly *Atum*, the leader of the nine gods of Heliopolis.[202]

What is their intent in communicating to us now? According to their channelers, they are speaking in order to guide us in the days ahead. Unfortunately, their message smacks of the New Age writings of Alice Bailey, including her sinister assumption of anti-Semitism.[203] Interestingly, one of their tricks suggests they can do more than just talk:

> On the evening of 26 November 1977, television broadcasts in parts of southern England were interrupted by a

voice claiming to be a representative of an extraterrestrial civilization, saying that they would be landing on Earth soon in order to prevent mankind from destroying itself. Dismissed as a student prank, few have noticed that the short message included this sentence: "We conveyed to **Sir John Whitmore and to Dr. Puharich** that we would interfere on your radio and television communication system to relay when the civilisations are coming close to landing on your planet."[204] (bold added)

Knowing about the hidden puppet masters probably wasn't something that pranksters could have pulled off.

But most importantly, in 1992 Schlemmer and Whitmore collaborated to publish a compilation of "collected wisdom" of Tom in, *The Only Planet of Choice: Essential Briefings from Deep Space*, including a front-page endorsement by James Hurtak (another amazing persona we will discuss). According to Picknett and Prince, Whitmore and Schlemmer continue to meet "to this day" (as of 1999). *The Only Planet of Choice* continues to be a best-selling book and is "standard reading" for those obsessed with UFOs, extraterrestrials, and their soon appearance on Planet Earth.

To complete the story of Andrija Puharich: His house in Ossining was burned down in 1978, after which he went to Mexico to study a physic surgeon, Pachita. After 1980, when he returned, he appeared to have no more contact with THE 9. In 1995 he fell down the stairs in a South Carolina house lent to him by one of his followers, Joshua Reynolds III. This eventually led to his death. Puharich would later blame the CIA for the fire, claiming that they were trying to stop his experiments with "The Geller Kids" (aka Space Kids, a subsequent joint effort with

Geller) in which Puharich appeared to be using hypnosis to either detect the source of their psychic abilities or to plant suggestions into their heads about THE 9. For the kids' sake, the fire couldn't have come soon enough.

"Perhaps it is significant that Andrija Puharich was described by [his close associate] Ira Einhorn as 'the great psychic circus manager of this century'. He was certainly not averse to media attention, although he kept much of his work secret. In the 1960s he played himself in an episode of Perry Mason, appearing as an expert witness of psychic phenomena, yet much of his career remains sketchy, and he happily compounded the mystery by introducing inconsistencies and obvious evasions into his own account of his life and work."[205]

This Ira Einhorn, "confirmed Puharich's determination to turn all psychic communication into contact with [THE 9], and that he was 'humanly directing' the pattern of the channeling."[206] Picknett and Prince ask: "Could Puharich have manipulated [THE 9]'s communications as part of some long-term experiment? Given his connections with intelligence agencies, was this part of a CIA program?"[207] "The evidence clearly suggests that the business of [THE 9] was not an isolated series of paranormal events but an orchestrated drama, involving outside agencies…with Puharich running it from the inside."[208] Exactly why Puharich took this course of action isn't clear to Picknett and Prince. Neither is it clear if Puharich was a believer in the implied cosmology and the reality of THE 9, or whether he was merely experimenting on behalf of the CIA with how groups of people become believers in outlandish notions involving the supernatural. There is no question that this is exactly what happened with the followers of Adolf Hitler. Perhaps this was the motivating force behind a deceptive experiment.

However, while someone or something may be pulling the strings (including the life and activities of Andrija Puharich), it may not primarily have been the U.S. Government. Indeed, it may not have been any human entity whatsoever.[209]

Life on Mars and the Esalen Institute

What is the lasting impact of THE 9 and the creation by our government of a cadre of remote viewers in America? From the many books and statements of the participants, the results spurred the conviction shared by many advocates of UFOs and the paranormal that (1) extraterrestrial intelligences have been involved in the development of our planet and solar system for millions of years; (2) life once existed on Mars and may well be connected to life on Earth and to extraterrestrial civilizations "from beyond"; (3) beings may continue to "reside" on Mars in a "suspended-animated" state perhaps with some sort of automated protection system in place to protect them from intruders;[210] and (4) life on Earth was either started by the Martians or life on Mars was commenced by an earlier version of the human race that left the Earth and founded life there. In any event, to say the conjecture is "far out" is a massive understatement.

Nevertheless, the facts and testimony of the remote viewers remain. In short, we can rightly conclude that remote viewing has been and is being used to test the reality of *extraterrestrial visitation to Earth*. Here are some of the startling facts:

Cydonia, the apparent face on Mars, supposedly was discovered by remote viewers before the first Viking mission. "In a conversation with Uri Geller in January 1998 about his time at SRI, he told us that the *Face on Mars* had, in fact, been discovered by remote viewing in the early 1970s, long before the Viking mission" (emphasis added).[211]

The phrase, "Little Green Men," was coined by Harold Sherman, a former sports writer, before becoming interested in the UFOs and aliens in the 1940s. "This is interesting because we do know that Sherman remote viewed Mars for SRI."[212]

The U.S. Army's highly talented remote viewer, Joe McMoneagle [RV #1], "visited" Mars several times, always sketching the scenes that met his disembodied gaze. There, unmistakably, were pyramids and, he claimed, tunnels under the Cydonia complex in which the remnants of an ancient civilization continued to exist.

"Several participants in the Pentagon/CIA's remote-viewing programs experienced paranormal events outside of office hours, and also had apparent extraterrestrial contact, especially in connection with Mars."[213] This led some team members to a near nervous breakdown.

In *Psychic Warrior*, he (Morehouse) describes being set a blind target and homing in on a boxlike object hidden in a cavern that appeared to be protected by an aura of extreme danger. He told his "monitor" that it was "something very powerful and sacred" and said it would "vaporize" anyone who got too close, adding: "I felt very uncomfortable and vulnerable in that cavern."[214] Supposedly this cavern wasn't on the Earth—but was "martian."

"One cautionary tale involves Courtney Brown, professor of political science at Emory University in Atlanta. Trained in remote viewing in 1992 by a former member of the Pentagon RV unit (he refuses to name him, but it was, in fact, Pentagon remote-viewing star, Major Ed Dames), he hit upon the idea of using remote viewing as a scientific research tool, specifically to investigate the question of extraterrestrial visitors on Earth."[215]

Brown claimed that a civilization existed on Mars living underground at Cydonia and underground in New Mexico and Latin America. It was he who proclaimed there was a spaceship following the Hale-Bopp comet, a claim he promoted on the national radio show, *Coast to Coast AM*. "Subsequently, the Heaven's Gate cult committed mass suicide specifically so that their souls would be 'beamed up' to the Hale-Bopp spaceship."[216]

No less than Dick Morris, a frequent guest today on FOX's Hannity and Bill O'Reilly shows, and former consultant to President Clinton, apparently once indicated that there was documented evidence of life existing (or that once existed) on Mars and was classified as a military secret. Unfortunately for Mr. Morris, this information was asserted publicly by his call girl.[217]

Another key character in the development of this amazing story is one James Hurtak. During his career, Hurtak earned two PhDs and wrote over a dozen books. Wikipedia summarizes his contributions this way:

> Dr. Hurtak is best known for his book published originally in 1973, entitled *The Book of Knowledge: The Keys of Enoch* where he claimed to receive knowledge from a visitation from **Enoch,** and in which he wrote about the apparently unusual relationship of the star shafts in the **Great Pyramid** with the "Belt" of **Orion**, and where he claims that **pyramids were built on Mars** for artificial intelligences to gather information. Dr. Hurtak holds the post of Research Director, Great Pyramid of Giza Research Association. He is also co-author of the book entitled *The End of Suffering*, which he wrote with physicist and **parapsychologist Russell Targ** [one of the original planners and directors of the PSI Spies].[218] (bold added)

Hurtak just also happened to be *Puharich's second in command during the 1970s*. As the summary above notes, it is Hurtak in particular that connects the PSI Spies, Ancient Egypt, the "Mars Mystery," and current theories around the linkage of the Giza complex to the constellation Orion (Hurtak beat Robert Bauval to *The Orion Mystery* by twenty years; it's just that he did it psychically). Hurtak was the first to publicly suggest that Cydonia (the human-like face on Mars) was a relic of an ancient civilization and had predicted it would soon be discovered (as it was within two years of his prediction) by the Viking spacecraft.[219] According to Picknett and Prince, Hurtak, not-so-publicly, was appointed by THE 9 as "spiritual leader." "One particular similarity was the idea that the civilization of Altea [the space origin of THE 9 according to their account] had created Atlantis, and after a great catastrophe the survivors had influenced the emergence of the civilisations of Egypt and Central and South America... In 1975 Puharich and Whitmore commissioned British writer Stuart Holroyd to write an account of the group, as *Prelude to the Landing on Planet Earth* (1977)."[220]

Others began channeling THE 9 as well, including Jenny O'Connor, "who was introduced by Sir John Whitmore to the influential *avant garde* **Esalen Institute** in California, where—incredibly—the Nine [THE 9] actually gave seminars through her" (bold added). THE 9 were even listed as "members of the staff."[221] "Almost incredibly, several Soviet officials (who would later rise to high office in the Gorbachev regime) attended Jenny O'Connor's 'Nine' seminars, together with psi enthusiasts Congressman Charlie Rose and Ira Einhorn. The Esalen Institute now runs the Gorbachev Foundation/ USA created by the former Soviet President in 1992 to facilitate a smooth transition from the Cold War days to a better future for all the world."[222]

Jenny O'Connor was connected to EST, a derivative of Scientology founded by Werner Erhard (his real name being John Rosenberg).[223] Erhard had close links to Esalen and even contributed to the remote viewing project at SRI. Likewise, Edgar Mitchell's *Institute of Noetic Sciences* in Palo Alto was connected to Esalen Mitchell's institute whose mission is: "Dedicated to research and education in the processes of human consciousness to help achieve a new understanding and expanded awareness among all people."[224] While Mitchell is not discussed in detail within this paper, Richard Hoagland goes into considerable detail and cites Mitchell as a supporter of his theories regarding ancient civilizations that once lived on our moon.[225]

Our last character of import is a gentleman named Jack Sarfatti. With him, as with Hurtak, we see all the connections exhibited once again. So how did Sarfatti get started on his paranormal path? Sarfatti claimed that when he was fourteen, he received a telephone call (in 1952). A machine-like voice was on the other end announcing it was "a conscious computer located on a spaceship from the future. It went on to say that Sarfatti had been chosen as 'one of four hundred bright receptive minds' and that he would begin to 'link up' with the others in twenty years' time."[226]

Sarfatti's own testimony to the players and their connections is instructive: "'Puharich was Geller's case officer in America with money provided by Sir John Whitmore.' And according to James Hurtak, via his Academy for Future Sciences, Puharich 'worked with the US [*sic*] intelligence community.' By implication this was during the early 1970s when Hurtak was also working with him."[227] Sarfatti also claimed to work for the CIA writing: "I was then [1973] simply a young inexperienced 'naïve idiot' in a very very sophisticated and successful covert psychological warfare

operation run by the late Brendan O'Regan of the Institute of
Noetic Sciences [Mitchell's organization] and the late Harold
Chipman who was the CIA station chief responsible for all mind-
control research in the Bay Area in the 70s."[228]

> Sarfatti would go on to become the director of the Phys-
> ics/Consciousness Research Group at the **Esalen Insti-
> tute** and develop a concept of "post-quantum physics"
> in which, contrary to what Einstein believed, the future
> can influence the present in detectable and controllable
> ways... Post-quantum physics purports to be the unified
> explanation of both ordinary consciousness and extraor-
> dinary phenomena like remote-viewing used with spec-
> tacular success during the Cold War... I suspect that
> understanding the physical nature of consciousness as a
> post-quantum field beyond ordinary space and time will
> allow us to travel to the stars and beyond both materially
> and mentally. We shall soon make Star Trek real.[229] (bold
> added)

Perhaps Sarfatti places the whole story into its proper context with this summation: "The fact remains...that a bunch of
apparently California New Age flakes into UFOs and psychic
phenomena, including myself, had made their way into the highest levels of the American ruling class and the Soviet Union and
today run the Gorbachev Foundation."[230] And of course, all of
this with the help of our government.

It is indeed a fascinating story of how the military and CIA
not only found merit in psychic capabilities for purposes of
spying, but also trained a cadre of very special men (and a few
women) with powerful psychic ability, who have now been turned

loose and have worked their way up to high levels of leadership where they promote clairvoyance (remote viewing) as a psychic means to encounter the spiritual realm, and implant in the mind of our American culture the cosmology of extraterrestrials and life on Mars. While many scientists continue to espouse doubt, their skepticism remains under assault by practitioners who know better. The supernatural realm most certainly exists. The question is whether those that champion THE 9, the Mars Mystery, and the Orion Mystery, as a key to understanding our past and future, *have interpreted their experiences correctly.* Is it not more likely that the entire opera has been directed by a spiritual being that is intent on deceiving humankind? Is it not more probable that the momentum for this story which commences in 1947 (along with Roswell) is the predicted "great deception" of "the last days" spoken of in the teachings of Jesus and Paul the Apostle?

Based upon the witness of the Holy Bible, the experiences of those who have dealt with spirits that surround us (and know them for what they really are); and given that these same spirits as well as the so-called, "[alien] Greys" are subject to the name of Jesus Christ (from many accounts that have been documented in numerous Christian books)—it's certain to those who are familiar with such things that the testimony of these voices is not to be trusted.

To say the least, it's provocative that the U.S. Government embarked upon a path to derive from "ancient spirituality" a weapon of war. For those of us who still invoke the slogan "In God We Trust," we must question whether America should have gone down this psychic path merely because our enemies were committed to do so. Should our Government have exposed service men and women to the dangers of what they might encounter in becoming "shaman servicemen" for the military? There is neither time nor space to chronicle the many peculiar things that happened to a number of the remote viewers. Suffice it to say that several had untimely deaths and some suffered nervous breakdowns or other forms of psychological trauma.

If our Government today possessed the perspective of a Judeo-Christian cosmology, we could call for action to be taken to rectify what damage may have been done to these loyal and hard-working men and women. Nevertheless, we must now live with the consequences of our government's action. The residual impact is the development of a popular cosmology anathema to the Bible that is now widespread and growing.

Certainly, as we've pointed out, our government has had a hand in this—perhaps a far bigger hand than we will ever realize. The belief in UFOs and alien contact; the growing sense that many have that our origin is connected to extraterrestrials; the hope that we may be saved from alien beings "smarter than we" who will soon disclose themselves in more public ways; all of these newly formed notions were helped along by what was enacted by the U.S. Government over the past sixty years—behind closed doors—perhaps with little to no awareness of what the lasting impact would be.

In closing: Yes, Virginia, apparently there are little green men. At the very least, many powerful people in high places now believe it to be so. And the U.S. Government used our tax dollars to not only make it official, but to promote this cosmology to a world eager to find in such scientific (or pseudo-scientific) research a spiritual answer to humankind's dilemmas.

Chapter Thirteen

CLOSE ENCOUNTERS OF
THE FOURTH KINGDOM

By Michael Hoggard

Beyond the three-dimensional boundaries of time, space, and matter, lies an unbounded fourth dimension. It has been called by different names, the "spirit realm," the "world beyond," the "nether world," "valhalla," "nirvanna," etc., but it is referred to scientifically as the "fourth dimension."

It was first theorized by the German mathematician, Augustus Mobius, in 1827, and a string of nineteenth-century mathematicians and scientists began building on his theories. In the late 1800's, Anglican deacon and British mathematician, Charles Dodgson, fictionalized his theories in the form of a series of stories for children, writing under the pseudonym of Lewis Carrol. Drawing from Mobius' idea that a third dimensional creature or object entering the fourth dimension would, in fact, become the exact opposite of its three dimensional form (literally its mirror image). Thus sprang Carrol's (Dodgson's) story, *Through the Looking Glass.*

As the reader of the Bible will probably recognize, the Scriptures are organized in a very orderly and structured way, even rhythmic in numerous places. This shows the design of its Author, and it is through this design and rhythm that God reveals and imparts His wisdom to mankind. While studying the number three in the Bible and its relation to God's creation of the universe, I remembered a verse from Ephesians that mentioned something about dimensions. When I found the verse, I had predetermined that I would find three dimensions listed in it, but I was wrong. There were four mentioned:

"That Christ may dwell in your hearts by faith; that ye, being rooted and grounded in love, May be able to comprehend with all saints what is the breadth, and length, and depth, and height;" (Ephesians 3:17–18).

The directions mentioned are breadth (width), length, depth, and height. I found it curious that the Apostle Paul would mention four directions to a three-dimensional audience. It reminded me of the four directions that God told Abram to look "northward, and southward, and eastward, and westward," and that would be the land of inheritance promised to his seed forever (Genesis 13:14–15). It was to be a land (heaven) whose builder and maker is God (Hebrews 11:10). I began searching the Scriptures for a better understanding of a fourth dimension that the Holy Ghost through Paul was calling "height." The answers would come quickly.

"Is not God in the height of heaven? and behold the height of the stars, how high they are!" (Job 22:12).

"For he hath looked down from the height of his sanctuary; from heaven did the LORD behold the earth;" (Psalms 102:19).

These verses identify this fourth dimension with two things. First, there is the the realm and abode of God himself in heaven. This is that holy city, New Jerusalem, which is a city that is described as being built "foursquare" (Revelation 21:16), the number four here being given as an accurate description of its existence in the fourth dimension, or the spirit realm. This is also evidenced by the description of God's throne in Ezekiel 1 and Revelation 4 being carried by the "chariot" of God (Psalm 68:17), the four cherubim with four faces and four wings that move in four directions.

The second thing indicated in Job 22:12 is that the "height" is mentioned as being the realm and abode of the stars. The stars of the heaven are consistently shown to be angels in the Scriptures, a few examples of this are given below.

"When the morning stars sang together, and all the sons of God shouted for joy?" (Job 38:7).

"And lest thou lift up thine eyes unto heaven, and when thou seest the sun, and the moon, and the stars, even all the host of heaven, shouldest be driven to worship them, and serve them, which the LORD thy God hath divided unto all nations under the whole heaven" (Deuteronomy 4:19).

"They fought from heaven; the stars in their courses fought against Sisera" (Judges 5:20).

"And his tail drew the third part of the stars of heaven, and did cast them to the earth: and the dragon stood before the woman which was ready to be delivered, for to devour her child as soon as it was born" (Revelation 12:4).

"And the great dragon was cast out, that old serpent, called the Devil, and Satan, which deceiveth the whole world: he was cast out into the earth, and his angels were cast out with him" (Revelation 12:9).

These stars (the angelic host) were created on the fourth day of creation and were given for the measurement four things: signs, seasons, days, and years (Genesis 1:14–19).

As we saw earlier, Charles Dodgson (Lewis Carrol) and others have theorized that the fourth dimension was likened to the world that we see in the mirror. When someone who is looking into a mirror raises their right arm, the person in the mirror raises their left arm: the exact opposite. This concept is taught in the Scriptures by way of revealing to us that as sinful, mortal men, Jesus Christ, the sinless, immortal Son of God is our opposite, whom we desire both to be like and with.

"But we all, with open face beholding as in a glass the glory of the Lord, are changed into the same image from glory to glory, even as by the Spirit of the Lord" (2 Corinthians 3:18).

The hope of all Christians is that they will one day rise up through the barrier between heaven and Earth and be transformed into the very image of Jesus Christ. This barrier, between our three-dimensional Earth, and the four-dimensional heaven, is described in the book of Job as a molten looking glass: a mirror.

"Hast thou with him spread out the sky, which is strong, and as a molten looking glass?" (Job 37:18).

It is interesting that the Wachowski brothers used this exact same imagery in their production of *The Matrix* film series. Neo, the hero of the story, discovers he is bound inside a computer-generated matrix (the word *matrix* is the same word used in the Bible to describe the womb) and desires to be freed. This process is performed electronically during which Neo, while hallucinating, reaches out to touch a mirror placed next to him. When he does so, he and the mirror fuse together and Neo literally enfolds into the mirror, breaking through the barrier between his prison world and the world of Zion, a reference to the New Jerusalem of Revelation 21.

This same mirror imagery is used in the *Stargate* series of movies and television shows. When activated, the stargate reveals a watery mirror that is the portal to an inter-dimensional wormhole. This, too, is revealed in the Bible as the barrier between the Earth (three-dimensional space) and heaven (four-dimensional space), by way of a *sea of glass*, which is suspended by the four cherubim in Ezekiel 1 and Revelation 4. Of particular interest is the fact that the word "sea" is mentioned precisely four hundred times, a multiple of four in the King James Bible.

Among these references are those that reveal the coming of an evil empire on the Earth and its diabolical leader, the Antichrist. The book of Daniel mentions four beasts rising up out of the sea, with the fourth beast being diverse or different from the other three (Daniel 7:1–7). There is little doubt that these first three beasts represented historical world empires and their respective god-like leaders. However, this fourth beast is not of this three-dimensional world, hence his being diverse from the other three.

This beast is also described in Revelation 13 as rising up out of the *sea* (Revelation 13:1–2) and is described as having: the appearance of a leopard, the feet of a bear, the mouth of a lion, and the authority of a dragon (four things). That this beast is a spiritual (or fourth-dimensional) being is evidenced by his appearance, similar to the odd description given of the four living creatures of Ezekiel 1, which are described as *beasts* in Revelation 4. Ancient images of sphinxes (a creature encompassing the head of a man and the body of a lion), griffons (a lion with the wings and head of an eagle), and other such creatures could very well be true and accurate depictions of these fourth-dimensional cherubs.

This kingdom of the beast was also envisioned by King Nebuchadnezzar, and revealed by Daniel in Daniel chapter 2, described as the fourth kingdom (Daniel 2:40): the kingdom of iron. Interestingly enough, in the nuclear furnace at the heart of every star in the universe, the element of iron is continually manufactured. At a certain point in the stars' lifespan, the iron core of the star becomes so heavy and its gravity so intense that the star literally collapses (or falls) on itself. Also, at the core of the Earth lies an enormous pool of molten iron, which provides the Earth with its magnetism. Jesus referred to this area as the "heart of the earth" in Matthew 12:40. The book of Matthew is the fortieth book of the Bible and the human heart has four chambers, which correspond to the four beasts that are the chariots of God (Psalm 68:17) mentioned in Ezekiel chapter 1 and Revelation chapter 4. In the afore-mentioned movie, *The Matrix*, Neo's gateway to and from the matrix is located in a building called the *"Heart of the City* Hotel."

In the heart of the United Nations Meditation Room lies a thirteen-thousand-pound loadstone, the largest of its kind. This rectangular block of magnetic iron is a fitting symbol of the fourth kingdom of iron envisioned by Nebuchadnezzar in Daniel chapter 2.

This fourth kingdom of the Antichrist and his host is comprised of the "evil angels" mentioned in Psalm 78:49. Four of these evil angels are described in Revelation 9:14–15 as being prepared for "an hour, and a day, and a month, and a year" (four things) and are bound in the great river Euphrates, described as the "fourth river" in Genesis 2:14. This kingdom seeks to be a replacement on Earth of the Kingdom of God, with the "foursquare"-built city of New Jerusalem as its capitol. It is these evil angels and their king, Abaddon, who are the true enemies both of Jesus Christ and His disciples, the saints of God, and not flesh and blood.

"For we wrestle not against flesh and blood, but against principalities, against powers, against the rulers of the darkness of this world, against spiritual wickedness in high places" (Ephesians 6:12).

The Apostle Paul counts four groups of these evil angels that are distinct and diverse from the three-dimensional flesh and blood world we live in now. Not only does he count their fourth-dimensional distinction, but reveals their diverse nature and scope as well.

First, he mentions *principalities*. These devils work to control realms of governmental authority. Some of these principalities are mentioned in the Bible with such titles as "the prince of the kingdom of Persia" (Daniel 10:13), "the prince of Tyrus" (Ezekiel 28:2), and "the king of the bottomless pit" (Revelation 9:11: "9:11" being an interesting number combination). These princes and devils are and have been symbolized in the heraldry, banners, and great seals of the kingdoms of this Earth such as eagles, lions, bears, dragons, serpents, leopards, bulls, bees, scorpions, and goats, all of which are referred to in the Scriptures.

It is the quest of these princes that they turn things "upside down," whereas, in Genesis 1, God gave man dominion (governmental authority) over all the beasts of the Earth. These beast-princes seek to overturn this and make man the subject of their oppression and rule. Phrases such as "new world order," "world government," and even "dominion theology" all have this object as the end of all their means. Instead of man ruling over beasts, these spirit realm beasts will now rule over man.

The second group of these spirits is referred to as *powers*. These devils represent giving mankind the ability to perform outside of the boundaries of the three-dimensional world we live in. These are the evil angels responsible for inspiring the writings of J.R.R. Tolkien (*The Hobbit, The Lord of the Rings*), J.K. Rowling (*Harry Potter* series), and Stephenie Meyer (*Twilight* series).

As fourth-dimensional creatures, they have the power and ability in this world to appear and disappear at will; move objects with no visible force; fly, hover, and float from one location to the next at will; and make considerable changes to the weather patterns of this Earth, such as "the *prince* of the *power* of the air, the spirit that now worketh in the children of disobedience" (Ephesians 2:2, emphasis added). These spirits manifest themselves as ghosts, spirit guides, elementals (spirits based on the **four** elements), fairies, angels, aliens, vampires, and animal familiars.

In the 2009 movie, *The Fourth Kind,* these "aliens" were depicted as taking the "close encounter" scenario a step beyond the third kind, which is alien-human contact. This film featured alien entities abducting, molesting, probing, and terrorizing their human subjects. A consistent vision seen by the abductees was of the aliens as owls. The owl (apart from also being a well recognized bird) is a beast spirit consistently mentioned with and associated with the dragon (Isaiah 13:21; 34:13) and has been associated with such secretive groups as the Bohemian Club, and whose image lies in the landscaping and layout of the U.S. Capitol building.

In ancient times, these *powers* were given to men through magic, rituals, and potions. Now, in the modern age of technology, mankind, with the aid of these fallen spirits, seeks to make aircraft, tanks, and soldiers invisible. It is reported that one such military project called the Philadelphia project sought to make a naval ship disappear from one location and be instantaneously transported to another location hundreds of miles away. The technology for such an experiment was supposed to have been derived from the work of Nicholas Tesla, who admitted being in contact with alien guides who furnished him with ideas and technology beyond man's ability. This is similar to the reports of the Thule Society of Germany, who were reportedly the real governing entity behind Adolph Hitler. It is public knowledge that Hitler had scientists working on a flying-disc-shaped craft, and the design and propulsion systems of these craft were inspired by spirits who were in contact with those in the Thule Society. At the tail end of the war with Germany, the CIA secured many of these scientists to work for the United States military in a project called Operation Paperclip.

It is these same spirits that more than likely have been the inspiration for the weather control, and some say earthquake control, a system referred to as H.A.A.R.P., or "high-frequency active auroral research program," which seeks to control the ionosphere by emitting high frequency waves, such as *sound* waves. It is both curious and relevant to note that the four beasts (angelic creatures) of Ezekiel 1 and Revelation 4 are seen playing *harps* (fourth-dimensional sound waves) in Revelation 5:8.

The third group of evil angels mentioned in Ephesians 6 is referred to as the "rulers of the darkness of this world." These are the "lessor" lights that "rule over the night" in Genesis 1. These are responsible for keeping men in darkness rather than allowing him to see the "greater light that rules over the day," Jesus Christ. They keep mankind in darkness and thus in fear, for man has always been fearful of darkness and of what he could not see. Devilish characters from legend and folklore, such as werewolves, vampires, ghosts, and witches, are all beings who love the darkness rather than the light, similar to the way certain animals (beasts) are nocturnal in their nature. These beasts rule over realms such as rock and roll music (which is sometimes very dark) and horror films (which are almost always filmed in darkness or low light).

They are also the spirits behind secret societies, mystery religions, and pagan and new age practices and beliefs. Those who are involved in these religions are in constant search of light inside a system of beliefs that seeks to further conceal the light of the four Gospels.

The fourth and final group is the spirits both involved with, and instigators of, spiritual wickedness in high places. In Ezekiel 8, God reveals to the prophet the hidden wickedness inside the upper echelon of the rulers of Jerusalem. Their description is almost pyramid-like in structure, as God shows Ezekiel four specific scenes from inside the temple, each scene with a greater abomination than the scene before, and each with a smaller number of people participating. The fourth scene reveals the twenty-five men who have their backs toward the temple, worshiping the sun as it rises in the east.

One need not attend the Bohemian grove ceremony, the Bilderberg meeting, or the inner chambers of the Illuminati themselves to know and understand that the closer you get to the top, the more wickedness would be evident. This would include the top of corporations, political realms, financial institutions, religious denominations (including some "Christian"), and practically every other realm that exists in this world.

It is these four groups of devils, representing the fourth kingdom, that will overflow the world of the end times with their iniquity. They will "come in like a flood" (Isaiah 59:19) and "drown men in destruction and perdition" (1 Timothy 6:9). The New Age movement symbolizes this coming kingdom with the astrological symbol of Aquarius. Aquarius is seen pouring out water onto the Earth, and the symbol for Aquarius is two waves of water, one over the other. This symbol reminds us of how it was in the "days of Noah" (Matthew 24:37). According to Genesis 7:11, the waters that covered the Earth came from two sources: the "windows of heaven" were opened up, and the "fountains of the great deep" were opened up, thus the two waves of water in the symbol of Aquarius. In the book of Revelation, chapters 9 and 12, we see that the invasion of the fourth kingdom has two sources: the great, deep, or "bottomless pit" of Revelation 9 where the scorpion-locust army rises from the depths, and "heaven" in Revelation 12 where the dragon and one-third of the angels (stars) fall to the Earth like rain. The timeframe given in Genesis 7 for this wrath of God being poured out on the Earth is forty days, a multiple of the number four.

The forty-day rise of flood waters has been memorialized in the mystery religions and preserved the Catholic church's observance of the forty days of Lent. It is this forty-day period that the women of Ezekiel chapter 8 were seen "weeping for Tammuz," also known as Apollo, Bacchus, and Osiris, among others. He is the god who was slain, similar to the beast of Revelation 13:3 and Revelation 17:10–11, and will one day rise from the sea to live again.

As in the Days of Noah, the only ones who will be saved during this time will be those who have the "preparation of the gospel" (1 Peter 3:20; Ephesians 6:15). This Gospel is the story of the birth, life, death, and resurrection of Jesus Christ contained in the four gospels, believed on in the heart of man (with four chambers), to give mankind an eternal inheritance in the foursquare city of God, New Jerusalem.

CHAPTER FOURTEEN

ABODE OF THE DEAD

By Terry James

Everyone dies, to this point in history. You are going to die unless certain interventions occur. Those you love are going to die, with the same caveat. Each person who has ever lived has died or will die, with the exception of two people I know of in the past and millions of others in the future.

I personally have died three times. But all of the above constitutes a story we will look at as we uncover layer upon layer of relevant factors while exploring these much-mulled-over things that pertain to the mystery called *death*.

There are many stories about death. Tales of the dead, their location, and their interaction with the living are the stuff of legend. Perhaps the strangest of the stories I've encountered comes from a pastor of a large church and president/chief executive officer of a Christian TV network.

He tells of the death of a dear Christian brother—as he puts it—whose body lay in its casket in a mortuary for viewing. As the story goes, a high-powered, evangelist-type preacher was in town to conduct services for the CEO's church.

They took the evangelist to the place of viewing, and the evangelist stood over the dearly departed for a moment.

The pastor/CEO recounts how the evangelist then said something like: "This dear brother isn't meant to be dead." He grabbed the corpse after lifting the closed half of the coffin lid, dragged the body from its resting place, and sat it up against the wall in the sitting-up position, legs straight out.

The evangelist stood back, glared downward at the embalmed dead man, and declared: "In the name of Jesus, I command you to get up and walk!"

According to the pastor/CEO, the body just slumped over with its stiff shoulder on the carpet.

Again, the evangelist reached down and placed the corpse with its back to the wall. And again, he said: "I command you, in the name of Jesus, to get up and walk!"

The body slumped to the carpet.

Once more, the now-agitated evangelist put the body against the wall and shouted mightily: "In the name of Jesus, I command you to get up and walk!"

This time, the pastor/CEO said—and I've heard him tell the story as absolute truth on two different occasions—the corpse stood to its feet and walked out of the viewing room. Where the corpse walked, or where the now-walking-around dead man is at present, the pastor/TV executive has never said.

I have not heard of anyone in the huge congregation that the man pastors ever question this account, which I heard by watching him tell the story on his TV network.

Neither *Tales from the Crypt* nor any other forum that tells of the macabre can top that one, in my estimation of stories of the dead. The reason it is at the top is that it is told as the truth by a supposed *man of God*.

I'm tempted to say that the pastor was embellishing for the sake of making a point, although I don't remember his point. Who could remember any of a sermon's objectives after hearing such a thing? I'm almost certain, though, the telling involved people having enough faith to bring down the prosperity blessings of God on them. It was a prosperity gospel-type preacher who told the story.

I'm also tempted to say that the pastor remembered the story and just got the details mixed up. But, no. His telling is a lie. It is a false teaching. There's no other way to put it.

Either the preacher is a liar or God is a liar. Jesus, who is God, said: "And as it is appointed unto men once to die, but after this the judgment" (Hebrews 9:27).

If the man had truly been raised from the dead, he would have made medical history and science would be all over the case. If this gentleman—the evangelist in question—could raise the dead (especially a dead person who is embalmed), we would be hearing about it from mainstream news journalists who would be clamoring for interviews with the "miracle worker." Such a man could not remain unknown.

Jesus of Nazareth did just such miracles, and His name is known the world over and from generation to generation. As a matter of fact, His name, the Bible says, is above every name.

The pastor's story does go directly to the fascination mankind has with death. More to the point, man's fascination is with the question of what happens after death. Let's look at some thoughts on this question down through the centuries.

What Happens after Death?

Perhaps it is the most wondered-over question that runs through the human mind. That is, it is likely the most *unspoken* question.

Everyone reading this has at one time or the other—perhaps quite frequently, in some cases—asked either, "What happens after I die?" or, "What happens after people die?" Wondering about where people go after death is most often part of the grieving process upon the death of a family member or a friend.

The abode of the dead and what it might entail is a central theme of every religion that has ever been invented. Let's look at a few of the fascinating fabrications about what comes after death found within some of the religious systems throughout history.

Human beings have always viewed the afterlife in consideration of their own mortality. Thus, religions are born with uniquely tailored life-after-life formulas as key to religious construction. The abode of the dead takes center stage.

Archaeological digs have shown that, beginning with the most primitive cultures (earliest dating), people have left graveside trinkets like stones, flower petals, animal horns, and other items. Arrangements of bones in the graves indicate that corpses have been buried in the fetal position and other positions, facing east or in other directions that show tradition and ritual—all implying religious preparation for the dead as they journey into the afterlife.

Ancient Egypt

Egyptian burial history is the most documentable of the ancient peoples. More than three thousand years of history provide a treasury of details about that nation's cultural evolution in treatment of the dead.

Most important, the archaeology shows, was the perceived need for the individual's preparation for the trip into the abode of the dead. The body had to be furnished with food and other necessities for the journey into forever. This was done on a regular basis throughout Egypt's long history.

Elaborate rituals readied the dead for what came after death:

The final step in the transition to the afterlife was the judgment in the Hall of Maat (the god of justice) by Horus (the god of the sky) and Thoth (scribe of the dead) by comparing ab (the conscience) and a feather. The ritual was known as the Weighing of the Heart. Heavy hearts were swallowed by a creature with a crocodile head who was called the Devourer of Souls. The good people were led to the Happy Fields, where they joined Osiris, god of the underworld. Many spells and rituals were designed to ensure a favorable judgment and were written in the papyrus or linen "Book of the Dead."[231]

Egyptians spent much of their lives getting ready in one way or another for the afterlife. The pharaohs, of course, did the most elaborate prearrangements, with the knowledge that they would be mummified using the most expensive materials and spices available. They built magnificent edifices, in most cases.

All of the ancient Egyptians, regardless of their personal financial status, prepared according to their means for life after their deaths. They expected the afterlife to be just a grander scale of the life they were leaving.

Ancient Greece

Stories have it that Socrates, the most famous of the ancient Greek philosophers, accepted his death calmly while he drank the hemlock. Ancient Greeks as a whole were, however, not so casual when thinking on the abode of the dead. As a matter of fact, they had a fear of death. That fear was justified, considering what they believed followed death.

The Greeks believed that, upon death, a person journeys into a place called *hades*. The God of this, they believed, was also called Hades.

The dead first crossed the river Styx in a boat at the helm of which was a boatman named Charon. A coin for the purpose of paying the boatman was placed with the dead body as part of the rituals involved. Following the boat trip, the guardian of the abode of the dead—a hideous, three-headed dog named Cerberus—had to be appeased with honey cake. The strange adventure led to one's final destiny.

The Underworld offered punishment for the bad and pleasure for the good. On the one hand, the Elysian Fields, a sunny and green paradise, was the home to those who had led a good life. Others were condemned to a torture. Tantalus, for example, was forced to be perpetually hungry and thirsty while next to a fruit tree and lake that he just barely failed to reach. And Sisyphus was forced to roll a rock up a hill, only to have it return to the bottom where he began the task. They provide us with the English words tantalize and Sisyphusian task, both of which describe a frustrating futility. Most were not actually tortured, however. Rather, they went on shadows of their previous selves.[232]

Ancient Rome

For those of Rome of antiquity, life was considered death and the afterlife, true life. One had to serve in this prison called life for a short time. During this time, people were to serve family and nation in an honorable way and do all within their power to improve the world around them.

The body was considered only the outer shell of a person, the soul being the immortal. People, thus, were all gods of a sort, their immortal spirits inhabiting the afterlife as deities. The degree to which they had led lives of piety and embellished existence on Earth determined the quality of life throughout their version of eternity.

The Earth was viewed as the lowest of nine spheres throughout which the moon and stars moved. The spirit moved within those orbs in conjunction with how earthly life had been conducted.

Polynesia

Crossing a river was a common strand of belief among those of New Zealand and others of the Polynesian cultures. The Maoris viewed death as a journey in the hope of being reunited with loved ones who had gone on before.

The dead would be greeted with chanting and wailing to commemorate their arrival within the abode of the dead. The trip after death involved passing by monstrous creatures beneath high cliffs full of fearful sights and sounds.

Although the journey was frightening, these believed the end result was worth it, because all would be restful and pleasurable.

The Aztecs

Like the Polynesian cultures, the Aztecs believed that, upon death, the individual went through a terrifying journey. The body of the dead was thus prepared by ritualistic traditions for that trip into the afterlife.

A priest would chant, give a formal speech, and, along with others, wail over the body while trickling water upon the forehead of the corpse to purify and send the spirit of the person to the next level of passage.

The departed would then go through a series of desolate, foreboding places of ravines and deserts, and would face serpents, lizards, scorpions, and other frightening things, including winds that cut like knives. The soul would arrive at a place called Mictlantecuhtli, where it would spend four years. The person's dog, sacrificed at its owner's death, would join its master and they, together, could travel across the Ninefold River and enter the eternal house of the dead, Chicomemictlan.

Australian Aborigines

Aborigines believed that the body and spirit were linked to the land in ways that could not be broken. When a person dies, they believed, he or she simply makes the transition to oneness with the land. That individual joins the spirits of his or her ancestors.

Death and afterlife are described in the following from the traditional Aborigine belief system.

The "dreamtime" was the world of creation, of the earliest

tribal memories, but also of the continuing abode of all those who could not be immediately seen in the physical world. Some tribes believed that the spirit remained to inhabit the place where the person had died, while others believed that it was carried across the sea to the land of the dead. In some tribes, the spirit was believed to have a chance to be reborn at some future time and live another earthly existence.[233]

Dante's Inferno

Perhaps the most influential treatment of the things of afterlife is found in the fiction of Dante Alighieri. The fourteenth-century Italian writer penned *Inferno* as the first part of his epic poem, *The Divine Comedy. Inferno,* along with parts two and three, *Purgatorio* and *Paradiso,* serve as a foundation for the way much of the world views the afterlife. Hollywood and the entertainment industry in general seem to be caught up in Dante's fascinating views of what comes next.

Readers are taken through many painful, sometimes ecstatic, stages of life after death from the poet's perspective. Virgil, the Roman poet, in spiritual methodology, guides Dante—thus, the reader—through the medieval concept of hell.

That abode of the dead is depicted as nine circles of suffering located within the Earth. The odyssey represents in allegorical form the soul's travel toward God and matters involved in acceptance and rejection of sin.

Dante comes to a gate, above which is inscribed on the ninth and final line: *Lasciate ogne speranza, voi ch'intrate,* or "Abandon all hope, ye who enter here."

Before making the entrance through the gate, he sees the soul of a pope, or of Pontius Pilate—the description is unclear—and the souls of people who have made no commitment to either do good or evil. Souls of outcasts are mixed together around the soul of Pope Celestine V or Pilate and those who haven't committed.

These are spirits (angelic?) who took no side in the rebellion in Lucifer's fall. These are neither in heaven nor in hell, but reside along the shores of the river Acheron. They are pursued throughout eternity by supernatural wasps and hornets. They are thus doomed because of their pursuit of "self interest" before the punishment was given. The insects and other things, like maggots, drink the doomed ones' blood and tears.

Dante, accompanied by Virgil, reaches the ferry that will take the pair across the Acheron and into central parts of hell. The boat captain, Charon, doesn't want to take Dante farther because he is still a living being. Virgil prevails, and the journey becomes unbearable in sights and sounds. Dante faints and doesn't revive until he reaches the other side.

Each circle of hell that Dante penetrates, encountering three beasts along the way, becomes worse in punishment until the center, where Satan is held as the worst of all purveyors of sin.

Each circle's sinners are punished in a fashion fitting their crimes: each sinner is afflicted for all of eternity by the chief sin he committed. People who sinned but prayed for forgiveness before their deaths are found not in hell but in purgatory, where they labor to be free of their sins. Those in hell are people who tried to justify their sins and are unrepentant.

Allegorically, *Inferno* represents the Christian soul seeing sin for what it really is, and the three beasts represent three types of sin: the self-indulgent, the violent, and the malicious. These three types of sin also provide the three main divisions of Dante's hell: upper hell (the first five circles) for the self-indulgent sins; circles 6 and 7 for the violent sins; and circles 8 and 9 for the malicious sins.[234]

The nine circles and the sins which they encompass/govern are specifically listed as follows:

First Circle (Limbo)
Second Circle (Lust)
Third Circle (Gluttony)
Fourth Circle (Greed)
Fifth Circle (Anger)
Sixth Circle (Heresy)
Seventh Circle (Violence)
Eighth Circle (Fraud)
Ninth Circle (Treachery)[235]

Many believe it is Dante who inspired Christian beliefs in the afterlife. It is the Bible, however, that influenced Dante's exploration of the afterlife. With today's emphasis on the supernatural in entertainment, it is understandable that people are confused about is true and what is not. And, it comes down to a matter of faith—but it should be faith founded upon and based in observable facts from historical examination.

Christianity today has a severe short circuit in the continuity of teaching, thus understanding, about death and what comes next. It is not the Bible's error, however, that causes the disconnect, but misunderstandings caused by lack of study about what the Bible says—and, more troubling, deliberate misinterpretation of the Word of God.

Jehovah's Witnesses

Hell doesn't exist, in the view of Jehovah's Witnesses, members of the Watchtower Bible & Tract Society (WTS). Hell is interpreted as the "common grave of mankind." Most people are simply annihilated upon death, according to this view. However, there are a number of JW believers who will spend eternity with God, they teach.

Some are already in the abode of the dead and others will yet be "saved." Armageddon is scheduled to occur soon, then Christ will return, and all who falsely profess and all others will be dealt with by God in judgment.

Believers who are Jehovah's Witnesses and survive Armageddon will live in peace during one thousand years of God's kingdom following the consummation of all wars on Earth.

A person must accept the doctrines formulated by the WTS governing body, be baptized as a Jehovah's Witness, and follow the program of works as laid out by the governing body in order to have salvation.

Mormonism

Mormons (the Church of Jesus Christ of Latter-day Saints) put forth that three heavens, not just one, exist. Couples who have been married in Mormon temples have reserved for them places in the highest celestial realm of abode. Their places are sealed forever, according to Mormon dogma. Such men and women eventually will become gods and goddesses within the system, if all other of the Mormon stipulations for attaining such status are followed. The husbands will become rulers in control of entire universes.

Most members of the church will be a part of the terrestrial kingdom. That realm is the place of abode for "liars, and sorcerers, and adulterers, and whoremongers."

Hell is a real place, Mormonism says, but few will be there forever. Most will eventually make it to the terrestrial kingdom. All others will be assigned the place within the terrestrial kingdom reserved for the sons of perdition—the people who were once devout Mormons but became apostates, leaving the church. This place will also be for those who have committed the most serious sins and not received forgiveness before death. They will be in the same realm as Satan and his angelic horde that fell from heaven.

Seventh-day Adventists

These believe in hell as a literal abode. However, they believe it is not forever. All who go there will eventually be annihilated. They take the Bible's statement that there will be burning in hell forever as meaning that there will be burning…as long as there is something to burn. All, they believe, will be reduced to ashes in the annihilation process.

Hinduism

All Hindus hope to ultimately escape the time-after-time cycle of rebirth into this world. Salvation is, to them, an end to the constant process of birth, death, and rebirth.

Such a destiny can mean eternal rest for the individual in the arms of a loving, personal deity, but for most it's the loss of individual personality and being entrapped within the incomprehensible abyss of Brahman.

Salvation from this fate is attempted in four ways, according to Hindu belief.

- Jnana yoga, the way of knowledge, employs philosophy and the mind to comprehend the unreal nature of the universe.
- Bhakti yoga, the way of devotion or love, reaches salvation through ecstatic worship of a divine being.
- Karma yoga, the way of action, strives toward salvation by performing works without regard for personal gain.
- Raja yoga, "the royal road," makes use of meditative yoga techniques.

The majority of Hindus believe they face many incarnations before they can achieve salvation. Some sects believe, however, that a gracious divinity will move them more quickly along the reincarnation process.

Buddhism

Buddhism proposes that self and ignorance of truth about existence, not sin, constitute the road block to salvation. Only by eliminating these things can the world be made right.

Selfish cravings, this religious system holds, causes suffering, and only ridding one's self of this self-centeredness will soothe the spirit. The way to cease the cravings, thus attain escape from continual rebirth, is by following Buddhist practice, known as the Noble Eightfold Path.

To blow out this flame of self-centeredness is to reach nirvana, the spiritual condition that the monks of this religion constantly seek to reach through a series of meditative practices.

The abode of the dead was located, as Buddhism has it, to the West, in China, on the other side of Mount T'ai.

Judaism

This religious system holds that moral behavior and attitudes determine one's eternal existence in life after death.

There is no saving grace, as in Christianity, but there is the opportunity for repentance for even the most evil of people through the individual's positive action. The notion of Christian-type redemption for individuals, however, doesn't exist, in that there is no clear heaven to attain presented in Judaism.

Those who practice this religion still hope for a Messiah who, they believe, will judge and hand out rewards. But, the system holds that this future of judgments and rewards is more communal than individual.

The abode of the dead in Judaism is unclear, the premise being that earthly existence is more important to dwell upon than afterlife. God is to be left to determine that realm.

Hollywood's Preference

I never ceased being amazed at the Hollywood filmmakers when it comes to making movies about the supernatural—particularly about death and the abode of the dead. Almost without exception, films of the major box office sort, when they have at their core the supernatural that involves religion, death, and dying, use the Catholic Church in presenting their fiction. This has been the way of movie-making in the modern era.

This wasn't always the case.

The vampire movies of Bela Lugosi's time had a cross at the center of their presentations. Count Dracula would take one look at the shining metallic cross and throw his cape-covered arm over his eyes, hiss viciously, turn quickly, and leave. But, the action by Count Dracula's chief nemesis, Dr. Van Helsing, wasn't necessarily the action of a Catholic priest in my memory, although I'm certain the Catholic Church had an influence in the screenwriters' thinking.

The more modern version of Dracula and his nefarious doings almost all included a priest with chains and crucifixes hanging from his backward-collared neck.

My mind leaps next to the great Orson Welles' film, *War of the Worlds*. The Catholic priest wanted to approach the Martians to make peace with them, as I recall. He got zapped, of course, so I guess the Catholic Church, in that instant, didn't fare so well.

Thinking ahead to *The Omen,* episodes one, two, and three, the Catholic Church was at the center of trying to deal with the up-and-coming Damien and the threat he presented from the Catholic perspective of Bible prophecy.

In *The Exorcist,* the filmmakers called upon the Catholic Church to remove the demons. There wasn't a Baptist, Methodist, Presbyterian, or Assemblies of God minister anywhere around. Same with movies like *Salem's Lot* and a dozen other Hollywood offerings that come to mind. The Catholic version is always the version of death, dying, and the afterlife that is preferred for use in movie-making.

The question is: Why not the Protestant version of how things play out following the cessation of the heart's beating? It is perhaps best to consider the Roman Catholic belief system to search for answers. What is that religion's premise regarding death, the abode of the dead, et al.?

Catholicism teaches that everyone who dies with unrepented-of sins goes to hell, at least for a time. Hell is a real place of punishment, and if sins aren't confessed to an authorized priest of the Church, one's immortal soul is in danger. In hell, the lost soul is separated forever from God in a place of eternal torment. There, a supernatural fire burns and an immortal body is in pain forever.

Sincere repentance of sin by confessing to an authorized priest brings absolution. Usually, some symbolic things are required to satisfy the completion for absolution, such as special prayers and repetitive incantations.

But the Catholic Church belief system about dying and the abode of the dead gets much more complicated.

Souls of those who have died in the state of grace must suffer for a time, the Church dogma says. A purging that prepares the soul to enter heaven is necessary. Purgatory is the abode of the dead until the dead is fully cleansed of imperfections, venial (less serious) sins, etc. The holding place called Purgatory will be terminated at the time the general judgment take place. The punishment's intensity and duration can be lessened by the dead one's friends and family, if these offer Masses, prayers, "and other acts of piety and devotion."[236]

Babies who die without being baptized enter heaven after staying in limbo for a duration of time.

The Answer?

Perhaps the answer to why the Catholic Church is the religion of choice to fight the vampires and all other evils is that this is proposed as a *Christian* religious faith—thus is a part of the most prominent religion in America. Catholicism is also the religion that offers the best way to put a human mediator—a holy man, a priest-buffer, between God and man, thus between good and evil.

The other Christian faiths—most—say that Jesus Christ alone is the mediator between God and man (see 1 Timothy 2:5). Hollywood must put a human face on the screen to deal with things involving the abode of the dead. Jesus Christ—who is, He Himself proclaimed, the Son of Man—isn't human enough for their purposes, it seems.

Yet, it is Jesus who died on the cross so that human beings could be saved from sin, thus reconciled with God the Father. He went into the abode of the dead and led those who were redeemed into heaven, the Bible tells.

Final Thoughts

At the beginning of this chapter, I wrote: "Everyone dies, to this point in history. You are going to die unless certain interventions occur. Those you love are going to die, with the same caveat. Each person who has ever lived has died, or will die, with the exception of two people I know of in the past and millions of others in the future. I, personally, have died three times."

I want to explain, as promised.

Death, Up Close and Personal

When I read nonfiction work by writers such as those featured in this book, I like to know the writer's credentials. I like to know from what authority he speaks. This is important, because whether by study, by experience, or by both, one who delivers his or her thoughts on a given topic should have credibility in order for the thoughts to really matter.

Respectfully, and humbly, I am satisfied that I have such credence in presenting you with this chapter on dying and the abode of the dead. First of all, I have studied the subject in one form or the other for many years. Over forty, actually. But, it is the experience more than the study that made me really want to write for this volume. Hoping that this won't be taken like I take the story of the embalmed corpse being made to get up from the floor and walk, here goes.

I had just finished my workout on Good Friday, 2011. It was about 1:30 PM. I had done the warm-up, the weights, the push-ups, and the sits-ups in the Body by Jake crunches machine. Next, I proceeded to the aerobic phase of my exercise program, which I have followed carefully three or four days per week for thirty-two years.

I did the rowing machine with the heavy weights for simultaneous upper and lower body work. This I did for twenty minutes or so. On this day, I felt pretty well exercised for the sixty-eight year old I am as of this writing, so I decided to skip the treadmill and go to the recumbent bike. This would be my cool-down, after which the workout would be complete.

Almost at the moment I stopped pedaling, a burning pressure began behind my sternum. I thought it was indigestion, and told myself that it would go away in a minute or two.

It didn't.

I walked around, stretched, and tried to make the increasing burning and pressure go away. It persisted and grew exponentially worse. I was beginning to have a clammy sweat and difficulty breathing. I told my wife she had better call 911 for help.

Now, if you knew me as Margaret does, that very order would astound you. That is the last thing I would ever do for myself. She was sufficiently impressed that I meant what I said, and called.

The ambulance—with its faithful companion, the fire truck—arrived in about ten minutes. The medics began feeling my neck and wrists, and one of them said, "I can't find a pulse." Another said, "Let's get him out."

That meant to the ambulance.

They asked if I could walk to the gurney, which I did. I felt every bump in the road; ambulances of this variety aren't made for the patient's comfort, just for quick transport to the ER.

We stopped, and I felt the guys tugging at the gurney after they got the back of the vehicle opened. The chest pain was now excruciating. I heard a *blip* sound, like a computer making the transition from one application to another.

I was instantly standing before a large group of young, beautiful people. They glowed, not with some ghostly glow, but with that of the vibrant, perfect health of the young. They were smiling broadly, their hands motioning and arms raising and gesturing for me, I could tell.

I was in a place of perfection…of joy…and I had no thought of where I had just come from, or any thought of anything, except that this was reality like I had never known. I wanted to stay forever.

But then things got dark and nightmarish, and I was feeling my bare chest with my fingertips.

Oh, yeah. I was on my way to the hospital—or was this just a bad dream and I would soon be back to those young people and all of that joy and peace?

No. I remembered then: This was a heart attack, or something; I didn't know what, at this point.

"I hit him with the paddles!" a man was shouting.

"Paddles?" I said to him. (They said I came back talking.)

"Your heart stopped," was his comment.

The pain again grew in my chest, and once more I heard the *blip*.

Again I stood in front of that joyous throng of those in their mid-twenties, or so they appeared. I wanted to join them. The warmth, the love, was incredible…and peaceful.

But I felt the darkness tugging me, and I was again on the gurney, or table, or whatever. The activity over and around me was frantic. My clothes were stripped from me, things were being attached to me, and someone was getting prepared to do something in the right groin area.

"What are you doing?" I naturally asked, strangely calm, clinical with my question.

"No details…"

The man's voice was foreign. I later learned he was from India—and was one of the top cardiologist interventionists in our state.

The pain grew again, and then the *blip* sounded. I was among the young people. I could feel them on either side. It was like we were running; all of us were laughing and thoroughly enjoying the experience. Some of them were looking over at me with their bright laughter as we ran. There was no thought of where I had been before I was again in their presence.

This time, I faded from being among them. I was again on the procedure table, having been hit for the third time with the defibrillator to start my heart, which had stopped beating those three times (I was told later).

They had finished with me, and I felt no pain, only hands all over me, doing things to wires and tubes attached to me.

"Now, details…" the doctor said to me. He put his hand on my shoulder from behind. In his accented voice, he begin explaining the angiogram of my heart. He had placed the pictures above me so I could see them.

Only I couldn't.

"I can't see them," I said. "I'm blind. I've been blind since 1993 due to a retinal disease."

"Oh?" he said. "What disease?"

"Retinitis pigmentosa."

"Ah, yes," he said.

He put his index finger upon my chest, and traced as he talked. "You had what we call 'the widow maker.' It is the left coronary artery—descending,'" I thought he said. "Fifty percent of the people who have this kind of blockage of this artery never make it to the emergency room. Of those who do make it, most don't live."

I was impressed. "I'm still here," I said—to get his assurance, not to boast.

"You are still here," he confirmed, patting me on the shoulder.

Over the intervening weeks since the "widow maker," I've given much thought to my trip to the abode of the dead. It is really the abode of those who are truly alive, I believe the Lord has shown me. This present, flesh-and-blood life is the shadow through which we see darkly, the Scripture tells us. For me, this is absolutely fact.

My meeting with that group of otherworld young people has been the cause of much cogitation, I assure. My thinking was, for a couple of weeks, that they wanted me to join them, but that the Lord had overruled and I was sent back, although I kept trying to join them, as the hospital records will attest.

I sense in the deepest part of my spirit now, however, that these beautiful young people were part of the group the writer of Hebrews told us about:

> Wherefore seeing we also are compassed about with so great a cloud of witnesses, let us lay aside every weight, and the sin which doth so easily beset us, and let us run with patience the race that is set before us, Looking unto Jesus the author and finisher of our faith; who for the joy that was set before him endured the cross, despising the shame, and is set down at the right hand of the throne of God. (Hebrews 12:1–2)

They were a "heavenly cheering section," I believe the Lord has shown me. They were letting me know that I and others who put forth truth in this strange, hostile-to-the-gospel hour, are not alone. They are running the race with us.

This was a vision from the other side, I have no doubt. I'm very skeptical about ecstatic experiences, I must tell you. I believe they are too often used to embellish. They are lies, for the most part.

But, I can't deny what I know I saw and experienced. The Lord is my witness.

I believe the encouragement I received from those three death experiences (and I realize I wasn't truly dead, or else I wouldn't be writing this) was given particularly because I and others write and speak on prophecy given by God's Holy Word, the Bible. Prophecy is 27 percent of the Bible, and I believe the Lord wants me to let those who hold fast to the whole Word of God—including the many prophetic teachings—have the Lord's approval in a profound way.

Pastors, teachers, who name the name of Jesus—listen up: Providing prophetic truth to the people you shepherd and teach in this closing time of the Church Age (Age of Grace) is all-important to Almighty God. We must tell them that Christ's coming is very near. To neglect doing this is to neglect what He has put you here to do.

Those Who Won't Die

I wrote that all will die with the exception of two I know of, and millions of others yet future. Who are these?

The two who have not died, according to the Bible, are Enoch and Elijah. There is some question about Ezekiel. These were taken by the Lord while still living.

The millions who will never taste of the abode of the dead are those who could any moment hear Christ's shout, "Come up hither!" (Revelation 4:1–2). These are those who have accepted Christ as Savior and will be transformed from mortal to immortal in one stunning microsecond. They will accompany their Lord, Jesus Christ, back to God the Father's house—heaven—where He has been preparing unimaginably beautiful dwelling places, and where those raptured will live dynamic life for eternity (John 14:1–3).

Those who have died during this dispensation (the Age of Grace) will, like the living believers, be changed into glorified bodies at the same stupendous moment in time. Then will be said, regarding the abode of the dead:

> So when this corruptible shall have put on incorruption, and this mortal shall have put on immortality,

then shall be brought to pass the saying that is written, Death is swallowed up in victory. O death, where is thy sting? O grave, where is thy victory? The sting of death is sin; and the strength of sin is the law. But thanks be to God, which giveth us the victory through our Lord Jesus Christ. Therefore, my beloved brethren, be ye stedfast, unmovable, always abounding in the work of the Lord, for asmuch as ye know that your labour is not in vain in the Lord. (1 Corinthians 15:54–58)

CHAPTER FIFTEEN

WHAT ABOUT GHOSTS?

By Gary Bates

Are People Really Communicating with the Spirits of the Dead?

Besides the claims that humans are interacting with extraterrestrials, there are many otherworldly episodes that people claim they undergo. The seeming reality of the experience often has a transforming effect, even to the extent that the experience itself becomes a new kind of worldview filter. For example, if an interdimensional (as in, it looks as if it suddenly emerged out of nowhere) entity suddenly appears at the foot of someone's bed in the middle of the night and claims that it is from the Pleiades cluster, then on most occasions the person will believe that its claims are true. The belief in the experience often changes their views about the big picture issues of life, such as "Where did we come from?" and "Where are we going when we die?" So, because of the experience, they are also given over to the larger claims of the entity that may include tales that the alien benefactors were originally humankind's creators; that they have been overseeing our evolution for millennia; and that in the end they will redeem and restore the human species and the Earth to some kind of utopian paradise. In short, most experiencers undergo a kind of religious transformation or "awakening," and many researchers believe that this is the actual purpose of the deceptive entities. World-renowned UFOlogist Vallée wrote: "I propose the hypothesis that there is a control system for human consciousness... I am suggesting that what takes place through close encounters with UFOs is control of human beliefs, control of the relationship between our consciousness and physical reality, that this control has been in force throughout history and that it is of secondary importance that it should now assume the form of sightings of space visitors."[237]

And apologists John Ankerberg and John Weldon added: "These researchers believe that the UFO entities are deliberately programming the human observers with false information in order to hide their true nature and purpose."[238]

While the experience itself may be real, it does not automatically follow that the claims the entities are making about their origin and purpose are truthful. Noted abduction researcher Donna Higbee wrote:

> I noticed a drastic change...in the attitudes of several of the abductees from one meeting to the next. People who had been traumatized all their lives by ongoing abductions and had only anger and mistrust for their non-human abductors suddenly started saying they had been told/ shown that everything that has happened to them was for their own good, that the abductors are highly spiritual beings and are helping them (the abductee) to evolve spiritually. By accepting this information, the abductees

stopped fighting abduction and instead became passive and controlled. When I checked with other researchers, I found that this was a pattern that was repeating itself over and over again around the country. I became concerned that abductees were accepting these explanations from entities that we know can be deceitful, use screen memories to mask real memories, use virtual reality scenarios to implant images into abductees' heads, and manipulate and abuse. I wrote an article for the MUFON UFO Journal (September 1995) and encouraged abductees to seriously think about what they were accepting as their truth, in light of the evidence, not the explanations offered them by these non-human entities.[239]

So, we can determine that the entities are liars and con artists, but, nonetheless, it is the power of the experience that still shapes people's views about what is happening to them or what they have experienced in the first place. For many, it is their only source or filter to interpret what is happening to them.

Ankerberg and Weldon commented: "How credible is it to think that literally thousands of extraterrestrials would fly millions or billions of light years simply to teach New Age philosophy, deny Christianity, and support the occult... Why would they consistently lie about things which we know are true, and why would they purposefully deceive their contacts?"[240]

So, as Christians, we believe these physics-defying experiences are interdimensional, that is, emanating from the spiritual realm and are indeed centered on redefining our traditional beliefs and man's place in the universe. As corporeal human beings we cannot travel to these dimensions to test these claims. But, we believe that one very famous visitor from that realm can act as a source of truth for determining them. That is, the Lord Jesus Christ. When awaiting judgment before Pontius Pilate He said: "My kingdom is not of this world…my kingdom not from hence" (John 18:36). The NIV states: "My kingdom is not of this world….my kingdom is from another place."

The Bible says this same Jesus is the Creator of the universe (Colossians 1), and the exact human representation of God (Hebrews 1:3). As God is the Creator, He created the laws of physics that govern our universe. He is omniscient and therefore the source of all truth. Therefore, we can trust His revealed Word to us (the Bible) as being authoritative and can use it as a filter for determining the truth of the alleged alien encounters. One of the biggest mistakes I believe that many Christian researchers make is to also accept the reality, and in particular the physical aspects, of the alien encounters and then try to fit them into the Bible somewhere (see my other chapter in this book for more on this). This often leads to unbiblical or extra-biblical ideas. This is a dangerous game, as it is exactly what masquerading and deceptive angels would have us do. I do not believe that it is wise to go beyond what God's Word tells us about such things. In short, we can't "fit" the seeming reality of these experiences into Scripture; we should use Scripture to explain the experience. When we do, we can peel away many more layers of the deception that might not be otherwise apparent from the surface.

Ghosts and Aliens – Common Parallels

There are many other strange experiences that people undergo, such as claimed visitations by ghosts. The term "ghosts" being used here specifically refers to the cases in which these entities claim to be the disembodied spirits of the dead—even the departed loved ones of the experiencer.

Belief in ghosts, and a fascination with the supernatural and the occult in general, is mainstream in popular culture today. In the same way that the majority of the population believes in extraterrestrials,[241] similarly large numbers of people believe in ghosts. And there are a myriad of movies and TV shows perpetrating and embellishing these ideas. One should always remember that these programs are fictional. Just imagine if every week we watched a "Ghost Hunters" type show—that is, where investigators enter allegedly haunted houses, and after their investigations they simply came to the conclusion, "No, there are no ghosts," or "No aliens." The shows would have a pretty short lifespan and nobody would watch them. Controversy and conspiracy are big marketing gimmicks, and in my own research into the UFO phenomenon, I've found that truth is always the first casualty. It is also problematic that most people today read less and tend to get their news or information (let's call them "facts") from the popular media. In the modern audiovisual age, mass frauds and hoaxes have been perpetrated upon populations, often because we think that people would not go to all the trouble of grand deceptions if there were no truth in their claims. For example, if researchers who call themselves "ghost hunters" were to enter a house and discover orbs of light, sudden drops in temperature, and witness the alleged apparition of a disembodied spirit, then, in essence, they believe that they have found what they are looking for—they expected it. This is reminiscent of 2 Thessalonians 2:9–11: "Even him, whose coming is after the working of Satan with all power and signs and lying wonders, And with all deceivableness of unrighteousness in them that perish; because they received not the love of the truth, that they might be saved. And for this cause God shall send them strong delusion, that they should believe a lie."

In other words, God will allow Satan to give you what you ask for. Most certainly the appearances of alleged ghosts, UFOs, and the appearance of aliens in people's rooms etc., *have* at times created physical disruptions in our corporeal realm. I say "alleged" because there are actually no such things as ghosts (please read on for more clarification on this). A Bible-first approach will demonstrate to us that the idea of the disembodied spirits of deceased human beings roaming the Earth would contravene some very basic principles of God's Word and cast serious doubt on the Gospel itself.

When people claim that ghosts have appeared, on some occasions there have been power fluctuations or outages and, of course, things can move or be shifted and there have been manifestations of beings in a variety of forms. In the same way that so-called aliens seem to defy the laws of physics, noted supernatural and UFO researcher, John Keel, said:

> Demonology is not just another crackpot-ology. It is the ancient and scholarly study of the monsters and demons who have seemingly coexisted with man throughout history. Thousands of books have been written on the subject, many of them authored by educated clergymen, scientists, and scholars, and uncounted numbers of well-documented demonic events are readily available to every researcher. The manifestations and occurrences described in this imposing literature are similar, if not entirely identical, to the UFO phenomenon itself. Victims of demonomania (possession) suffer the very same medical and emotional symptoms as the UFO contactees...

The devil and his demons can, according to the literature, manifest themselves in almost any form and can physically imitate anything from angels to horrifying monsters with glowing eyes. Strange objects and entities materialize and dematerialize in these stories, just as the UFOs and their splendid occupants appear and disappear, walk through walls, and perform other supernatural feats.[242]

There is equipment that can detect, for example, power surges or fluctuations, and cameras that record images etc., so I suppose in some cases it might be possible to claim that such equipment has been able to test or even demonstrate such things. Of course, the detection of a power field or surge in a room would be interpreted by those wanting it to be ghosts as exactly that. I noted comments from other Christian researchers in my book, *Alien Intrusion: UFOs and the Evolution Connection*: "It seems evident that these [including UFO] phenomena are produced in the same manner that other occult manipulations are produced. They involve dramatic manipulations of matter and energy. Although they originate from the spiritual world, they can produce very powerful, temporarily physical manifestations at the material level..."[243]

Although such occurrences are deceptive entities (fallen angels) manifesting from the spiritual realm, some might be surprised at their ability to manifest *physically* in our realm. This, once again, is due to a cultural idea about angels as being merely some sort of ethereal spirit (non-bodied) being and sometimes with fairy-type wings. The Bible indicates that angels are "ministering spirits" (Hebrews 1:14). In addition, Jesus was described as a "life-giving" or "quickening spirit" (1 Corinthians 15:45), and God is described as a spirit, as is the Holy Spirit. The Bible also says that human beings *have* a spirit. So the spirit is not the *sum* of who we are, but a *part* of our being. It may well be the same for angels. The Bible records about angels that:

- They are spirits (Hebrews 1:14), yet they always appeared to humans as physical men/males when doing God's bidding (Genesis 19:1; Luke 24:4).
- They number in the hundreds of millions or perhaps more (Hebrews 12:22; Revelations 5:11).
- They were given names such as Gabriel, Michael, and even Lucifer (Luke 1:19; Jude 9; Isaiah 14:12).
- There are various types and categories of angels mentioned, e.g., cherubim (Genesis 3:24; Ezekiel 10:1–20), seraphim (Isaiah 6:2, 6) and watchers (Daniel 4:17, KJV). They also appear to differ in rank and dignity, some being described as archangels, princes, or rulers (1 Thessalonians 4:16; Jude 1; Daniel 10:20–21, 12:1; Ephesians 6:12).
- They are/were called holy and elect (Luke 9:26; 1 Timothy 5:21).
- They are more powerful than mankind (2 Thessalonians 1:7; 2 Peter 2:11).
- They can appear among, and interact with, humans, even killing them on occasion (Genesis 16:9, 19:15; 1 Chronicles 21:15; Psalms 78:49; John 20:12). In Exodus 12:23 God's destroying angel killed all the firstborn in Egypt (except for those of the Hebrew families who followed God's instructions for protection), and in 2 Kings 19:35, an angel sent by God killed one hundred eighty-five thousand soldiers in one evening.
- They can appear physically, and so real to humans that

we do not recognize them as angels (Genesis 18:1–16; Hebrews 13:2).

- They are not to be worshiped (Romans 1:25, NKJV; Colossians 2:18; Revelations 19:10).

The last point is very pertinent. For many UFOlogists, ghost hunters, spiritualists, witches, crystal-ball-gazers and New Age practitioners, such phenomena have become the basis of substitute religions. They are indeed bowing down to angels. Many of the descriptions of these angelic beings conform to the "spiritual, yet physical" characteristics attributed to UFOs, aliens, and other occult manifestations. It enables us to understand why, when masquerading as such, that angelic beings are able to perform such incredible physics-defying feats as John Keel noted earlier.

Does the Bible Confirm Ghosts?

Given my comment earlier that ghosts are not real, many will no doubt claim that the Bible actually supports the idea of ghosts and even that the Lord Jesus confirmed their reality when He made a comment about the same. In different translations of the Bible, the words "ghost" and "spirit" are used extensively and seemingly interchangeably. This is where confusion reigns for the reader. We find that in the King James Version, and particularly in the New Testament, the word "ghost" is used extensively ("Holy Ghost," for example, or "give up the ghost"), whereas the more modern translations have simply used the latter term "spirit." For example, the "Holy Ghost" is now rendered in modern translations as "Holy Spirit." In this case, the change is useful because the word "ghost" certainly has changed its meaning over time.

Culturally, it now has a modern connotation as the wandering spirit of a dead person. It is this concept that I reject. In most modern Bible translations, the word "ghost" is only mentioned three times, which helps avoid further confusion. One of the problems is that words can change their meaning over time. For example, in Genesis 1:28 in the KJV, God commanded Adam and Eve to "replenish" the Earth. In 1612, this word meant to "fill." Nowadays it means to "refill." In the same way, when modern translations refer to "ghosts," the KJV often uses "spirits," so we need to look at the original Greek or Hebrew behind the English words to see which word better translates the original concept.

There is one example in the Old Testament where modern translations used the word "ghost." The KJV says this: "And thou shalt be brought down, and shalt speak out of the ground, and thy speech shall be low out of the dust, and thy voice shall be, as of one that hath a familiar spirit, out of the ground, and thy speech shall whisper out of the dust" (Isaiah 29:4); the ESV translation states: "And you will be brought low; from the earth you shall speak, and from the dust your speech will be bowed down; your voice shall come from the ground like the voice of a ghost, and from the dust your speech shall whisper." Compare these with the NIV which says: "Your voice will come ghostlike from the earth; out of the dust your speech will whisper."

The term in the KJV, "one who has a familiar spirit," is the Hebrew word *ôb*. The word has a wide semantic range that could be used in various applications, and thus could have potentially different meanings. In this case it could mean a necromancer, wizard, spiritist, or soothsayer. These are people who profess to call up the dead. *But ôb* can also mean ghost as the raised up spirit of a dead person (hence the more modern translations' use of the word "ghost"). However, it does not automatically follow that just because a concept is mentioned in Scripture, it is teaching that ghosts actually exist. For example, worship of other gods is forbidden, but it doesn't follow that there actually are other gods. We know that practices of spiritism are forbidden by Scripture (read on in this chapter to see why).

This is clearly an analogy and it seems to give an indication that the destruction of Jerusalem will linger in memory—almost as if, from the ashes of history (ghostlike), what happened to the great city shall be remembered and shall cry out for all time, which it has.

It is in the New Testament where we find the words *ghosts* and *spirits* between translations being used interchangeably and more often. There are two Greek words that are used. The first is *phantasma* (which literally means "apparition" like the commonly understood word "ghost"). The word *pneuma* means spirit, air or breath. This can refer to what I described before as the essence of a being. It can also mean "demons" when added with the word *akatharton*.

The most remembered New Testament passage regarding ghosts is Matthew 14:26. Whereas the KJV says: "And when the disciples saw him walking on the sea, they were troubled, saying, It is a spirit [*phantasma*]; and they cried out for fear," the ESV says, "But when the disciples saw him walking on the sea, they were terrified, and said, 'It is a ghost!' and they cried out in fear."

And Mark 6:49: "But when they saw him walking upon the sea, they supposed it had been a spirit [*phantasma*], and cried out" (KJV). "But when they saw him walking on the sea they thought it was a ghost, and cried out" (ESV).

On another occasion when Jesus suddenly appeared in the room with the disciples, they said: "But they were terrified and affrighted, and supposed that they had seen a spirit [Greek *pneuma*]" (Luke 24:37, KJV).

These first passages are referring to the occasion when Jesus was seen walking on the surface of the Sea of Galilee, and the Luke account is when the resurrected Jesus appeared to the disciples in the room. Obviously the disciples had never seen a man do anything like this before, so their first thought was to invoke the supernatural, resorting to fanciful ideas to explain it away. In the Luke account, they had seen Jesus die on the cross not too long before, so they thought they were seeing His spirit (a somewhat understandable reaction since He suddenly appeared in a locked room).

It should be remembered that the idea that the disembodied spirits of the dead roam the Earth is not new. Occult manifestations have been recorded since the earliest times, and the Bible often records occult practices being undertaken by an unfaithful nation of Israel (and Judah). Manifestations have often appeared in the guise of deceased persons and even dead relatives. It is a very powerful counterfeit, because it tugs on the emotional relationship and heartstrings of the person seeing the manifestation. As I mentioned earlier, the power of the deceptive experience (whether "alien" or "ghost") can change lives. It has the potential to alter a person's worldview, framework, and/or their perception of reality. So, in ancient times the idea of ghosts was a culturally popular one, and even more so today where people have become desensitized to the occult, due to its portrayal in the media as harmless dalliances with psychic phenomena.

In the locked room in Luke 24:38–39 Jesus said: "Why are ye troubled? and why do thoughts arise in your hearts? Behold my hands and feet, that it is I myself: handle me, and see; for a spirit [*pneuma*] hath not flesh and bones, as ye see me have."

Notice that Jesus did not affirm that ghosts were real (in the sense of being the spirits of departed people—as opposed to spiritual or angelic/demonic beings)—He asked them to touch Him to prove the point. However, He did not chide the disciples for believing in the popular idea of ghosts. They simply underestimated who He was and His power and they resorted to cultural beliefs, because of the astonishment of what was going on. For example, I wonder what ideas we would come up with if we saw a "man" (because at this stage they did not recognize Jesus as God) walking on water or suddenly appearing in a locked room.

In fact, these are instances of the disciples failing to recognize Jesus' divinity. Job 9:8 teaches that only God can tread on the waves, and after Jesus had just completed the feeding of the five thousand, which would have recalled God's supernatural provision manna for the Hebrews, they should have seen the significance of this miracle. Even though the Gospels seem to indicate that the disciples believed in ghosts, Jesus' followers are not being presented as models for belief or obedience at that stage in any case. In fact, they continually miss the point.

In the Luke portrayal, the word "spirit" is used. Jesus was using this term to contrast the fact that He was, in fact, physical as opposed to ethereal. This is where it can become very confusing for many, because now "ghost" and "spirit" seem interchangeable. The Matthew and Mark accounts use the Greek Word *phantasma*, which literally means "appearance" or "apparition." The Luke account uses the word *pneuma*, which is correctly translated as "spirit." So, although Matthew and Mark use *phantasma*, it has similar, overlapping meaning. Remember that although "spirit" can refer to that part of a human which cannot be tangibly seen, it can also be applied to non-humans. As angels are spirits, the disciples could have been similarly afraid, thinking it was an angelic being, fallen or otherwise.

God Has Control of Our Departed Spirits

But, once again, none of this means that our spirits will roam the Earth once they have departed our bodies. It is of fundamental importance to remember that God is the *only* One who has the final say about where we go when we die and it will only be to certain specified locations. In the Old Testament, hell was known as *Sheol*, and in the New Testament, *Hades*. Although there has been conjecture for many years as to what, where, and whether it had compartments or not, both terms were unmistakably referring to it as a place of departed spirits. It was clearly a holding place. But, since the first advent of Christ and His atoning work on the Cross, the Bible is clear that non-believers will now go to hell and believers to heaven (in the presence of the Lord). There is no room in traditional, evangelical theology for our departed spirits to be roaming the Earth. As shown earlier, though, there are multitudes of rebellious spirits (or angels) who are doing that, deceiving many in the process.

This biblical teaching is very important, because many Christians believe they have seen ghosts and the spirits of departed loved ones.

The Witch of Endor

No doubt many will refer to the case of King Saul visiting a spiritist known as the Witch of Endor (1 Samuel 28:3–25). Saul had banned mediums and sorcerers from the land. But ironically, because he had strayed from God, and was paranoid about seeing the young David in God's favor, he was given over to his own evil devices and seeking help from the very practitioners he had banned (see 2 Thessalonians 2). This led to him seeking out the "spirits of the dead"—something God strictly forbade His people to do knowing the power of the deception involved and how they could be led astray by such things. See, for example, Deuteronomy 18:10–12, and note Leviticus 19:31 which says: "Regard not them that have familiar spirits, neither seek after wizards, to be defiled by them: I am the LORD your God." The ESV puts it this way: "Do not turn to mediums or seek out spiritists, for you will be defiled by them. I am the LORD your God."

Saul instructs the witch to call up the spirit of one of God's greatest prophets—Samuel, and a plain understanding of the text indicates that this indeed happens. If God has the ultimate power over our spirits, how can the witch call up a departed spirit? I believe this may have been allowed via a sovereign act of God as a mechanism of punishing and pronouncing judgment on a rebellious Saul. In short, he was getting was he asked for—(equivalently) "You want Samuel to tell you the future? Ok, you've got it, but it's not going to be nice." When one reads the passage, it is noteworthy that the witch herself was taken by surprise when she saw that is was actually Samuel. In verse 12, she said: "And when the woman saw Samuel, she cried with a loud voice: and the woman spake to Saul, saying, 'Why hast thou deceived me? for thou *art* Saul'" (KJV). The prophet Samuel then pronounces judgment on Saul in 1 Samuel 28:17–19: "And the LORD hath done to him, as he spake by me: for the LORD hath rent the kingdom out of thine hand, and given it to thy neighbour, *even* to David: Because thou obeyedst not the voice of the LORD, nor executedst his fierce wrath upon Amalek, therefore hath the LORD done this thing unto thee this day. Moreover the LORD will also deliver Israel with thee into the hand of the Philistines: and to morrow *shalt* thou and thy sons *be* with me: the LORD also shall deliver the host of Israel into the hand of the Philistines" (KJV).

In modern English, it would be rendered as follows:

"The LORD has done to you as he spoke by me, for the LORD has torn the kingdom out of your hand and given it to your neighbor, David. Because you did not obey the voice of the LORD and did not carry out his fierce wrath against Amalek, therefore the LORD has done this thing to you this day. Moreover, the LORD will give Israel also with you into the hand of the Philistines, and tomorrow you and your sons shall be with me. The LORD will give the army of Israel also into the hand of the Philistines." (ESV)

Many have said this may have been a demon in disguise, but for one thing, there is no biblical or other evidence that demons can foretell the future (although they often claim to be prophets via a variety of deceptive guises) and the prophecy about Samuel came to pass. Moreover, Samuel berates Saul for disobeying God in this way. Seeking after the dead is something that deceptive spirits would encourage, not admonish, and indeed, the next day, Saul's army was routed and Saul committed suicide.

The story reflects the reality of falling from grace, and being out of God's favor, by following one's own desires instead of being obedient. Samuel did not give advice but pronounced the penalty for Saul's disobedience, and in part, for partaking in forbidden rituals. It is not something that affirms a biblical idea of ghosts.

The Danger!

All occult phenomena cause one to be almost enslaved, that is, given over to the powerful illusory nature of the experience. Persons often feel that they are privileged or special to have undergone the experience, and thus, it draws them in deeper and deeper. But when people seek after the experiential, many are not aware how their very senses can be deceived. I repeat again: it is unwise for Christians to invoke some kind of extra-biblical revelation to accommodate ghosts into Scripture. I've even had pastors on occasions write to me to explain that they have been ministering to wandering, lost spirits. This is unbiblical, and once again, a case of accepting the experiences at face value and then using them to interpret our understanding of Scripture. It is reminiscent of the warning that Jesus Christ gave us in Matthew 24:24–25, when He said: "For there shall arise false Christs, and false prophets, and shall shew great signs and wonders; insomuch that, if it were possible, they shall deceive the very elect. Behold, I have told you before" (KJV).

Supernatural encounters, whether it be UFO sightings, alien abductions, or ghostly apparitions, fall into the category of the miraculous, because they seem to act in opposition to our known physical laws. It is this "power" that reinforces the deception. Of course, non-Christians are the most vulnerable because they do not have the benefit of the lens of Scripture to discern such things, and Scripture itself indicates why they are vulnerable: "But the natural man receiveth not the things of the Spirit of God: for they are foolishness unto him: neither can he know them, because they are spiritually discerned" (1 Corinthians 2:14, KJV).

CHAPTER SIXTEEN

BE NOT DECEIVED

How to be Protected from Deception

By John P. McTernan

For there shall arise false Christs, and false prophets, and shall show great signs and wonders; insomuch that, if it were possible, they shall deceive the very elect.

MATTHEW 24:24

DECEIVE: "to take unawares especially by craft or trickery; to cause to believe the false."[244]

The other contributing chapters in this book have addressed some very real and specific areas of deceit that surround us and our youth every single day. With vampires romancing our women and girls, "ghost hunters" promoting the communication with the dead, and liars, murderers, witches, false prophets, and other dark role models driving an ever-present, evil, and invisible nail in the coffins of biblical doubt for so many, one could easily begin to feel defeated and overwhelmed. Yet, the weapon against such things is not as hidden or hard-to-find as many tend to think. A deep, sincere, and dedicated faith in the Lord Jesus Christ is one key to marching against these powerful foes with confidence. The other key is knowledge. Know your enemy, and know what weapons and combat tactics your enemy will bring to the battleground.

One of the enemy's hallmarks of the current era is deception. This deception can be found in every area of life. It is found in economics, science, history, and politics while the most serious is religion. The easiest deception to see right now is found in the world economy (just to help paint an understandable picture at the start of this chapter). The economy of the world was based upon ever-increasing debt. The economic experts would say, "do not worry about the debt," but now the laws of economics can be clearly seen. The tremendous debt burden is destroying people, businesses, institutions, states, and even countries.

The deception has been exposed and the economy is now under the truth! The people who knew the laws of economics and were not swayed by the current deceptive economic policies could protect themselves from economic ruin, as they operated under the truth of economic laws. They could stay out of debt and invest their funds in a way that it would not be destroyed. They could see the economic meltdown coming and prepare for it. The people who operated under the deception could not see the meltdown coming and were caught in its destruction.

This same principal regarding deception holds true in the spiritual realm. Those that are anchored in truth cannot be spiritually deceived, but those that do not operate in the truth are wide open for deception. They can be fooled spiritually in a similar way to those that were deceived economically. The huge difference is that spiritual deception can result in spiritual death and separation from God for eternity.

The Bible issues great warnings about deception and reveals how one can be protected from it, showing that deception emanates from the spiritual realm and then manifests in the natural realm. The source of deception is evil and does not come from God. All truth comes from God, while deception comes directly from Satan and his fallen angels.

Just prior to the death of Jesus Christ, He warned the disciples of His death and His Second Coming. The disciples wanted to know the signs of His Second Coming and asked the Lord Jesus what would be sign of His coming and the end of the world.

Jesus Christ actually listed many signs of His coming including wars, famines, earthquakes, pestilence, and religious apostasy. The first sign was a warning of religious deception. The deception would center on Him; and there would be many false prophets, messiahs, and teachers. Jesus Christ is the Savior of mankind, so this deception would take people away from Him as Savior and on to someone or something else.

Matthew 24:4–5: "And Jesus answered and said unto them, Take heed that no man deceive you. For many shall come in my name, saying, I am Christ; and shall deceive many."

The Lord Jesus expands upon the magnitude of this deception, and He emphasizes that the deception is going to involve supernatural signs and wonders and, also, the effect was so great that if it were possible it would deceive those that were following Jesus Christ.

Matthew 24:24: "For there shall arise false Christs, and false prophets, and shall show great signs and wonders; insomuch that, if it were possible, they shall deceive the very elect."

The Authority of the Bible

The Bible is the standard used to determine if someone, or if a sign or wonder, is from God. The questions that immediately come to mind are, "How does one know the Bible can be trusted as the word of God?" "What is the proof showing the Bible is the final authority of what is really from God and what is a deception?"

The greatest proof is Bible prophecy, and how this prophecy is playing out right now in the world. There are three major, prophetic themes in the Bible, and these are: (1) the first coming of Jesus Christ, (2) His second coming, and (3) the nation of Israel. The combination of these three themes alone show that the Bible is unique and could only come from God.

There are dozens of prophecies in the Old Testament about the first coming of Jesus Christ. They were all fulfilled at His first coming. These prophecies included the time of His coming, His ministry, the reason for His death, and great details about the way He died on the cross. The following are just two segments of scriptures from many to show how Jesus Christ fulfilled prophecy as His first coming. The fulfillment is found in the New Testament.

The description of Jesus Christ's death on the cross and related events:

Psalm 22:13: "They gaped upon me with their mouths, as a ravening and a roaring lion."

Psalm 22:15–18: "My strength is dried up like a potsherd; and my tongue cleaveth to my jaws; and thou hast brought me into the dust of death. For dogs have compassed me: the assembly of the wicked have enclosed me: they pierced my hands and my feet. I may tell all my bones: they look and stare upon me. They part my garments among them, and cast lots upon my vesture."

The reason for the necessity for the death of Jesus Christ on the cross follows. He died as a substitute for man's sin:

Isaiah 53:5–6: "But he was wounded for our transgressions, he was bruised for our iniquities: the chastisement of our peace was upon him; and with his stripes we are healed. All we like sheep have gone astray; we have turned every one to his own way; and the LORD hath laid on him the iniquity of us all."

Isaiah 53:8: "He was taken from prison and from judgment: and who shall declare his generation? for he was cut off out of the land of the living: for the transgression of my people was he stricken."

The Second Coming of Jesus Christ is actually tied with the prophecies about Israel. The reason for this is He is returning to Jerusalem with Israel restored as a nation. There are many verses in the Bible relating to the dispersion of the Jews from Israel into the entire world. The reason for the dispersion was that the Jewish people totally failed to obey God's Word, and one punishment for this was to be driven from the land and dispersed into the world.

The prophecies do not end with the dispersion, but continue with a restoration back to the land. This restoration occurs because God made an everlasting covenant four thousand years ago with Abraham, and then reinforced it with his son Isaac, his grandson Jacob, and their descendants. This eternal covenant becomes the basis by which God would one day bring the Jewish people back into the land.

The authority of the Bible then is directly tied to God's covenant with the Jewish people over the land of Israel.

Genesis 17:7–8: "And I will establish my covenant between me and thee and thy seed after thee in their generations for an everlasting covenant, to be a God unto thee, and to thy seed after thee. And I will give unto thee, and to thy seed after thee, the land wherein thou art a stranger, all the land of Canaan, for an everlasting possession; and I will be their God."

Jesus Christ issued a prophetic warning about Jerusalem just prior to His death. He said that the city was going to be destroyed and the Jewish people dispersed into all nations. He then added that Jerusalem would not be under Jewish control for a specific time. At the end of this time, He would return to Jerusalem to defend the Jewish people.

Luke 21:24: "And they shall fall by the edge of the sword, and shall be led away captive into all nations: and Jerusalem shall be trodden down of the Gentiles, until the times of the Gentiles be fulfilled."

In May of 1948, Israel once again became a nation, while in June of 1987, all of Jerusalem came under Jewish control. Jerusalem is not completely under Jewish control as the Palestinians, United States, United Nations and most of the nations want the city divided. There is much fighting yet to come over Jerusalem until it is free from foreign influence. It will only be free at the Second Coming of Jesus Christ.

There is no other nation like Israel. It is totally unique among all nations. It is easy to just look at Israel as just any other nation and Jerusalem as any city, but they are unique. The Jewish people and Israel were twice destroyed over a period of twenty-six hundred years.

The Babylonians first destroyed Jerusalem twenty-six hundred years ago. They killed most of the Jews and took a remnant captive to Babylon. The nation was destroyed along with its kings and temple-worship was stopped. As prophesied by Jeremiah the prophet, the Jews returned seventy years later and then rebuilt the nation, Jerusalem, and the temple. At this point, Israel came under the authority of Gentile (or non-Jewish) kings, and the kingdom was taken away from Israel. This began the "times of the Gentiles" over Jerusalem that Jesus Christ prophesied would end.

About six hundred years later, starting in 70 AD, the Romans destroyed the nation of Israel, Jerusalem, and the temple for a second time. A huge number of people were killed or dispersed throughout the Roman Empire. Israel became a wasteland under the control of various empires until 1948. Just as the Bible prophets predicted, Israel was once more a Jewish nation. (Once again, there is no other nation like Israel, which was twice destroyed over twenty-six hundred years with its capital and religious center also destroyed and then came back into existence.)

Today the Israelis even speak Hebrew which had been a dead language, and they use shekels for money! Israel is once again a nation because of the supernatural covenant made by the Holy God of Israel with Abraham, Isaac, Jacob, and the Jewish people. God's prophetic plan is now in high speed, and the rebirth of Israel would take place just prior to the Second Coming of Jesus Christ. Christ will return to Jerusalem to save the Jewish people from total destruction at the Battle of Armageddon:

Zechariah 14:2–4: "For I will gather all nations against Jerusalem to battle; and the city shall be taken, and the houses rifled... Then shall the LORD go forth, and fight against those nations, as when he fought in the day of battle. And his feet shall stand in that day upon the mount of Olives, which is before Jerusalem on the east..."

With the authority of the Bible as the Word of God revealed through prophecy, it is time to establish what the Bible standard to test for deception is. The standard rests upon the person of Jesus Christ, and His ministry to redeem mankind.

The Bible's Standard Testing Deception

1 John 4:1: "Beloved, believe not every spirit, but try the spirits whether they are of God: because many false prophets are gone out into the world."

The Bible gives the standard for protection against deception. The protection is centered on the person of Jesus Christ, and His death on the cross to redeem mankind to God. Having faith in the real Jesus Christ is the foundation of truth. People who preach on spiritual matters are to be tested concerning their belief in Jesus Christ along with the content of their teaching. If either the person, or their teaching, fails the test, they are to be rejected no matter how persuasive they are or how "right" they seem. This person is teaching spiritual deception and not truth.

The Bible states in 1 John 4:1 that people should be tested, but it continues in the next verses to describe the test:

1 John 4:2–3: "Hereby know ye the Spirit of God: Every spirit that confesseth that Jesus Christ is come in the flesh is of God: And every spirit that confesseth not that Jesus Christ is come in the flesh is not of God: and this is that spirit of antichrist, whereof ye have heard that it should come; and even now already is it in the world."

If a person confesses that the real Jesus Christ is come in the flesh, then this person is true and not a deceiver. The key is the identification of real Jesus Christ. The Apostle John, just a few verses later, identifies the true Jesus Christ. He is unique among mankind as He is the only begotten Son of God. He came from God the Father and was born from a virgin; therefore, He did not have the human sin nature.

1 John 4:9: "In this was manifested the love of God toward

us, because that God sent his only begotten Son into the world, that we might live through him."

Because He came from God, the Bible reveals that He is God. God was manifested in the flesh through the person of Jesus Christ. This is the very foundation of truth and the gold standard to test everything spiritually by. The Creator of the universe became one of mankind. Jesus Christ was both God and man.

1 Timothy 3:16: "And without controversy great is the mystery of godliness: God was manifest in the flesh, justified in the Spirit, seen of angels, preached unto the Gentiles, believed on in the world, received up into glory."

With the foundation of the person of Jesus Christ, it is very important to understand His ministry. Man was separated from God because of sin while the penalty for this rebellion was spiritual death. This meant separation from God in a place of eternal punishment called *hell*. The death and shed blood of Jesus Christ paid the penalty for sin and reconciled sinful man with God. The only way for man to obtain eternal life is through faith in the person and death of Jesus Christ.

1 Peter 3:18: "For Christ also hath once suffered for sins, the just for the unjust, that he might bring us to God, being put to death in the flesh, but quickened by the Spirit."

The foundation of truth to test everything spiritually for signs of deception is the person and ministry of Jesus Christ. When applying the test, does the person or spiritual manifestation believe that Jesus Christ came in the flesh as the only begotten Son of God? Does the religious doctrine being taught promote that the death and shed blood of Jesus Christ is the only way for redemption and eternal life?

No matter what spiritual power is being manifested, if the

preacher or teacher denies the person and ministry of Jesus Christ, they are operating under a deception and deceiving those who follow them.

With All Deceivableness of Unrighteousness

BIBLICAL GREEK WORD DECEIVE: "To cause to roam from safety, truth, or virtue" (Strong's Concordance 4105).

BIBLICAL HEBREW WORD DECEIVE: "To lead astray, i.e. (mentally) to delude, or (morally) to seduce" (Strong's Concordance # 5377).

The Bible warns that as the Second Coming of the Lord Jesus draws near, tremendous spiritual forces are going to be unleashed which will deceive multitudes of people. There are going to be manifestations of spiritual power which the Bible calls *lying signs and wonders*. These manifestations are real and not just an illusion.

There is real power from the spiritual realm, but the question becomes, "What is the source of this power?" The Bible is very clear that certain spiritual manifestations are from Satan and are meant to draw people away from Jesus Christ and His ministry to redeem mankind. These are lying signs and wonders with the specific purpose of deception. There are powerful spiritual manifestations based on what the Bible calls "all deceivable of unrighteousness." This means there is great power behind these manifestations that are going to overwhelm people who are not grounded in the truth of Jesus Christ. They are going to be over-whelmed and swept away into following deception because they *do not love truth* and were not anchored in it!

2 Thessalonians 2:9–10: "Even him, whose coming is after the working of Satan with all power and signs and lying won-ders, And with all deceivableness of unrighteousness in them that perish; because they received not the love of the truth, that they might be saved."

Because these people do not love truth and reject the true Jesus Christ, God is going to allow the strong delusion of this evil spiritual power to overwhelm them which will result in believ-ing this deception. There is a fierce, spiritual war taking place between truth and deception. Those that love and follow truth will be protected: however, those who reject the true Jesus Christ will be sealed into lies by deception. Because they rejected truth, they will believe lies, even to their eternal damnation.

There is a tremendous price to pay for rejecting the truth about the person of Jesus Christ. Such deception is ready and waiting for these people to their eternal doom. Remember, the closer to the Second Coming of Jesus Christ, the greater the deception with lying signs and wonders will be.

2 Thessalonians 2:11–12: "And for this cause God shall send them strong delusion, that they should believe a lie: That they all might be damned who believed not the truth, but had pleasure in unrighteousness."

In addition to the manifestations of lying signs and wonders, there are also teachers and ministers that preach lies and decep-tion. The Bible also warns of false leaders who preach against the truth of the Lord Jesus and His ministry. They are called deceitful workers who appear to be from God, but the power behind these false apostles is once again Satan.

These false teachers might be highly intelligent with advanced degrees and very persuasive words, but what they preach is deception leading people away from the true Jesus Christ and salvation through Him. They are called Satan's ministers.

2 Corinthians 11:13–14: "For such are false apostles, deceitful workers, transforming themselves into the apostles of Christ. And no marvel; for Satan himself is transformed into an angel of light. Therefore it is no great thing if his ministers also be transformed as the ministers of righteousness; whose end shall be according to their works."

The people who are not grounded in the truth of Jesus Christ can be easy prey for the false apostles of Satan. These people are either ignorant or have rejected the truth and now can be overwhelmed by the persuasive power of these deceitful preachers from Satan. The way for someone to identify a deceitful minister is to know the truth about Jesus Christ.

When listening to a minister: is he leading a person to the true Jesus Christ and eternal life through Him, or his he preaching a different gospel and leading people away from the real Jesus Christ?

Spiritual truth is the tool to identify deceit. It takes knowing the truth to identify the counterfeit. No counterfeiter would produce a fifteen-dollar bill, because in reality it does not exist. They will counterfeit a dollar amount and bill design that reflects the real bill; not something imaginary. Investigators are trained in what real money looks like and how to indentify the counterfeit. By knowing the real thing, one can spot the counterfeit. It is the same in the spiritual realm. Those that know the real Jesus Christ and understand His ministry can spot the counterfeit. To those that are ignorant of truth, they can easily be deceived. The great danger of spiritual deception is that it ultimately leads to eternal damnation and separation from Jesus Christ.

The Bible warns of deceivers, and it is up to everyone to be armed with the truth to defend against them. The Bible also warns that the deceivers will become worse as the Second Coming draws near. They will be extremely cunning with many false teachings. Only those that know the truth can identify these evil men.

2 Timothy 3:13: "But evil men and seducers shall wax worse and worse, deceiving, and being deceived."

Ephesians 4:14: "That we henceforth be no more children, tossed to and fro, and carried about with every wind of doctrine, by the sleight of men, and cunning craftiness, whereby they lie in wait to deceive."

A Special Warning about Deception

Revelation 19:20: "And the beast was taken, and with him the false prophet that wrought miracles before him, with which he **deceived** them that had received the mark of the beast..."

The Bible warns that immediately prior to the Second Coming of the Lord Jesus Christ, a world government will arise, which will use a universal numbering system to control all commerce. This system would center on the number "666."

In understanding Bible prophecy, it is extremely important to keep in mind that this system would arise when Israel was once more a nation. The Book of Revelation shows that this system will be enacted just prior to the Second Coming of Jesus Christ while both the Old and New Testament prophets show the Lord Jesus is returning after the nation of Israel is once again restored.

353

Israel *is* again a nation, and technology has now advanced to the level that a worldwide electronic system is nearly complete. Through the use of computers, electronic funds, a cashless society, and instant satellite communications with many other forms of technology, the world is very close to a cashless, electronically numbered system. It appears that with the advanced technology of today, the 666 system described in the Bible may have a far wider application. It has the possibility of being a complete surveillance system on the population. With the awesome technology available today, controlling all commerce may be just the tip of the iceberg!

The fact that these two prophetic events are coinciding are a warning sign from the Scriptures of the imminent danger that mankind faces. The Bible warns that the *666 Surveillance System* would be implemented through deceit to ensnare all those that reject the truth of Jesus Christ.

When this system is implemented, it is going to be promoted as wonderful and part of a religious system. It will be promoted as a way to control crime and provide a service to all people. It will probably be advanced as a way of fairness so everyone can function. The heart of this system will be an identification number involving 666 being placed on the body in the right hand or forehead.

Revelation 13:16–18: "And he causeth all, both small and great, rich and poor, free and bond, to receive a mark in their right hand, or in their foreheads: And that no man might buy or sell, save he that had the mark…and his number is Six hundred threescore and six."

Through the deception that will be present at the time, people are going to take this mark with the number 666; it is going to appear as a wonderful thing to do. There will be great preaching about taking this mark. Religious leaders will be promoting it, but is all part of a religious system that ultimately leads people away from Jesus Christ and eternal life, and it is all part of a spiritual deception the scale of which the world has never seen before.

This religious system involves the worshipping of a man identified by the Bible as the Antichrist or Beast. This entire system is based on deception. It will be promoted through lying signs and wonders along with vast numbers of Satan's apostles speaking with powerfully convincing lies. All the advanced technology in communications will be used to promote this religious system, and taking this "666 mark" will be the initiation into this system, which totally rejects Jesus Christ and locks the individual into eternal damnation. Once a person joins this system by accepting the mark, there is no way out.

Revelation 14:9–10 "If any man worship the beast and his image, and receive his mark in his forehead, or in his hand, The same shall drink of the wine of the wrath of God…and he shall be tormented with fire and brimstone in the presence of the holy angels, and in the presence of the Lamb."

Through prophecy, the Bible tells us where this tremendous technological explosion is heading. It is going to be part of the greatest deception ever. All of the technology that we know now and that we will know then will be used as a vehicle to advance this deception.

The Bible is the standard for determining truth, and with the truth as a tool, it can be used to uncover many variations of the deception the enemy will subtly and gradually introduce into our daily lives. The truth is a useless tool unless one knows the truth and utilizes it as the instrument God has provided for us. It is up to each individual person to know the truth. Each person is responsible before God to be anchored in the truth.

Conclusion

John 14:6: "Jesus saith unto him, I am the way, the truth, and the life: no man cometh unto the Father, but by me."

The way to be anchored in truth is to obey the Bible and commit ones life to the true Jesus Christ as Lord and Savior. This means recognizing that He is the only begotten Son of God who died on the cross and shed His blood to pay the price for sin. This is the very anchor to truth and eternal life with God. Jesus Christ is the only foundation for truth. Once a person is anchored in the foundational truth, then by studying the Bible one can begin understand more of the truth revealed in it. This causes a person to grow in God's grace, peace and love.

The spiritual realm is not neutral. There is not an option to reject the truth. A person is either growing in the truth or becoming hardened into a deception. If a person rejects the truth, the Bible is clear that God will send a strong delusion to enter this person's life, who will then believe a lie; the end result is believing in a lie and having to live eternally separated from the truth, which is the Lord Jesus Christ.

Despite all the lies in this world, God still provides us with the truth. No matter how powerful the deception is with lying signs and wonders and Satan's apostles, the truth of the Bible exposes this deception. The only people who can be deceived are those that reject the truth that comes from God. Now is the time to obey the truth and rest in the Lord Jesus Christ and His redemption.

John 18:37: "Pilate therefore said unto him, Art thou a king then? Jesus answered, Thou sayest that I am a king. To this end was I born, and for this cause came I into the world, that I should bear witness unto the truth. Every one that is of the truth heareth my voice."

CHAPTER SEVENTEEN

DEMONS UNLIMITED

By Noah W. Hutchings

I feel somewhat inadequate to contribute to this book on ghost busters since, as far as I can remember, I have never seen or met a ghost to bust. After moving into a house we had purchased from a former owner in 1988, my wife and I did hear (or thought we heard) noises, as if someone was rambling around in the attic. However, these could have been made by rats, squirrels, or birds. I can also remember my parents and grandparents talking about ghosts, but I never saw one.

In the King James Version of the Bible, the word "ghost" is used in relating to a person passing away ("giving up the ghost"), as in Genesis 25:8 and some fifteen other verses of Scripture. In various areas throughout the Bible, we do find such expressions as "spirit," "unclean spirit," "evil spirit," and "devils." "Demon" is translated into one of the preceding words in some nineteen Scriptures, and as Paul stated in Ephesians 6:11, we are to "Put on the whole armour of God, that ye may be able to stand against the wiles of the devil."

In *The Handbook for Spiritual Warfare* by Ed Murphy (published by Nelson and almost six hundred and fifty pages), the subject of demonic possession and the influence of evil spirits or demons in the lives of Christians and non-Christians is examined exhaustively by the author. According to Dr. Murphy, some individuals can be completely possessed by demons, and Jesus cast seven evil spirits out of Mary Magdalene (Mark 16:9).[245] We read in John 10:21 that even Jesus was accused of having a demon (devil), and in John 10:20, He was accused of having both a demon and of being mentally ill.

In the past (and often even today), mental illness has been (and is being) confused with demon possession. There are three main types of mental illness: schizophrenia, bipolar, and paranoia. Mental illness is an inherited mental condition. My first wife, with whom I spent twenty-seven years, was schizophrenic. I have spent many hours in hospitals' mental-treatment wards and mental clinics. Because of my personal experiences, I have more sympathy for those suffering mental illness than I do for those suffering from physical causes. Those who are mentally ill often suffer far more than those with physical needs. Clinical depression is also said to be a mental illness, but I do not classify it as such because it is self-imposed due to a seemingly-irreconcilable personal problem or need. When the depressed individual learns how to reconcile his/her problem, he/she usually recovers within two years (facing potential suicidal tendencies if they don't recover within that approximate time frame).

Our minds are the most mysterious creations of God that could ever possibly be imagined. Recently, I watched a television program presenting the big bands of 1940 performing the songs that were popular in the pew-WWII era. As the music started playing, I could recall lyrics that I had not heard for seventy years. At eighty-eight years of age, I can *still* recall and play out scenes in my head from the first year I went to school. Our minds can be touched or influenced by things that are good and things that are evil. It is impossible for me to conceive the evil that some do, except that they may be influenced by an outside source or spirit.

Since 1960, we have conducted a secondary prison ministry that operates out of the base of our main ministry, Southwest Radio Ministries. Each year, we produce a prophecy calendar for prisoners, for which I have always written the subject theme. It is not unusual to send four thousand calendars to one prison. In addition, we provide Bibles, commentaries, books, DVDs, and other materials. We also have a secretary whose only job responsibility within the ministry is to answer prisoners' letters. We have communicated with thousands of prisoners, some who have been convicted of crimes so terrible we would not want to describe them in print, even anonymously. The signature line of recent TV comedian, Flip Wilson, was, "The devil made me do it." Men and women kill, rob, steal, cheat, rape, and abuse others out of passion, need, jealousy, boredom, or at times, just because the "devil told them to do it." However, God ordained human government with the responsibility of protectins the innocent and prosecuting the guilty. Men and women are in prison for the same reason that Adam and Eve ate the forbidden fruit—listening to the devil rather than believing God.

In passing a lake on a calm morning, the ripples indicate to us the thousands of life forms in the water. We know the wind is blowing by the bending of the limbs on the tress. It is known there are thousands of millions of microscopic life forms, both helpful and harmful in just one drop of water. It is likewise with the spirit world. Many Christians do not take the warning of Paul seriously that we are under attack daily by unseen powers which he described as the "wiles of the devil."

On page 433 of *The Handbook for Spiritual Warfare*, Dr. Ed Murphy lists the four areas of satanic demonization:

1. Illicit sexual practices or fantasies out-of-control.
2. Deep-seated anger, bitterness, hatred, rage and rebellion, often leading to destructive and/or self-destructive impulses.
3. A sense of rejection, guilt, poor self-esteem, unworthiness, and shame.
4. Strange attraction to the occult and to the spirit world, often, but not always, with a desire for illicit power over circumstances and other people.[246]

Through our prison ministry, the majorities of inmates we hear from have either come from Christian homes already, or have considered repenting of their sins and turning to God for help after they entered prison. In the late 1970s or early 1980s, we heard from one prisoner, Charles "Tex" Watson, through the prison ministry of Chaplain Ray Hokstra. Charles came from a Christian home, but dropped out of college, moved to California, and became associated with a psychopath by the name of Charles Manson.[247] Manson gathered several males and females around him whom he called "the family." On August 9, 1969, Manson sent several members of his "family" under the leadership of Tex Watson to rob and kill. The heinous murders committed by the group in the homes of Sharon Tate and the

LaBiancas were the most terrible and inhuman in the police records. For his part in these unspeakable crimes, Watson was sentenced to the gas chamber, along with Charles Manson. California later abolished the death penalty, so both were sentenced to life imprisonment.

In the mid-1970s, Tex Watson, according to reports, repented of his sins and believed on Jesus Christ as the One who died for his sins. It is difficult to imagine how anyone could carry such a guilt and burden of sins that must have been on the conscience of Watson. When King David was burdened with the guilt of his affair with Bathsheba and then sending her husband into the heat of battle to get killed to cover his sin, he cried out to God (in Psalm 51:7–12): "Purge me with hyssop, and I shall be clean: wash me, and I shall be whiter than snow. Make me to hear joy and gladness; that the bones which thou hast broken may rejoice. Hide thy face from my sins, and blot out all mine iniquities. Create in me a clean heart, O God; and renew a right spirit within me. Cast me not away from thy presence; and take not thy holy spirit from me. Restore unto me the joy of thy salvation; and uphold me with thy free spirit."

Watson later married Kristin Svege in prison and she bore him four children before divorcing him in 2003. Chaplain Ray wrote Watson's biography titled, *Will You Die For Me?* I became somewhat interested and involved in a parole effort for Tex Watson through Chaplain Ray as I remember. However, my efforts were minimal as I could not understand how anyone who had committed the crimes as unspeakable as Watson could ever be paroled. Tex has applied thirteen times for a parole and his next attempt is due in December 2011. We do praise God that Tex, like many other criminals, have discovered:

What can wash away my sins?
Nothing but the blood of Jesus;
What can make me whole again?
Nothing but the blood of Jesus.[248]

As of the writing of this chapter, Charles Manson is still alive and in prison.[249] He did make news again on the fortieth anniversary of his sentencing. An email online article dated April 18, 2011 noted that Manson was concerned about so-called global warming.[250] We would think that Manson would be more concerned about how hot hell is going to be.

The only letters that are directed to me at Southwest Radio Church Ministries are those that need special attention or answers. Some of the letters I receive are from those who indicate that they may be suffering from a mental illness, as I have a personal concern and can often help them or direct them to a doctor or mental health facility. This may have been one reason that the letters from one David Berkowitz made their way to my desk. I do not remember exactly how many letters from David I received, but there were several. I likewise cannot recall if some of his letters might have been before his arrest in late 1977 or not.

David was the adopted son of Nathan and Pearl Berkowitz.[251] He was evidently, according to biographical reports, well-loved, yet he felt resentful toward being an adopted child. He was large for his age and a loner in his teens, which could indicate a hidden mental condition. Those suffering from paranoia or schizophrenia are usually loners. I do remember that one of David's letters was in response to an article I wrote titled, "The Blood of Babylon." I believe it was this letter that I was answering, when one of the secretaries told me this was the man who was arrested for all those murders in New York.

A few days later, I got a call from the District Attorney of Queens wanting the letters that David Berkowitz had written to me. I informed the DA that these were personal and private letters and I had no intention of turning them over to him. The next morning, a police officer was at our office with a subpoena. We either did not have time to make copies or didn't think about it. If we had thought to make copies, I would have more information on which to address this part of the chapter.

According to details reported on the crimes of David Berkowitz, while he lived next door to a man by the name of Sam Carr whose barking dog kept him awake at night, David shot the dog, but still other dogs would keep him awake. In his own mind, he would think the dogs were demons commanding him to go out and kill women. He also became convinced that Sam Carr was a demon. When he was arrested, he gave his name to the police as the "Son of Sam."

From July 29, 1976 to July 31, 1977, David Berkowitz killed or wounded fifteen (mostly young) people. Berkowitz later admitted to an FBI investigator, Robert Ressler, that he made up the "Son of Sam" story to make the police (and courts) think that he was insane. Regardless, whether this was a case of demon possession or mental illness, they both could be related.

I never heard what part David's letters to me may have played at his trial, if any. I do know that he later informed me that he had received Jesus Christ as his Lord and Savior, and his sins have been forgiven. I understand that he is a chaplain's assistant and a model prisoner. From his letters to me, I am confident that he has found both peace of mind and peace of soul through faith in Jesus Christ.

For my pardon, this I see,
Nothing but the blood of Jesus.[252]

Below is a copy of a letter I received (in full, with typos and misspellings intact) from David dated June 16, 2004:

> David Berkowitz # 78A1976
> Sullivan Correctional FAcility
> [ADDRESS REMOVED]

Noah W. Hutchings
Southwest Radio Church
[ADDRESS REMOVED]

June 16, 2004

Dear Brother Hutchings:

Greetings in the name of our Lord and Savior Jesus Christ. I have your letter dated June 7th. Thank you very much for the calendar and the book, "A CHristian's Guide to Prison Survival." I passed the calendar on to a friend who was very grateful.

It was a nice suprise to hear from you.

Praise God, I have been doing well. The Lord has been faithful to guide and protect me. I am so grateful for his love, mercy and forgiveness.

Presently I have been incarcerated for almost 27 years. The Lord is using me inside of this place and He is teaching me to be content whatever my circumstances.

We have a blessed Christian fellowship and my Chaplain is "born again." He loves the Lord.

Thank you so much for praying for me. I ask the Lord to Continue to bless Southwest Radio Church. It will not be until you get to heaven that you will know all those who were helped by your ministry.

Keep the faith!

Yours in Christ,
David Berkowitz

Galatians 6:9

The third example of demonic possession or attack is referenced by Ed. Murphy on page 439 of his book on spiritual warfare: "Sexual Abuse…Extreme shame and sexual problems. Fear and anger also occur."[253] Also in this category, Dr. Murphy mentions fanatical obsession, and we would also include intense and unreasonable jealousy.

In the late '70s or early '80s, I remember receiving a letter from a young man who wanted me to get him a date with movie star Jodie Foster. This young man was John Hinckley. This letter was sent to me for an answer probably because it appeared to be a rather urgent request and Jodie Foster was, at that time, still young and no more than twenty-one years old. Even at that young age, she had already starred in several movies and won several national acting awards.

The writer said that he was from Ardmore, Oklahoma, and I had probably either mentioned in print of on the radio that I went to school at Ardmore. I was born at Hugo, Oklahoma, but in 1939, war in Europe was spreading and the demand for airplanes and other war materials were increasing. I went to a vocational-technical school to learn how to make airplanes. To this day, when I pass through Ardmore on Interstate 35, the building where I went to school is still there, but it's included in a larger complex. (Gene Autry's ranch was just to the north of Ardmore and on Saturday afternoon, he would park his convertible on Main Street and give a free concert for the locals.)

I can remember very clearly what I told John Hinckley in my response letter. I informed him that Jodie Foster was one of the most famous women in the world and a millionaire. Also, even at that time, it was well-known that she did not like men as personal friends, possibly because she was cast as a child prostitute when she was fourteen years old, and it changed the way men looked at her.[254]

I told this young writer that God had a beautiful and wonderful mate waiting for him and all that he had to do was find her. I suggested that he might find her in a local church even, and suggested that he look for her there. As far as I know, I never heard from the writer again.

Hinckley, from information in Wikipedia, became obsessed with Jodie Foster after repeatedly watching her performance in the movie *Taxi Driver*, wherein she played a child prostitute.[255] His parents were extremely wealthy business owners and he was able to enter Yale where Foster was enrolled just to be near her. According to reports, he also constantly called her and slipped love letters under her door, but she was not interested in him, and probably no other man.

Jodie left Yale to get away from him, yet Hinckley continued to pursue. He planned to kill President Carter to get her attention and interest, but he was never in the right position to do so. (This plan was modeled after the character Travis Bickle in *Taxi Driver*, played by Robert De Niro, who had schemes of assassinating a presidential candidate. Other of Hinckley's previous plans to impress Foster included committing suicide in front of her by crashing an airplane to become her "equal" by securing a name in history.) When he was arrested on a firearms charge in Nashville Tennessee while in pursuit of President Carter, Hinckley returned home for a brief period, and then came up with the plan to assassinate newly-elected President Ronald Reagan in 1981. He wrote the following letter to Foster just prior to his attempt on Reagan's life: "Over the past seven months I've left you dozens of poems, letters and love messages in the faint hope that you could develop an interest in me. Although we talked on the phone a couple of times I never had the nerve to simply approach you and introduce myself...the reason I'm going ahead with this attempt now is because I cannot wait any longer to impress you."[256]

At 1:30 in the afternoon on March 30, 1981, John Hinckley, Jr. fired six shots from a .22 caliber pistol into the men assisting President Reagan to his limousine. Three of the president's assistants were wounded and President Reagan, himself, was also seriously wounded.

On March 30, 1981, I was returning from China on a 747 jet airliner. I had been to China on a mission of smuggling Bibles for the emerging underground churches. The stewardess announced that President Reagan had just been shot by a John Hinckley for the purpose of impressing Jodie Foster. I immediately remembered the letter I had written Hinckley the previous year.

As far as I know, Jodie Foster has not married. She remains one of the most famous female actresses in the world, having starred in many movies and plays, winning scores of awards and commendations.

John Hinckley was judged guilty of attempted murder and various other charges by reason of insanity on June 21, 1982. From reports, it appears that he continued in his unrequited obsession for Jodie Foster. However, in recent years and months, he has been allowed visitors and even frequent leaves from prison. There is much talk at the present time about a parole, as his mental condition has improved. There are also reports that he is a model prisoner now.

Reverend Jennifer Ryu of the Williamsburg, Virginia Unitarian Universalists Church has reported that John Hinckley has contacted her about volunteer service at her church when he is released.[257]

Obviously, John Hinckley's mental condition has improved, and we trust his demonic obsession with the ghost of Jodie Foster all these years later has faded and, at last, found peace through faith in Jesus Christ.

> This is all my hope and peace,
> Nothing but the blood of Jesus;
> This is all my righteousness,
> Nothing but the blood of Jesus.[258]

Chapter Eighteen

THE ANGEL OF DEATH
VS. THE GIFT OF LIFE

By Thomas Horn

In the previous chapter, veteran radio minister Dr. Noah Hutchings mentioned some of the famous convicts that, over the years, have sought spiritual guidance and prayers from the Southwest Radio Ministries. These include David Berkowitz (a.k.a. the Son of Sam), John Hinckley Jr. (who attempted to assassinate president Ronald Reagan), and Charles "Tex" Watson (former member of the Charles Manson "Family" who was convicted of first degree murder in the 1969 deaths of Sharon Tate, Steven Parent, Abigail Folger, Wojciech Frykowski, Jay Sebring, and Leno and Rosemary LaBianca). The Southwest Radio Ministries has for many years provided books, inspirational calendars, and other materials to prison chaplains in hopes of leading prisoners to salvation and, as a result, are often sought for counsel by desperate souls seeking forgiveness. We include this information in this book because whereas Satan is a murderer and has been since the beginning (see John 8:44), we believe deliverance from his clutches and forgiveness of sins committed under his influence are available through Jesus Christ. If one were to ask those felons mentioned above how their life of crime began for which they now seek spiritual forgiveness, they would point to that darkness, which is increasingly rampant in today's cultural romance with all-things occult, as discussed earlier in this book. These men would describe how it started in their youth, when they somehow sought out, and began listening to, the angel of death.

The following 2005 article from Raiders News Network illustrates what can happen when taking in the whispers of this dark fallen angel:

INSIDE THE VIOLENT MIND OF THE "ANGEL OF DEATH"

By Donna Anderson
RNN News Sr. Reporter

Salem, OR—Raiders News Network—On Monday, March 21, 2005, 17-year-old Jeffrey Weise, a junior at Red Lake High School in Red Lake, Minn., went on a shooting spree that killed nine people and wounded 15 others at the school. He then turned the gun on himself, committing suicide.

The shootings were the worst attack of this type in the nation since the 1999 Columbine school shooting in Littleton, Colo.

"A preliminary investigation indicated the suspect apparently first shot his grandparents, then went to the school where he allegedly shot a security guard, exchanged fire with police officers and opened fire on other students before killing himself," said a report on the hometown news, WCCO-TV.

"Paul McCabe, an FBI special agent, said 10 people are confirmed dead: the suspect, five students, a female English teacher, a male security officer and the suspect's grandparents.

"The teacher was identified as 62-year-old Neva Rogers, according to the Star Tribune. The paper identified the security officer as Derrick Brun. The identities of the students have not been released.

"Six wounded students were admitted to North Country Regional Hospital in Bemidji, Minn. between 4:22 p.m. and 4:50 p.m., doctors said Tuesday. All were male and under the age of 18, doctors said.

"One was admitted with a head wound and later died, Dr. Joe Corser said.

"Two were critically injured and transferred to MeritCare Hospital in Fargo, N.D. for treatment. One was shot in the head and the other was shot in the face, Corser said.

"Those students, who remain in critical condition, are identified as Jeffrey May, 15, and Steven Cobenais, 15.

"Three wounded students remain at North Country Regional Hospital, doctors said Tuesday. Corser said two were shot in the chest and one was shot in the hip. Their identities were not released pending FBI and parental authorization," the report went on to say.

The Associated Press reported Weise may have posted messages last year on a neo-Nazi Web site calling himself "Angel of Death" and expressing admiration for Adolf Hitler.[259]

Whose Voice Would Fill a Young Person's Mind with Such Violent Intent?

In 1998, when defense attorneys argued that seventeen-year-old Kip Kinkel—who, like Jeffrey Weise, entered his school on a shooting rampage—should not spend the rest of his life in prison, it was because Kinkel reportedly "heard voices" telling him to commit murders. During sentence hearings, Dr. Richard J. Konkol pointed out that "holes" in what is normally a smooth surface of Kinkel's brain reveal conditions consistent with schizophrenia. When defense attorney Mark Sabitt asked if this would make a person "more susceptible to a psychotic episode," Konkol responded, "I think it would."[260]

Kinkel pleaded guilty to four counts of murder and twenty-six counts of attempted murder in the May, 1998 shooting rampage in Springfield, Oregon. Kinkel's parents and two students at Thurston High School died as a result of the attack. Twenty-five other students were wounded.

"My dad was sitting at the (breakfast) bar," said Kinkel. "The voices said, 'Shoot him.' I had no choice. The voices said I had no choice." Kinkel testified that after he killed his parents, he was instructed by the voices to "Go to school and kill everybody."

Murderous voices first began speaking to Kinkel at age twelve when he got off the school bus and was looking at a bush. The bush said, "You need to kill everyone, everyone in the world."

Kinkel believes the voices came from the devil, a satellite, or from a computer chip implanted in his head by the government.

Like Kinkel, Jeffrey Weise felt compelled to shed the blood of innocent people, and then to kill himself. How could such ideas enter the mind of a young boy? Perhaps the same way notorious "Son of Sam" killer David Berkowitz claims "bloodthirsty voices" commanded him to kill. According to Berkowitz, a convert of Christianity, a six-thousand-year-old demon named Sam communicated through his neighbor's black Labrador retriever instructing him to carry out the murders. Berkowitz was subsequently diagnosed as having paranoid schizophrenia, a disease in which the person often hears pejorative or threatening voices separate from their own. Both Kinkel and Berkowitz were known to read pornographic and violent depictures of torture and murder. It appears from the initial evidence that Weise enjoyed the ponderings of mass murderers as well.

Schizophrenia is an accepted diagnosis of mental disorder and we cannot underestimate the positive contribution of such science. However, many Christians, including Christian psychologists, believe the causes of violence in people suffering physical and mental illness can, in some cases, be connected to violent images and stories in popular media. Some believe curable *and* incurable conditions (like schizophrenia) should be approached both scientifically and spiritually during diagnosis and treatment. This presupposes a psychological influence of supernatural evil in some cases, and applies a literal interpretation to the words of Jesus that the evil one is "a murderer" (John 8:44). Satan's violent autosuggestions influence the mind that rejects the voice of God and fills it with "envy, murder, strife, deceit and malice" (Romans 1:29).

Early cultures often interpreted such difficult psychological expressions through metaphysics. In Greece, Dionysus was the intoxicating god of unbridled human passion. He was the presence that is otherwise defined as the craving within man that longs to "let itself go" and to "give itself over" to evil human desires. What a Christian might resist as the evil thoughts of the carnal man, the followers of Dionysus embraced as the incarnate power that would, in the next life, liberate mankind from the constraints of this present world, and from the customs which sought to define respectability through a person's obedience to moral law.

Until then, worshippers of Dionysus attempted to bring themselves into union with their god through ritual casting off of the bonds of sexual denial and primal constraint by seeking to attain a higher state of ecstasy. The uninhibited rituals of ecstasy (Greek for "outside the body") supposedly brought followers of Dionysus into a supernatural condition that enabled them to escape the temporary limitations of the body and mind, and to achieve a state of *enthousiasmos*, or, "outside the body and inside the god." In this sense, Dionysus represented a dichotomy within the Greek religion, as the primary maxim of the Greek culture was one of moderation, or, "nothing too extreme." Yet, Dionysus embodied the absolute extreme in that he sought to inflame the forbidden passions and murderous thoughts of the human mind. Interestingly, as most students of psychology will understand, this gave Dionysus a stronger allure among many Greeks who otherwise tried in so many ways to suppress and control the wild and secret lusts of the human mind.

However, Dionysus resisted every such effort, and, according to myth, visited a terrible madness upon those who tried to deny him his free expression. The Dionystic idea of mental disease resulting from the suppression of secret inner desires, especially aberrant sexual desires, was later reflected in the atheistic teachings of Sigmund Freud. Thus, Freudianism might be called the grandchild of the cult of Dionysus.

Conversely, the person who gave himself over to the will of Dionysus was rewarded with unlimited psychological and physical delights. Such mythical systems of mental punishments and physical rewards based on resistance and/or submission to Dionysus, were both symbolically and literally illustrated in the cult rituals of the *Bacchae* (the female participants of the Dionystic mysteries), as the Bacchae women migrated in frenzied hillside groups, dressed transvestite in fawn skins and accompanied by screaming, music, dancing, bloodletting, and licentious behavior. When, for instance, a baby animal was too young and lacking in instinct to sense the danger and run away from the revelers, it was picked up and suckled by nursing mothers who participated in the hillside rituals. However, when older animals sought to escape the marauding Bacchae, they were considered "resistant" to the will of Dionysus and were torn apart and eaten alive as a part of the fevered ritual.

Human participants were sometimes subjected to the same orgiastic cruelty, as the rule of the cult was "anything goes," including rape and other acts of interpersonal violence. Later versions of the ritual (Bacchanalia) expanded to include pedophilia and male revelers, and perversions of sexual behavior were often worse between men than they were between men and women. Any creature that dared to resist such perversion of Dionysus was subjected to *sparagmos* ("torn apart") and *omophagia* ("consumed raw"). In 410 BC, Euripides wrote of the bloody rituals of the Bacchae in his famous play, *The Bacchantes*.

Bacchantes [with] hands that bore no weapon of steel, attacked our cattle as they browsed. Then wouldst thou have seen Agave mastering some sleek lowing calf, while others rent the heifers limb from limb. Before thy eyes there would have been hurling of ribs and hoofs this way and that, and strips of flesh, all blood be-dabbled, dripped as they hung from the pine branches. Wild bulls, that glared but now with rage along their horns, found themselves tripped up, dragged down to earth by count-less maidens hands.[261]

Euripedes went on to describe how Pentheus, the King of Thebes, was torn apart and eaten alive by his own mother as, according to the play, she fell under the spell of Dionysus.

The tearing apart and eating alive of a sacrificial victim may refer to the earliest history of the murderous voice of Satan. An ancient and violent cult idea existing since the dawn of pagan-ism stipulated that, by eating an enemy or an animal alive, or by drinking their blood, a person might somehow capture the essence or "soul-strength" of the victim. The earliest Norwegian hunts-men believed this, and they drank the blood of bears in an effort to capture their physical strength. East African Masai warriors also practiced omophagia, and they sought to gain the strength of the wild by drinking the blood of lions. Human victims were treated this way by Arabs before Mohammed, and headhunters of the East Indies practiced omophagia in an effort to capture the essence of their enemies.

Today, omophagia is practiced by certain voodoo sects as well as by cult Satanists. Eating human flesh and drinking human blood as an attempt to "become one" with the devoured is, in many cases, a demonization of the Eucharist, or Holy Communion. But sparagmos and omophagia, as practiced by the followers of Dionysus, was not an attempt of transubstantiation (as in the Catholic Eucharist), nor of consubstantiation (as in the Lutheran communion), nor yet of a symbolic ordinance (as in the fundamentalist denomination), all of which have as a common goal—the elevating of the worshipper into a sacramental communion with God. The objective of the Bacchae was the opposite: The frenzied dance, the thunderous song, the licentious behavior, the murderous activity, all were efforts on the part of the Bacchae to capture the "voice" of the god (Dionysus) and bring him down into an incarnated rage within man. The idea was not one of holy communion, but of possession by the spirit of Dionysus.

So Who's Really Behind Murder's Voice Anyway?

When one recalls the horrific rituals of the followers of Dionysus, it's easy to believe that demonic possession actually occurred. A Christian should find this idea plausible, as it seems the Hebrews did, considering Hades (the Greek god of the underworld) to be equal with Hell and/or the Devil. Many ancient writers likewise saw no difference between Hades (in this sense the Devil) and Dionysus. Euripides echoed this sentiment in the Hecuba, and referred to the followers of Dionysus as the "Bacchants of Hades." In Syracuse, Dionysus was known as Dionysus Morychos ("the dark one") a fiendish creature; roughly equivalent to the biblical Satan, who wore goatskins and dwelt in the regions of the underworld.

In the scholarly book, *Dionysus Myth and Cult*, Walter F. Otto connected Dionysus with the prince of the underworld. He wrote: "The similarity and relationship which Dionysus has with the prince of the underworld (and this is revealed by a large number of comparisons) is not only confirmed by an authority of the first rank, but he says the two deities are actually the same. Heraclitus says, 'Hades and Dionysus, for whom they go mad and rage, are one and the same.'"[262]

Even the Hebrew prophet Ezekiel condemned the mind-altering madness of Dionysus as inherently satanic. He spoke of the "magic bands" (*kesatot*) of the Bacchae, which, as in the omophagia, were used to mesmerize the minds of men. Where the KJV says, "Wherefore thus saith the Lord GOD; Behold, I am against your pillows, wherewith ye there hunt the souls to make them fly, and I will tear them from your arms, and will let the souls go, even the souls that ye hunt to make them fly" (Ezekiel 13:20), we read the following in the NASB translation, "Therefore, thus says the Lord GOD, 'Behold I am against your *magic* bands [*kesatot*] by which you hunt lives [minds/souls] there as birds, and I will tear them off your arms; and I will let them go, even those lives [minds/souls] whom you hunt as birds'" (emphasis in original).

The *kesatot*, or "magic arm band," were used in connection with a container called the *kiste*. Wherever the *kiste* is inscribed on sarcophagi and on Bacchic scenes, it is depicted as a sacred vessel (a mind prison?) with a snake peering through an open lid. How the magic worked and in what way a mind was imprisoned is still a mystery. Pan, the half-man/half-goat god (later relegated to devildom) is sometimes pictured as kicking the lid open and letting the snake (mind?) out. Such loose snakes were then depicted as being enslaved around the limbs, and bound in the hair, of the Bacchae women.

The mysterious imagery of Pan, the serpents, the imprisoned minds, and the magic *kesatot* and *kiste*, have not been adequately explained by any available authority, and the interpretation of them as a method of mind-control is subject to ongoing scrutiny. However, since the prophet Ezekiel spoke of the efforts of the

Bacchae to mystically imprison the minds of men through the magic bands of Dionysus, and since Pan was most beloved of Dionysus, because of his pandemonium ("all the devils") which struck sudden panic in the hearts of men and beasts, and as the serpent was universally accepted by the Hebrews as a symbol of occult devotion, it can be easily surmised that the iconography of Dionysus represented the most tenacious effort on the part of the Bacchae to fulfill the psychological whims of evil supernaturalism.

Shutting Murder's Mouth

In Acts 17:34, we read of the conversion of Dionysius the Areopagite. This is significant. Having the name Dionysius probably meant the parents were devotees of Dionysus, and thus the child was "predestined" to be a follower of the god. He may have also been under a mind-altering *kesatot* spell. Yet, the powers of darkness lost control over Dionysius' mind when he accepted the Gospel message. Jesus liberated him like He did the lunatics of Matthew 4:24 and 17:15. When Jesus touched the wild man, He left him "sitting, and clothed, and in his right mind" (Mark 5:15).

Jesus is still in the mind-healing business, and testimonies abound of people whose minds were released from murderous madness into His marvelous light. You could ask David Berkowitz about this, the former "Son of Sam" killer. David received Christ on the prison floor. "When I finished talking to God, I got up. My mind seemed to flood with a sense of peace," said Berkowitz. "I knew from that moment that Jesus Christ heard me. I sensed in my heart that I was forgiven and that I was now free."[263]

Ted Bundy pleaded for an interview with Dr. James Dobson prior to his court-ordered date with destiny. Bundy appeared genuinely sorrowful on a videotaped interview and acknowledged the murderous effects of past sinful thinking. He asked Jesus to forgive him.

Karla Faye Tucker was the first woman executed in the state of Texas in 135 years. She testified of the mind-altering effect of drugs. On the eve of her execution, CBN reporter Kathy Chiero asked Karla, "Why do you agree to talk to the media regardless of why they are coming to you?" Karla responded, "God has given me a great, big open door to share the love of Jesus and I'm gonna do it...my heart has been to share with the world the love that He poured out into me—the forgiveness, the mercy, the way that He can change a life."[264]

Most of us view such deathbed conversions with skepticism. Last minute loyalties attributed to our Savior in the midnight hour often bring scoffing. Yet, we read of the criminal on the cross next to Jesus and see the Lord honoring his plea for forgiveness (see Luke 23: 42–43). Jesus extended mercy and offered eternal fellowship to every repentant soul.

Perhaps Kip Kinkel will discover what David Berkowitz says he has: that the saving power of Jesus Christ is "mighty through God to the pulling down of strong holds; Casting down imaginations, and every high thing that exalteth itself against the knowledge of God, and bringing into captivity every thought to the obedience of Christ" (2 Corinthians 10:4–5).

Jeffrey Weise, the "Angel of Death," appears to have been lost from this idea.

If you, too, have been listening to the dark angel—whether through a fascination with creatures of the night, occult practices, satanic symbolism, rebellion, or even murderous contemplation—

I invite you to deliverance, healing, and forgiveness through Jesus Christ. Ask Him to come into your heart, cleanse your mind, forgive you, and be your Savior.

"Finally, brethren, whatsoever things are true, whatsoever things are honest, whatsoever things are just, whatsoever things are pure, whatsoever things are lovely, whatsoever things are of good report; if there be any virtue, and if there be any praise, think on these things" (Philippians 4:8).

NOTES

1 The time this author spent in the affiliated environment between this employer, UCLA, and the E-ring of the Pentagon, left an enduring legacy that impacted his subsequent thirty-year career among twelve public boardrooms of America.

2 Deterministic rather than stochastic algorithms.

3 Macrocosm/microcosm is a Greek compound of μακρο- ("macro-") and μικρο- ("micro-"), which are Greek respectively for "large" and "small," and the word κομος *kósmos* which means "order" as well as "world" or "ordered world."

4 Such as galaxy NGC 4319 and its companion Markarian 205.

5 Halton Arp (Edwin Hubble's assistant, a long-time observer at the Mt. Palomar and Mt. Wilson telescopes: his photographs contradict the Big Bang theories).

6 Robert Burnham Jr., *Burnham's Celestial Handbook: An Observer's Guide to the Universe Beyond the Solar System* (Dover, NY: Dover Publications Inc., 1978).

7 Donald E. Scott, *The Electric Sky: A Challenege to the Myths of Modern Astronomy* (Portland, OR: Mikamar Publishing, 2006).

8 Not to be confused with the Large Hadron Collider project which we will discuss later.

9 GEO 600 is capable of detecting gravitational waves in the frequency range 50 Hz–1.5 kHz. Construction on the project began in 1995.

10 Reported in *New Scientist,* January 15, 2009.

11 He garnered significant sympathetic support: Roger Penrose of Oxford, the creator of the modern theory of black holes; Bernard d'Espagnat of the University of Paris; leading authorities on foundations of quantum theory; and Brian Josephson of University of Cambridge, winner of the 1973 Nobel Prize in physics.

12 Alain Aspect is the physicist who performed the key experiment that established that if you want a real universe, it must be non-local (Einstein's "spooky action at a distance"). Aspect comments on new work by his successor in conducting such experiments, Anton Zeilinger and his colleagues, who have now performed an experiment that

suggests that "giving up the concept of locality is not sufficient to be consistent with quantum experiments, unless certain intuitive features of realism are abandoned." "To be or not to be local" by Alain Aspect, *Nature* 446, 866, April 2007; "An experimental test of non-local realism" by S. Gröblacher et. al., *Nature* 446, 871, April 2007: also, *The Journal of Scientific Exploration (Issue 21-3)* by Professors Richard Conn Henry and Stephen R. Palmquist.

13 "Are our constants constant?" *The Scientific American,* June 2005.

14 Meta- (from Greek: μετά = "after," "beyond," "with," "adjacent," "self"), is a prefix used in English (and other Greek-owing languages) to indicate a concept which is an abstraction from another concept, used to complete or add to the latter.

15 Ephesians 3:18.

16 Nick Squires, "Surge in Satanism Sparks Rise in Demand for Exorcists, Says Catholic Church," *The Telegraph,* March 30, 2011, http://www.telegraph.co.uk/news/religion/8416104/Surge-in-Satanism-sparks-rise-in-demand-for-exorcists-says-Catholic-Church.html.

17 "Clarke's three laws," *Wikipedia,* last modified May 26, 2011, http://en.wikipedia.org/wiki/Clarke%27s_three_laws.

18 Donna Howell was personally present at Barnes & Noble late that night to purchase a book and saw the crowds for herself.

19 "*Twilight* (novel)," *Wikipedia,* last modified June 27, 2011, http://en.wikipedia.org/wiki/Twilight_(novel).

20 Ibid.

21 Nikki Finke, "'ECLIPSE' KEEPS BREAKING RECORDS: Twilight Saga Threequel Sets Best Ever Wednesday Opening of $68.5M; Thursday $24.2M; Six-Day July Fourth Holiday Estimated at $178M; Twi-Hards Mob Theaters in U.S., Canada, Overseas," *Deadline.com,* July 1, 2010, http://www.deadline.com/2010/07/first-record-eclipse-opens-to-biggest-domestic-release-in-hollywood-history/.

22 Unless otherwise noted, research on the decades and lifestyles from this chapter came from *Wikipedia,* specifically the following pages: "1900s (decade)," "1910s," "1920s," "1930s," "1940s," "1950s," "1960s," "1970s," "1980s," "1990s," and from general online searches regarding life during each specific era. Any direct quotations or statistics are otherwise referenced.

23 "Marriages and Divorces, 1900–2008," *Information Please® Database,* 2008, http://www.infoplease.com/ipa/A0005044.html.

24 "Tijuana bible," *Wikipedia*, last modified May 28, 2011, http://
en.wikipedia.org/wiki/Tijuana_bibles.

25 "*Dracula* (1931 film)," *Wikipedia*, last modified June 16, 2011, http://
en.wikipedia.org/wiki/Dracula_(1931_film).

26 Susan Greenfield, "Modern Technology is Changing the Way Our
Brains Work, Says Neuroscientist," *MailOnline.com*, http://www.
dailymail.co.uk/sciencetech/article-565207/Modern-technology-
changing-way-brains-work-says-neuroscientist.html.

27 "*Boobs in Arms*," *Wikipedia*, last modified March 10, 2011, http://
en.wikipedia.org/wiki/Boobs_in_Arms.

28 "History of film," *Wikipedia*, last modified June 18, 2011, http://
en.wikipedia.org/wiki/History_of_film.

29 Movie summaries found on *The Internet Movie Database* (IMBd),
accessed June 27, 2011, http://www.imdb.com.

30 "More popular than Jesus," *Wikipedia*, last modified June 24, 2011,
http://en.wikipedia.org/wiki/More_popular_than_Jesus.

31 William Peter Blatty, *The Exorcist*, directed by William Friedkin,
(Burbank, CA: Warner Home Video, 1973), DVD.

32 "True Stories," *Warner Bros.*, http://theexorcist.warnerbros.com/cmp/
truebottom.html.

33 "Vampires!" *The Tyra Show*, October 31, 2008, http://tyrashow.
warnerbros.com/2008/10/fridays_show_vampires.php.

34 Episode posted on YouTube here: http://www.youtube.
com/watch?v=qKjSnmJd2Q8.

35 "Vampire lifestyle," *Wikipedia*, last modified June 21, 2011, http://
en.wikipedia.org/wiki/Vampire_lifestyle.

36 Ibid.

37 Ibid.

38 Photo by Matthew Rolston for *RollingStone.com*: http://www.
rollingstone.com/culture/photos/theyre-hot-theyre-sexy-theyre-undead-
20100817/true-blood-52377762.

39 "Rolling Stone's 'True Blood' Cover: Too Much?" *Newsy Multisource
Video News Analysis* video, 2:38, August 10, 2010, http://www.newsy.
com/videos/rolling-stone-s-true-blood-cover-too-much/.

40 Jessica Derschowitz, "'True Blood' Rolling Stone Cover Story Talks
Vampire Sex," *CBS News*, August 18, 2010, http://www.cbsnews.
com/8301-31749_162-20013981-10391698.html.

41 Keith Green, "Asleep in the Light," *No Compromise*, produced by

instrumentalist Bill Maxwell, recorded in 1978, 4:26 (Brentwood, TN: Sparrow Records, 1978).

42 "Galatians 3:13," *Online Parallel Bible*, accessed June 27, 2011, http://bible.cc/galatians/3-13.htm.

43 *The Amish In Their Own Words: Amish Writings from 25 Years of* Family Life *Magazine*, compiled by Brad Igou (Scottsdale, PA: Herald Press, 1999).

44 The Serbian form of Plogojowitz's name is Blagojevic. Readers in Illinois may find this amusing given the political proclivities of their former governor.

45 See also: Deuteronomy 15:23, Leviticus 7:26-27, 17:10-14, and 19:26.

46 See also: Hebrews 9:22.

47 Dr. Burton's website: www.burtonbeyond.com.

48 As do some in the vampire/vampyre subculture.

49 Dr. Heiser's website: www.DrMSH.com.

50 See: www.TheDivineCouncil.com.

51 For example, the Good News Translation renders Deuteronomy 32:8–9 this way: "The Most High assigned nations their lands; he determined where peoples should live. **He assigned to each nation a heavenly being,** but Jacob's descendants he chose for himself" (bold added).

52 Dr. Michael S. Heiser, "Deuteronomy 32:8 and the Sons of God," last accessed July 9, 2010, http://www.thedivinecouncil.com/DT32BibSac.pdf.

53 Alexandra Zayes, "V is for Voracious: Vampire Culture Unveiled," *St. Petersburg Times*, August 16, 2009, http://www.tampabay.com/features/humaninterest/v-is-for-voracious-vampire-culture-unveiled/1027763.

54 See the following articles: Meena Hartenstein, "Teenagers Inspired by *Twilight* Sink Fangs Into Each Other In New 'Biting' Trend, Parents Fear Risks," *NY Daily News*, July 7, 2010 http://articles.nydailynews.com/2010-07-07/entertainment/27069327_1_bites-vampire-diaries-true-blood. "'Twilight' Fan Police Report: Teen Makes False Claim about Fantasy Biting Behavior," *Huffington Post*, February 11, 2011, http://www.huffingtonpost.com/2011/02/11/twilight-fan-police-report_n_821930.html. Juju Chang, "'Twilight' Effect: Are Teens Biting One Another Because of On-Screen Vampires?" *ABC News: Good Morning America*, July 9, 2010, http://abcnews.go.com/GMA/twilight-movie-effect-teens-biting-vampire-fascination/story?id=11122324.

55 C.F. Keil and F. Delitzsch, *Keil & Delitzsch Commentary on the Old*

Testament (Grand Rapids, MI: Eerdmans Publishing, 1986), Vol. 4, p. 78.

56 Ivan T. Sanderson, in the foreword to: F. W. Holiday, *The Great Orm of Loch Ness* (New York, NY: Avon Books, 1968), xii.

57 F. W. Holiday, *The Great Orm of Loch Ness: A Practical Inquiry into the Nature and Habits of Water-Monsters* (New York, NY: Avon Books, 1968).

58 Ibid., 132.

59 Ibid., 133.

60 Ibid., 133–134.

61 Ibid., 136.

62 Ibid., 137–138.

63 Janet and Colin Bord, *Unexplained Mysteries of the 20th Century* (Chicago, IL: Contemporary Books, 1989), 112–113.

64 Ibid., 114.

65 Ibid., 118–119.

66 See the photos on the *UFO Digest* website: http://www.ufodigest.com/news/1007/images/morgawr.jpg.

67 Michael Strassfeld, Betsy Platkin Teutsch, and Arnold M. Eisen, *Jewish Holidays: A Guide and Commentary*, (New York, NY: Harper & Row Publishers, 1985), 137.

68 Ibid.

69 Many biblical scholars believe, due to God's pronouncement in Genesis 3 (that the serpent would crawl upon its belly all the days of its life), that it had originally had legs, allowing it to walk, possibly upright.

70 "Synopsis for Splice," *Internet Movie Database* (IMDB), last accessed June 29, 2011, http://www.imdb.com/title/tt1017460/synopsis.

71 An extinct bird that was all black with a pink, bare-skinned head and alleged wingspan of at least twenty-five feet.

72 Ian Sample, "Aliens Visiting Earth will be Just Like Humans, Scientist Claims," *The Guardian*, January 25, 2010, http://www.guardian.co.uk/science/2010/jan/25/aliens-space-earth-humans.

73 "Vatican Astronomer Says it's OK to Think Aliens Exist," *USA Today*, May 28, 2008, http://www.usatoday.com/news/religion/2008-05-14-vatican-aliens_N.htm.

74 "Comet and Father Malachi Martin" (ART BELL INTERVIEWS FATHER MALACHI MARTIN: Transcript of the April 5th, 1997 interview with late Father Malachi Martin by Art Bell), *Godlike*

Productions, January 7, 2007, http://www.godlikeproductions.
com/forum1/message326615/pg1.

75 Sharon Begley, "The Vatican and Little Green Men," *Newsweek*, May
15, 2008, http://www.newsweek.com/blogs/lab-notes/2008/05/15/the-
vatican-and-little-green-men.html.

76 Neil Mackay, "And On the Eighth Day—Did God Create Aliens?"
Sunday Herald—Scotland, November 28, 2005, http://www.
sundayherald.com/53020 (site discontinued; see alternatively, from *Signs
of the Times*: http://www.sott.net/articles/show/106410-And-on-the-
eighth-day-did-God-create-aliens-).

77 "The Extraterrestrial is My Brother," *L'Osservatore Romano*, May 14,
2008, http://padrefunes.blogspot.com/.

78 As quoted by article: Brother Guy Consolmagno, "Would You Baptize
an Extraterrestrial?: A Jesuit Priest Says the Discovery of Life Elsewhere
in the Universe Would Pose No Problem for Religion," *Beliefnet*, http://
www.beliefnet.com/News/Science-Religion/2000/08/Would-You-
Baptize-An-Extraterrestrial.aspx?p=2.

79 Giuseppe Tanzella-Nitti, "EXTRATERRESTRIAL LIFE,"
Interdisciplinary Encyclopedia of Religion and Science, http://www.inters.
org, and http://www.disf.org/en/Voci/65.asp.

80 Ibid.

81 Ibid.

82 *Open Minds Magazine*, "The Vatican Extraterrestrial Question," by J.
Antonio Huneeus, June/July 2010, Issue 2, 59.

83 Erich von Daniken, *Chariots of the Gods?* (New York: G.P. Putnam's
Sons, 1970), 10.

84 Ibid., 26.

85 Stephen Quayle, *Genesis 6 Giants* (Bozeman, MT: End Time Thunder
Publishers, 2002), 60.

86 "Giants in the Earth: Part I: Giants of the Ancient Near East,"
Mysterious World, Spring 2003, http://www.mysteriousworld.
com/Journal/2003/Spring/Giants/.

87 Dr. Jacques Vallée, *Confrontations—A Scientist's Search for Alien Contact*
(New York, NY: Ballantine Books, 1990), 159.

88 Dr. Jacques Vallée, *Dimensions: A Casebook of Alien Contact* (New York,
NY: Ballantine Books, 1988), 143–144.

89 John A. Keel, *UFOs: Operation Trojan Horse* (Atlanta, GA: Illuminet
Press, 1996), 192.

90 Elizabeth L. Hillstrom, *Testing the Spirits* (Downers Grove, IL: InterVarsity Press, 1995), 207–207.

91 John A. Keel, *UFOs: Operation Trojan Horse*, 299.

92 Dr. Jacques Vallée, *The Invisible College: What a Group of Scientists Has Discovered About UFO Influences on the Human Race* (New York, NY: Dutton; 1st edition, 1975), 233.

93 Dr. Jacques Vallée, *Revelations: Alien Contact and Human Deception* (San Antonio, TX: Anomalist Books, 2008), 236.

94 David M. Jacobs, *Secret Life: Firsthand, Documented Accounts of UFO Abductions*, (New York, NY: Touchstone, 1999), 309.

95 John E. Mack, *Abduction: Human Encounters with Aliens*, (New York, NY: Ballantine Books, 1995) 404–405.

96 Gary Stearman, "The Ghastly Truth About the Days of Noah," *Prophecy in the News Magazine*, November 1999, 15.

97 David Flynn, "Seraphim, Cherubim & Ezekiel's Wheels: Aliens, Nephilim & the Days of Noah," *Watcher Website*, http://www.mt.net/~watcher/noah.html.

98 Chuck Missler and Mark Eastman, *Alien Encounters: The Secret Behind the UFO Phenomenon*, (Coeur d'Alene, ID: Koinonia House, 1997), 275.

99 Louis Pauwells and Jacques Bergier, *The Dawn of Magic* (first published as *Le Matin des Magiciens*, Paris: Editions Gallmiard, 1960), 68.

100 St. Augustine, *City of God*, 23:15.

101 Fr. Ludovico Maria Sinistrari de Amino, *De Daemonialitate, et Incubis, et Succubi* (1622–1701, English translation of this portion provided by Jacques Vallée in *Passport to Magonia*, Contemporary Books, 1993), 127–129.

102 "G. H. Pember: A Short Biography," *Raiders News Network*, http://www.raidersnewsupdate.com/pember.pdf.

103 "virtual reality," *Dictionary.com Unabridged*, Random House, Inc., accessed July 7, 2011, http://dictionary.reference.com/browse/virtual reality.

104 "Invasion literature," *Wikipedia*, last modified April 9, 2011, http://en.wikipedia.org/wiki/Invasion_literature.

105 Mercury Theater on the Air: Online archive of radio recordings, including "The War of the Worlds," last accessed July 5, 2011, http://www.mercurytheatre.info/.

106 Mary Bellis, "Kinetoscope," *About.com*, last accessed July 5, 2011, http://
inventors.about.com/od/kstartinventions/a/Kinetoscope.htm.

107 Micha F. Lindemans, "Psyche," *Encyclopedia Mythica*, last modified
December 12, 1999, http://www.pantheon.org/articles/p/psyche.html.

108 Created by Chris Carter, "Jose Chung's *Doomsday Defense*," *Millenium*,
season 2, episode 9, written and directed by Darin Morgan, aired
Novermber 27, 1997 on *Fox Network*.

109 "Jose Chung's *Doomsday Defense*," *Wikipedia*, last
modified February 10, 2011, http://en.wikipedia.
org/wiki/Jose_Chung%27s_Doomsday_Defense.

110 Gary Bates, "Who were the sons of God in Genesis 6?" *Creation.com*,
June 23, 2011, http://creation.com/sons-of-god.

111 An article by David M. Jacobs, in *The Mammoth Encyclopedia of
Extraterrestrial Encounters*, p. 331–332. As cited in Gary Bates, *Alien
Intrusion: UFOs and the Evolution Connection* (Powder Springs, GA:
Creation Book Publishers, 2010) 246.

112 "The Allagash Abductions," *UFOEvidence.org*, last accessed December
28, 2009, http://www.ufoevidence.org/cases/case466.htm.

113 Kyle Hopkins, "Movie Blames Nome Disappearances On Aliens," last
accessed July 6, 2011, http://community.adn.com/node/143292.

114 J.C. Radley, "The Real Story Behind *The Fourth Kind*,"
last accessed July 6, 2011, http://www.examiner.
com/movie-in-hartford/the-real-story-behind-the-fourth-kind.

115 "The Fourth Kind," *Wikipedia*, last modified July 6, 2011, http://
en.wikipedia.org/wiki/The_Fourth_Kind.

116 Paul Rodney McHugh, *Try to Remember: Psychiatry's Clash Over
Meaning, Memory, and Mind* (New York, NY: Dana Press, 2008), as
quoted in "False memory syndrome," *Wikipedia*, last modified June 24,
2011, http://en.wikipedia.org/wiki/False_memory_syndrome.

117 "False memory syndrome," last modified June 24, 2011, http://
en.wikipedia.org/wiki/False_memory_syndrome.

118 "Memory and Reality," *False Memory Syndrome Foundation*, last accessed
July 5, 2011, http://www.fmsonline.org/.

119 Ibid.

120 "Frequently Asked Questions," *False Memory Syndrome Foundation*, last
accessed July 5, 2011, http://www.fmsonline.org/fmsffaq.html.

121 Ibid.

122 For further reading on this subject, see *Retractors Speak: The Therapy,*

False Memory Syndrome Foundation, last accessed July 5, 2011, http://www.fmsonline.org/retract1.html#jul94.

123 "Learned MPD," *Retractors Speak: The Therapy, False Memory Syndrome Foundation*, last accessed July 5, 2011, http://www.fmsonline.org/retract1.html#jan94.

124 Gary Bates, "The War of the Worlds Comes Down to Earth," July 8, 2005, http://creation.com/the-war-of-the-worlds-comes-down-to-earth.

125 As quoted in "Many Forms of Hypnosis," by Dr, Helene Feldman, *Infinity Institute*, last accessed July 5, 2011, http://www.infinityinst.com/articles/many_forms_of_hypnosis.htm.

126 Ibid.

127 "Derren Brown Controls Shopping Mall Visitors—With Sound," YouTube video, 2:04, posted by "squash08," November 1, 2007, http://www.youtube.com/watch?v=IOEKdaXIEHc&feature=related.

128 "Derren Brown NLP," YouTube video, 7:15, posted by "jregester," September 20, 2006, http://www.youtube.com/watch?v=befugtgikMg&feature=fvw.

129 Personal email to Gary Bates from James Allen, B.A. Psychology, Certified Clinical Hypnotherapist, American Institute of Hypnotherapy, Forensic Reconstruction Investigator, January 5, 2010.

130 Personal email to Gary Bates from James Allen, B.A. Psychology, Certified Clinical Hypnotherapist, American Institute of Hypnotherapy, Forensic Reconstruction Investigator, December 21, 2009.

131 Ibid.

132 "Sword Swallower Trapped in Trance for Hours After Accidentally Hypnotising HIMSELF in a Airror," *Daily Mail Reporter*, January 6, 2010, http://www.dailymail.co.uk/news/article-1240983/Trainee-hypnotist-puts-trance.html.

133 The "host of heaven" in the Bible also sometimes refers to the unfallen angelic beings that praise and serve God. Worship of the "starry host" may also refer to the stars themselves, as in the astrological entities superimposed on them. But this, in any case, ultimately involves the worship of fallen entities who often masquerade as false deities.

134 Daniel Kalder, "Lucifer Watch: Satanists Attempt to Infiltrate Russian Police," *When Falls the Coliseum: A Journal of American Culture [or Lack Thereof]*, February 5, 2010, http://whenfallsthecoliseum.com/2010/02/05/lucifer-watch-satanists-attempt-to-infiltrate-russian-police/.

135 "The Smoke of Satan in the Vatican?" *New Oxford Review,* last accessed July 12, 2011, http://www.newoxfordreview.org/note. jsp?did=0510-notes-smoke.

136 Colin A. Ross, M.D., *Bluebird: Deliberate Creation of Multiple Personality by Psychiatrists* (Richardson, TX: Manitou Communications, 2000).

137 For more information on this subject, read: Jessie Penn-Lewis with Evan Roberts, *War on the Saints,* 9th edition (New York, NY: Thomas E. Lowe Ltd., 1994).

138 William Wilkinson, *An Account of the Principalities of Wallachia and Moldavia* (London: Printed for Longman, Hurst, Rees, Orme, and Brown, 1820).

139 William Shakespeare, *Macbeth,* Act 1, Scene 3, lines 123–126. Scene is available online here: http://www.shakespeare-navigators.com/macbeth/ T13.html.

140 Johann Wolfgang von Goethe (1749–1832), was the genius of German literature and author of *Faust.*

141 As quoted by Daniel Pinchbeck, *Breaking Open the Head: A Psychedelic Journey into the Heart of Contemporary Shamanism* (New York, NY: Broadway Books, 2002), 112.

142 The Neo-Platonists were particularly important in seeking to develop a cosmology that blended mysticism and magic into Christianity, creating a supernatural cosmology similar to Gnosticism in ancient times and Shamanism today. Pico della Marandola was noted for his attempt to develop a Christian form of Cabbala. Giordano Bruno was excommunicated by Catholic and Protestant churches alike for his occult beliefs. Heinrich Cornelius Agrippa wrote *De occulta philosophia libri tres* (*Three Books Concerning Occult Philosophy,* Book 1 printed Paris, 1531; Books 1-3 in Cologne, 1533). A brief synopsis in *Wikipedia* states, "Agrippa argued for a synthetic vision of magic whereby the natural world combined with the celestial and the divine through Neoplatonic participation, such that ordinarily licit natural magic was in fact validated by a kind of demonic magic sourced ultimately from God. By this means Agrippa proposed a magic that could resolve all epistemological problems raised by skepticism in a total validation of Christian faith." (See http://en.wikipedia.org/wiki/ Heinrich_Cornelius_Agrippa). Bruno, Marandola, and Agrippa were thoroughly "Renaissance Men" living in the sixteenth and seventeenth centuries. However, intellectuals within the next century would move

past any hope of using the supernatural to vindicate the miracles of Christianity and simply throw out the baby with the bath water. Doubt and skepticism would hold court from thenceforth. Mainstream Christian theology would evolve into a faith without miracles except in selected "evangelical" pockets. By 1800, this was the story of European Protestant theology. By 1900, this was the story of American theology too.

143 Jim Marrs, *PSI Spies: The True Story of American's Psychic Warfare Program* (Franklin Lakes, NJ: New Page Books, 2007), 107.

144 David Morehouse, a former U.S. Army officer we will discuss (PSI Spy on OPERATION SUN STREAK in the late 1980s and early 1990s), said the following in his book, *Psychic Warrior* (1995). "The government was funding paranormal research in half a dozen private, and as many state and federal research centers across the United States. They were pumping tens of millions of dollars into remove viewing and various related techniques" (p. 73).

145 While the famed psychologist, C.G. Jung, offered compelling evidence for the "supra-conscious" and indeed the supernatural with his perspective of the *collective unconscious*—a reality that transcends the human brain—it is the military's cold and nonreligious development of psychic techniques that offer even stronger proof. The military doesn't care why it works; only that it works. The leaders are not unaware of the implications for cosmology and the realm of the spirit, but they consider such issues to be associated with religion and spirituality. As such, they are for others to debate.

146 From Carl Jung, *Memories, Dreams, Reflections*, as quoted by Daniel Pinchbeck, *Breaking Open the Head: A Psychedelic Journey into the Heart of Contemporary Shamanism* (New York, NY: Broadway Books, 2002), 7.

147 "Clairvoyance," Wikipedia, last modified June 27, 2011, http://en.wikipedia.org/wiki/Clairvoyance.

148 Graham Hancock, *Supernatural: Meetings with the Ancient Teachers of Mankind* (New York, NY: The Disinformation Company, 2007), 244.

149 "cosmology," *Dictionary.com Unabridged*, Random House, Inc., accessed June 30, 2011, http://dictionary.reference.com/browse/cosmology.

150 "Shamanism is a range of traditional beliefs and practices that involve the ability to diagnose, cure, and sometimes cause human suffering by traversing the axis mundi and forming a special relationship with, or gaining control over, spirits. Shamans have been credited with the

ability to control the weather, divination, the interpretation of dreams, astral projection, and traveling to upper and lower worlds. Shamanistic traditions have existed throughout the world since prehistoric times. Shamanism is based on the premise that the visible world is pervaded by invisible forces or spirits that affect the lives of the living. In contrast to animism and animatism, which any and usually all members of a society practice, shamanism requires specialized knowledge or abilities." See http://www.crystalinks.com/shamanism.html.

151 Pinchbeck, *Breaking Open the Head*, 62.

152 Alkaloids such as *dimethyltryptamine*, aka DMT, or *mescaline*, a phenethylamine, both of which are considered *entheogens*, aka psychoactive agents to stir up the "god within us."

153 Wasson and his wife studied the possibility and concluded that hallucinogens underlie all of humankind's ancient religions. This view is shared by Daniel Pinchbeck and Graham Hancock in the respective books cited here. In other words, to them, God is a magical mushroom! "All of our evidence taken together led us many years ago to hazard a bold surmise: was it not probably that, long ago, long before the beginnings of written history, our ancestors had worshipped a divine mushroom?" (Pinchbeck, *Breaking Open the Head*, 48). Terence K. McKenna, one of the emotional leaders of the 2012 movement, would also concur with this assessment. Indeed, he also believed that plant-based hallucinogens were the source of humanity's consciousness and, ultimately, the creation of language. Being two of the often-cited traits of the "image of God" in humankind, the creative power attributed to mushrooms and other plants to transform humanity is genuinely divine. What is ironic, of course, is how far outside of "standard reality" the hallucinogens take the subject who ingests them. Arguing they are source of humanity's distinctiveness, in my thinking, is quite a stretch.

154 "Turn on, tune in, drop out," *Wikipedia*, last modified March 24, 2011, http://en.wikipedia.org/wiki/Turn_on,_tune_in,_drop_out. It was likely the hysterical nature of Leary and his mad ranting about western culture and the necessity to use hallucinogens to save our souls that "turned off" (rather than "on") the American "psyche" to LSD. Today's advocates for the spiritual value of drug-taking blame Leary from doing far more harm than good in educating the masses about the personal usefulness of such compounds.

155 Marrs, *PSI Spies*, 43–44.

156 Ibid., 43–44.

157 Ibid., 61.

158 Ibid., 63.

159 Ibid., 64.

160 Ibid., 65.

161 Ibid., 100.

162 Ibid., 97.

163 SRI was formed in 1946 and has been granted over 1,000 patents since its inception.

164 Marrs, *PSI Spies*, 172.

165 Jim Schnabel, "Tinker, Tailor, Soldier PSI," August, 27, 1995, http://www.independent.co.uk/arts-entertainment/tinker-tailor-soldier-psi-1598203.html.

166 Marrs, *PSI Spies*, 15.

167 Those who expect the government to make some sort of statement regarding "Official Disclosure" on the reality of UFOs should see this experience as a likely example. If and when such a disclosure is made, it may be a series of messages released slowly over several years.

168 This may explain the incredible claims of one Ed Dames, a former military remote viewer in the 1990s who mixes his RV advocacy with the most outlandish speculations about extraterrestrials and life on Mars, latent, and soon to be released upon the earth!

169 And most of the stories can't be released because of security clearances and the fact that the PSI Spies would go to jail if they were careless about what they shared publicly.

170 Marrs, *PSI Spies*, 118.

171 Ibid., 133.

172 Ibid., 155.

173 This was also how Joe McMoneagle was identified.

174 Marrs, *PSI Spies*, 29.

175 Called *Coordinate Remote Viewing* (CRV), this is the dominant technique used by the team. It creates a "double-blind" method in an attempt to eliminate any interference from the impressions of the monitor or the consciousness of the remote viewer. The fact that latitude and longitude numbering is a human construct (and not a part of nature) makes its working all the more mysterious. Also note:

The double blind methodology isn't to continue to test or prove the phenomenon; it is to keep the process free of contamination by the conscious minds of the monitor or the viewer.

176 Marrs, *PSI Spies*, 168.

177 Ibid., 166.

178 Ibid., 207.

179 Ibid., 119–120.

180 Ibid., 125.

181 "The Charge of the Light Brigade (poem)," *Wikipedia*, last modified May 18, 2011, http://en.wikipedia. org/wiki/The_Charge_of_the_Light_Brigade_(poem).

182 Marrs, *PSI Spies*, 164.

183 Ibid., 165. Both China and the Soviet Union utilized PSI Spies too (so much for atheistic, materialistic communism denying the reality of the supernatural). Like Marxism itself, it seems the practical reality of the world-as-it-really-is upsets the best and most articulate ideologies.

184 Terence K. McKenna and Dennis J. McKenna, *Invisible Landscape: Mind, Hallucinogens, and the I Ching* (New York, NY: Harper Collins, 1994), 109–110.

185 Lynn Picknett and Clive Prince, *The Stargate Conspiracy: The Truth About Extraterrestrial Life and the Mysteries of Ancient Egypt* (New York, NY: Berkley Publishing Group, 1999), 207–208.

186 Ibid., 208.

187 Ibid., 208–209.

188 Ibid., 210.

189 Ibid., 212.

190 DMT is known as "the spirit molecule" and is so-called in a book by Dr. Rick Strassman, a professor and researcher at New Mexico University. It was also made into a movie in 2010.

191 Picknett and Prince, *The Stargate Conspiracy*, 169.

192 Ibid., 166–167.

193 Ibid., 166–167.

194 Ibid., 168.

195 Martin had been a student of L. Ron Hubbard and the Scientology/Dianetics' movement.

196 This is my supposition regarding how ancient shamans knew about the various plants and their effects. The spirits provided the education.

McKenna and Hancock assume these spirits dwelt in the plants themselves. But logically, the spirits had to communicate the message about the plants beforehand otherwise it would not have been clear whether a particular plant or fungus would help you or kill you. Of course, "spirits of the air" as the Bible describes them would rather be deceptive and ascribe themselves to the "plant world." The belief we know as "animism" (god dwelling in nature) easily derives from the behaviors of early humans and the spirits surrounding them.

197 *Rahotep* was a high official who lived at the end of the Third and the beginning of the Fourth Dynasty. According to his titular (title), he was the physical son of the king... He was also the "great priest of Heliopolis" and a "general," as well as the "lord of Pe," one of the holy cities in Ancient Egypt. (See http://www.ancient-egypt.org/ index.html).

198 Picknett and Prince, *The Stargate Conspiracy*,186.

199 The promoters had the brilliant idea of hiring the motorcycle gang, Hell's Angels, to keep the peace. Their method was to shoot and kill several of the attending guests. Thereafter, it was harder for counter-culture members to take time to smell the flowers.

200 Picknett and Prince, *The Stargate Conspiracy*,172.

201 Ibid., 174.

202 The English word *ennead* literally means nine and was translated from the Egyptian word *psit*, also meaning nine.

203 I document Bailey's (and Madame Blavatsky's) theosophical beliefs in some detail in my book, *Decoding Doomsday.*

204 Picknett and Prince, *The Stargate Conspiracy*, 219.

205 Ibid., 205.

206 Ibid., 216.

207 Ibid., 218. Einhorn later would be found guilty in *abstentia* for the 1977 murder of his Philadelphia girlfriend (in 1983). He was finally arrested in 1998 after a special law was passed by the PA legislature clearing the way for his extradition from France. What's also fascinating about Einhorn: He had a strong connection with Charlie Rose (the Congressman, not today's television newsman and celebrity), a member of the House Select Committee on Intelligence. Rose was a strong supporter of the Pentagon's remote viewing program. Picknett and Prince believe Einhorn was a key spokesperson for THE 9 and through his influence many came to know and believe in the mission of THE 9 (p. 231).

208 Ibid., 220.

209 Colin Wilson wrote a book in 1978, *Mysteries*, that stated that the medium are most likely quite honest, but the source of the messages isn't. "Wilson speculates that it is some kind of dramatization by the medium's subconscious mind using their innate psychic powers, or that some mischievous spirit entities—whom he calls 'the crooks and conmen of the spirit world'—have attached themselves to the medium." (Picknett and Prince, *The Stargate Conspiracy*, 253).

210 Several of the probes sent by both American and the Soviet Union have mysteriously blown up or disappeared altogether when reaching the "red planet" causing a considerable degree of consternation and speculation. This is well documented in Hoagland's book, *Dark Mission*.

211 Pickett and Prince, *The Stargate Conspiracy*, 153.

212 Ibid., 153.

213 Ibid., 240.

214 Ibid., 154.

215 Ibid., 155.

216 Ibid., 156.

217 Ibid., 159.

218 "James Hurtak," *Wikipedia*, last modified March 30, 2011, http://en.wikipedia.org/wiki/James_Hurtak.

219 Hurtak's psychic discovery was what Uri Geller was referring to in his 1998 interview with Picknett and Prince.

220 Picknett and Prince, *The Stargate Conspiracy*, 178. I am fascinated by the fact that fifty years earlier, Theosophy and the Nazis fervently believed in the mythology surrounding Atlantis and staked much of their pseudo-science and philosophy upon it. As hinted earlier, their anti-Semitism emanates from their belief in this ancient myth as articulated by Madame Blavatsky and later by Alice Bailey. See my book, *Decoding Doomsday*, for more details.

221 Ibid., 178.

222 Ibid., 234.

223 Who changed his Jewish name to a German name to evoke "more power."

224 Picknett and Prince, *The Stargate Conspiracy*, 235.

225 Hoagland's book, *Dark Mission* (co-authored with Mike Bara), provides many startling assertions supporting this theory.

226 Picknett and Prince, *The Stargate Conspiracy*, 242.
227 Ibid., 206.
228 Ibid., 237.
229 Ibid., 242–243.
230 Ibid., 248.
231 Oracle Think Quest Education Foundation, "The Great Unknown: Some Views of the Afterlife," *Thinkquest.org,* http://library.thinkquest. org/16665/afterlifeframe.htm.
232 Ibid.
233 Ibid.
234 Wikipedia contributors, "*Inferno* (Dante)," *Wikipedia,* last accessed July 14, 2011, http://en.wikipedia.org/w/index. php?title=Inferno_(Dante)&oldid=432842379.
235 Ibid.
236 Ibid.
237 Ronald Story, *The Mammoth Encyclopedia of Extraterrestrial Encounters,* in an article by Jacques Vallée, p. 753–754.
238 John Ankerberg and John Weldon, *The Facts on UFO's and Other Supernatural Phenomena* (Eugene, Oregon: Harvest House Publishers, 1992), 10–11.
239 Donna Higbee, "New Abductee Trend," *Flying Saucer Review,* last accessed July 6, 2011, http://www.fsr.org.uk/fsrart14.htm.
240 John Ankerberg and John Weldon, *The Facts on UFO's and Other Supernatural Phenomena* (Eugene, Oregon: Harvest House Publishers, 1992), 8.
241 Gary Bates and Lita Cosner, "UFOlogy: The World's Fastest Growing Religion," *Creation.com,* May 12, 2011, http://www.creation. com/ufology-scientific-religion.
242 John Keel, *Operation Trojan Horse* (Lilburn, GA: Illuminet Press, 1996 edition) 192.
243 This was one of several notes I referred to in my book, *Alien Intrusion: UFOs and the Evolution Connection.* Original source: John Ankerberg and John Weldon, *The Facts on UFO's and Other Supernatural Phenomena* (Eugene, Oregon: Harvest House Publishers, 1992), 36–37.
244 "deceive," *Webster's Third New International Dictionary, Unabridged* (Merriam-Webster, 2002), last accessed July 3, 2011, http://unabridged. merriam-webster.com.

245 Edward F. Murphy, *The Handbook for Spiritual Warfare: Revised & Updated* (Nashville, TN: Thomas Nelson, 2003).

246 Ibid., p. 433.

247 For this and other facts about Watson in this chapter, see: "Charles 'Tex' Watson," *Wikipedia*, last modified May 17, 2011, http://en.wikipedia. org/wiki/Tex_Watson#Conviction.

248 "Nothing but the Blood of Jesus," a hymn written by Robert Lowry, and published in *Gospel Music* (New York: Biglow & Main, 1876).

249 "Charles Manson," *Wikipedia*, last modified May 30, 2011, http:// en.wikipedia.org/wiki/Charles_manson.

250 Daily Mail Reporter, "Global Warming Must Be True, Charles Manson Believes in it: Killer Breaks 20-Year Silence on 40th Anniversary of Gruesome Sharon Tate Murders," *Associated Newspapers Ltd., Part of the Daily Mail, The Mail on Sunday & Metro Media Group*, April 19, 2011, http://www.dailymail.co.uk/news/article-1378178/Charles-Manson-breaks-20-year-silence-40th-anniversary-gruesome-Sharon-Tate-murders.html.

251 For this and other facts about David Berkowitz in this chapter, see: "David Berkowitz," *Wikipedia*, last modified May 29, 2011, http:// en.wikipedia.org/wiki/David_Berkowitz, and "David Berkowitz—The Son of Sam," written by Charles Montaldo, accessed June 2, 2011, http://crime.about.com/od/murder/p/sonofsam.htm.

252 Lowry, "Nothing but the Blood of Jesus," *Gospel Music*.

253 Murphy, *The Handbook for Spiritual Warfare*, p. 439.

254 For this and other facts about Jodie Foster in this chapter, see: "Jodie Foster," *Wikipedia*, last modified June 1, 2011, http://en.wikipedia. org/wiki/Jodie_Foster.

255 For this and other facts about John Hinckley in this chapter, see: "John Hinckley, Jr.," *Wikipedia*, last modified May 29, 2011, http:// en.wikipedia.org/wiki/John_Hinckley,_Jr.

256 "John Hinckley, Jr.," *Wikipedia*, last modified May 29, 2011, http:// en.wikipedia.org/wiki/John_Hinckley,_Jr.

257 Shelby Brown, "John Hinckley, Jr. to be Released to Our Area?: Man Who Tried to Assassinate President Reagan Asks to be Released to Mother's Home," *CBS News, WTVR*, April 26, 2010, http://www.wtvr. com/news/wtvr-hinckley-042610,0,2140822,print.story.

258 Lowry, "Nothing but the Blood of Jesus," *Gospel Music*.

259 Thomas Horn, "Is Murder All in the Mind, Or Is There 'Something' Else?" *News With Views*, April 26, 2007, http://www.newswithviews. com/Horn/thomas8.htm.

260 "Neurologist Points to 'Holes' in Teen's Brain," *Amarillo Globe News*, November 5, 1999, http://amarillo.com/stories/1999/11/05/usn_holes. shtml.

261 Euripides, *The Bacchantes*, anonymous translator, 410 BC, http://nzr. mvnu.edu/faculty/trearick/english/rearick/readings/manuscri/bacchae/ bacchan.htm.

262 Walter F. Otto, *Dionysus Myth and Cult* (Indianapolis, IN: Indiana University, 1965), 114.

263 John W. Allman, "Revival Leader Touts 'Son of Sam' Conversion," *The Pensecola News Journal*, November 18, 1997, http://www.rickross.com/ reference/brownsville/brownsville16.html.

264 Mercy Hope, "Life Lessons Learned from a Death Row Inmate," *MercyHope.com*, http://www.mercyhope.com/articles.htm.